PIMLICO

405

ESSENTIAL ENGLISH FOR JOURNALISTS, EDITORS AND WRITERS

Harold Evans was editor of the *Sunday Times* from 1967 to 1981 and editor of *The Times* from 1981 to 1982. His account of these years, *Good Times, Bad Times*, was a national bestseller. He won a European gold medal for his efforts for the thalidomide children. He is the author of *Pictures on a Page*, which has been acclaimed around the world as the bible of photo-journalism, and the celebrated *The American Century: People, Power and Politics – An Illustrated History*. In America, he has been editor-in-chief of *Conde Nast Traveler* magazine, and president and publisher of the Random House trade group in New York. He has most recently been editorial director and vice-chairman of *US News and World Report*, the *Daily News*, *Fast Company* and *Atlantic Monthly*. He lives in New York with his wife Tina Brown and their two children.

Crawford Gillan is a former editor of the *Evening Star*, Ipswich, and of the *Essex County Standard*. Before that he was deputy editor of the *Cambridge Evening News*. He has also worked as a sub-editor on the *Daily Express* and the *Guardian*. He chaired the editorial training committee of the Guild (now Society) of Editors for three years in the mid-1990s. He now works as a freelance editor and consultant.

ESSENTIAL ENGLISH

For Journalists, Editors and Writers

HAROLD EVANS

Fully Revised by Crawford Gillan

PIMLICO

Published by Pimlico 2000

14 16 18 20 19 17 15

First published in Great Britain as
Newsman's English by
William Heinemann 1972
Revised edition first published in Great Britain by
Pimlico 2000

Pimlico
Random House, 20 Vauxhall Bridge Road,
London SW1V 2SA

The Random House Group Limited Reg. No. 954009
www.randomhouse.co.uk

A CIP catalogue record for this book
is available from the British Library

ISBN 978-0-712-66447-9

The Random House Group Limited supports The Forest Stewardship
Council (FSC), the leading international forest certification organisation.
All our titles that are printed on Greenpeace approved FSC certified paper
carry the FSC logo. Our paper procurement policy can be found at
www.rbooks.co.uk/environment

Mixed Sources
Product group from well-managed
forests and other controlled sources
www.fsc.org   Cert no. TT-COC-2139
© 1996 Forest Stewardship Council
FSC

Typeset by Deltatype Ltd, Birkenhead, Merseyside
Printed in the UK by CPI William Clowes
Beccles NR34 7TL

Contents

Foreword
to the Pimlico Edition

Hugh Cudlipp was the journalists' journalist of the 1940s and 1950s. Harold Evans was the journalists' journalist of the 1960s and 1970s. Both remain journalists' journalists for the new millennium.

It was fitting, therefore, that Cudlipp, in his Foreword to the first edition of Evans's *Newsman's English* (as it was first called) should describe the book as unique. The word unique is too often misused. That it is still so often misused confirms the need for this welcome return of a masterful treatise on the English language.

A good English sentence is still a good English sentence. And a cliché remains a cliché. As the information available to the ordinary man, woman and child continues to multiply enormously each year, the need for good English not only persists, but becomes of increasing importance. Everyone needs a good editor. And it is the consumer who needs a good editor more than most as this eruption of knowledge threatens to overwhelm all in its unrelenting wake.

There are those who predict that content above all else will be king. I disagree. Context, provided by expert users of the language, will rule and shape people's lives in the future. Hence the need for this adroit revision of this *unique* book.

In the years since it went out of print no other text has come close to fulfilling its role. Thus the Society of Editors, in its inaugural year following the amalgamation of the Guild of Editors and the Association of British Editors, enthusiastically welcomes its re-publication.

Many of its members grew up on Evans. They not only appreciated what Evans preached, they also understood that Evans practised what he preached. He was not merely a teacher telling us what ought to be done. He was a practitioner who showed us what was done. The book was required reading for all those who became journalists in the 1970s. This new edition must become required reading for all those who will become journalists in the new millennium.

It has become far too fashionable for the use of good English to be derided. Indeed our own profession has not always helped the matter. Newspapers, radio stations and television broadcasters have all contributed to sloppy usage of the language. That is not to say that English should not be dynamic and move forward. Of course it should. But it must also be correct. There is a virtue in all language being correct and the journalist who believes otherwise is a poor journalist.

In the new millennium the Society of Editors sees its main goal as supplying a community at ease with itself with as free a flow of information as possible. But that information is of no use at all if it is obscured by poor, jargon-ridden and dense English. Clear English should be a priority for all those who use the language in this new millennium. And news English at its best is the clearest English of all.

This book remains not only essential reading for those who enjoy clear language. It remains essential reading for all those who pass knowledge to others. All editors and fellow journalists should devour this book. All writers, readers, listeners and viewers need to use the language in the same way. We should all aim to use the English language well and there is no better guide than Harold Evans.

NEIL FOWLER
President, Society of Editors
Editor, *The Western Mail*
January 2000

Editor's Preface

When I was chairing the editorial training committee of the Guild of Editors (now the Society of Editors) in the mid-1990s one of the big concerns among editors was the poor grasp of written English by recruits into journalism.

It seemed to matter little whether the trainees had come straight from school or, as most of them do these days, had entered the media industry as university graduates. So rife was the problem it was even suggested that the initial training programme for journalists should start with a compulsory course in remedial English. Assuming that students recruited into journalism could be expected to be among the most articulate and literate of their generation, it did not say much for the rest of their peer group.

It was while contemplating this problem – and how to tackle it – that we began to realise how much we regretted the disappearance from print of Harold Evans's powerful guide to the written word, *Newsman's English*.

As editor of the *Sunday Times* in the late 1960s and through to the 1980s, Harold Evans was an inspiration and role model for a generation of journalists, not least for those of us lucky enough to become editors ourselves. Who can forget the tingle of excitement on turning to the *Sunday Times* each week to follow the latest instalment in the paper's battles to fend off attempts to gag it in its many public-spirited campaigns – such as the one on behalf of the victims of the thalidomide drug – or simply to discover the truth behind one of the big stories of the day, arrived at only through the painstaking research of the *Sunday Times* team of investigative reporters.

It was not surprising, therefore, that when Harold Evans chose to share some of the secrets of the trade with a wider audience, in a series of instructional books, 'Editing and Design', the result was equally inspirational and influential for those of us cutting our first teeth as journalists. For not only were his books working manuals in every sense, packed with practical techniques for sharpening skills of communication, they reflected the very essence of what successful newspapers should be all about – that everything in them should relate to human beings; the abstract word should always be given flesh and the abstract story spiced with examples.

As Harold Evans says in *Newsman's English*: 'People can recognise themselves in stories about particulars. The abstract is another world. It requires an effort of imagination to transport ourselves there. The writer should bring it to us.'

What better template to ensure the reader is always at the centre of everything a newspaper does? And what better way to spread the message about how the use of good English is essential to achieve this vital rapport between writer and reader than by resurrecting *Newsman's English*, Book One in the original series?

Fortunately, Harold Evans was happy to agree to the Guild's suggestion that the book be republished. The result is an updated version now entitled *Essential English for Journalists, Editors and Writers*, a title that not only avoids accusations of gender bias in these changing times, but that seems to sit comfortably beside *Essential Law for Journalists*, the work that has served so well and so long as a legal bible for journalists.

This new edition is a marriage of two books, *Newsman's English* and *News Headlines*, the third book in the original series. It seemed sensible to extend guidance on the written word to include the advice on headlines. Good sub-editors have always been worth their weight in gold but nowadays there is a temptation, in some quarters, to imagine that computerisation means anyone can be instantly transformed into a text editor. Computers have certainly made it much easier to handle the mechanics of type than in the days of hot metal. But sticking the uninitiated in front of a screen does not account for the multitude of skills and knowledge needed to edit a story so that it reads swiftly, logically, vividly, economically and, of course, accurately. Nor does it prevent sub-editors from writing wordy, vague or confused headlines when what is called for is examples that are attractive, imaginative and full of vigour. The art of headline writing can be developed and this book establishes the principles for a sound approach.

Although the book is aimed mainly at journalists – both the experienced and the inexperienced can benefit from it – the many helpful suggestions for improving clarity of meaning will be invaluable for anyone who has to communicate through the written word.

New examples of contemporary articles are included, mainly from American newspapers, but much of the original content remains. References to events at the time the book was first published give a slightly anachronistic feel, but the examples fit the bill so precisely that it seemed churlish to change them. The important point is that the message is still valid today – perhaps even more so, given the concern expressed by editors about the use of English by today's trainees.

Editing this edition has been an extremely worthwhile refresher course and a reminder of how easy it is to slip into sloppy habits. I commend it to all writers and editors, experienced or otherwise.

CRAWFORD GILLAN

Essential English

CHAPTER ONE

The Making of a Newspaper

The news is thrown at him in huge miscellaneous masses, which, but for his labours, would kill the reader stone-dead with mental indigestion. He has to cook this mass, having first trimmed it into reasonable proportions, keeping one eye on the probable accuracy of the facts as stated, another on the law of libel, another on various other considerations which crop up from time to time, such as the law relating to elections, and yet a fourth, which must be no less vigilant than the other three, upon the clock. Sub-editors, when I meet them, seem to have only two eyes just like other people; where they keep the other two I cannot say, but I know they must have them.

EDWARD SHANKS

Enough news is arriving today at any large newspaper office to make four or five fat novels and fill the news columns many times over. This raw material of the newspaper is as diverse as the human race. There is an earth tremor in Brazil, and another kind of tremor on Wall Street; strawberries are expensive in London, and the peace talks in Kosovo have broken down; a famous film director has died in Hollywood, in Iraq a new military build-up is under way. The international news has been transmitted by satellite to the national offices of the major news agencies. It has been checked, rough-edited and flashed electronically to one focal point: the copydesk.

The Copydesk

The newspaper's staff reporters have been busy, too, and the newspaper's correspondents, some professional and some very amateur, have been dictating on the telephone; and all that, too, comes as 'copy' to the same focal point.

This news-gathering is a prodigious if familiar achievement; so is the multiplication of the message by the rotary machines. But the selection, condensation and presentation of the flood of news, which must occur before a line of type is finalised or a press can turn, is less well understood.

It is the work of men and women with bewildering titles; in the larger newspapers there are as many potentates as in Old Baghdad. But essentially it is the work of the copydesk, of copyreaders or copy-editors in the United States, and sub-editors in many guises in Britain and elsewhere. These production journalists, humble and exalted, work in private. Everybody knows about reporters. They have the excitement of being on the spot at banquets and world series and conventions and coronations (and they have hours of frustration, too, on false scents). But few of the public know anything about the copydesk, the creative fulcrum of the modern newspaper.

This concentrated huddle of checkers and revisers at their terminals conveys nothing of the responsibilities and romance of the work. These are the human sieves of the torrent of news. They make the judgments, they prepare the written word for conversion into mass reproduction, and they, by their choices and presentation, fashion the identity of a newspaper.

Simply in volume, this can be a stupendous task. The *New York Times* receives two million words on an average day. It publishes 185,000. When they appear as the *New York Times*, they have been transformed from mere words on a computer screen. They have become, in that newspaper's assessment, the most important words in the world. They have been fished expertly from the erratic torrent, weighed, assessed, revalued in the light of later catches, and finally prepared for public display in a setting which, hopefully, will exactly reflect their significance. More than 1.8 million words have been discarded, most rejected as complete stories, many rejected as paragraphs, some excised a word at a time. It is this process of scrutiny and then of presentation which every day creates the *New York Times* and every other newspaper, and the skills it requires are the subject of this book.

They are skills of editing and revision. They cannot create a newspaper which does not have a flow of news, but their absence can ruin a newspaper however good the flow. Titles and procedures change from country to country; standards of judgment change from newspaper to newspaper. But the skills required are the same whether the newspaper is grounded in high politics or low farce. All newspapers are born from a process of editorial selection, text editing and presentation. It may be well done or badly done, but done it must be. Words have to be read and assessed, types assigned, pictures selected, headlines written, news and entertainment organised in time for it to be printed and in forms that people will read.

Of course there is no universal agreement about the details of this craft of newspaper-making, or the way the basic skills should be acquired. Almost all copy-editors begin as reporters and want to come in from the rain or see the desk as the route to an editorship. It is assumed that the copydesk skills are transferable and to some extent they are. Good clear English is the stock-in-trade for newspapers and broadcasting. But there are excellent gatherers of news who have trouble organising a story, or collating one from several different sources, or compressing the excitements they have experienced into half a column. Compression is the antithesis of reporting. How is it best to learn? Most copy-editors would probably declare themselves graduates of the College of Osmosis. They sat around a newsroom long enough to absorb the essentials. The philosophy of this little book is that there are some principles and that these can be passed on more quickly or, at least, passed on after a few arguments.

The Text Editor

The first task must be to define the area of craft under discussion and the journalistic roles. Editing a newspaper or producing a news broadcast is team work; journalists can play different bits of different roles and there is no common international term for the basic one of text editing. In Britain the text editor is a 'sub-editor' who 'subs' copy; there may be twenty or thirty sub-editors on a newspaper. In the United States the text editor is a 'copyreader', and the same work luxuriates under other titles elsewhere. The term 'text editing' will be used in this book and the journalist who does it will be called a 'text editor'.

The text editor's work begins after stories have been selected for publication or broadcast. There are minor variations here. Some offices have separate teams editing home and foreign news or home and business sections. American dailies often divide the editing functions between national and foreign news from the agencies and city copy which is produced locally and often edited at the city (i.e. local) desk by the city editor or assistant city editor. 'Give me rewrite!' is still a valid command from 'Front Page'. Often enough in one issue of a paper the same name will occur in a byline, shared with others, on a fire in Brooklyn, a road accident in Manhattan, the Mayor's latest row, a graduation ceremony. He's been everywhere! Actually, he hasn't been anywhere. He (or she) shares the byline by virtue of having been nowhere but the newsroom.

Rewrite journalists may have earned a share of the byline because they have simply recast the language of the story; they may have elicited some of the information by prodding the reporter or using their computer to search for back-up data. They are most useful when reporters are filing in haste from several sources. Rewrite pulls it all together. Whatever the variation between different newspapers, the important thing is that in all systems the three stages of selection, presentation and detailed editing have to be organised, and all the advantages of division of labour accrue from appointing one specialist to select copy.

The Copy-taster

On a one-section paper of moderate size (say up to 24 broadsheet pages) one person can select news from several agencies and staff. On a multi-sectioned newspaper, especially one with specialist sections, there may have to be specialist selectors (e.g. five separate copydesks for foreign, national, metropolitan, sport and business).

There is no better title for this work than the British one of 'copy-taster': the old name perfectly describes the work. Copy-tasters must have a sensitive news palate. They savour all the news. On a big daily newspaper they will have to make a thousand snap rejections. Of course they cannot read every one of the hundreds of thousands of words that come at them. They skim the copy and because they are up to the minute with the news and in tune with the wants of their newspaper and its readers they can detect, at a taste, what is suitable. They are like professional wine-tasters. They do not have to drink the whole bottle; a tablespoonful or the mere bouquet will do to declare whether it is palatable for that particular paper at that particular moment.

The copy-taster rejects or 'spikes' what is not required. In days gone by the rejected material was quite literally impaled on the basic tool of the trade – a sharp metal spike. Nowadays the term 'spiked' means it has gone into electronic trash. Rejected copy that is 'dead' in one office may, of course, be very much alive in another office: the rescued cat-up-a-tree rejected on the serious daily but lovingly rescued from the flood on the popular paper. Copy-tasters will tell the news department when they detect a potentially good local angle in a few lines of a national report. They may give out short paragraph fillers to text editors for editing. They may do some text editing themselves when it is quiet. But their basic job is preliminary selection, and what they select is normally passed to another executive journalist, a chief sub-editor or a foreign editor; let us call them 'projection editors'.

The Projection Editor

Here is the pivot of the whole operation. It is the projection editor's job to refine the process of selection by deciding an order of priorities and expressing them with space and type and illustration. Projection editors may act alone or they may consult a galaxy of senior executives and designers, but their basic task is judicial projection. Should this story be allowed to run to a column of type on page one, or is it really a rather windy message which can be edited down to a quarter of a column? Should it be on the front page at all? Should it be discarded entirely, perhaps, so as to make a great deal of space for that picture? Which of all the possibilities tells the day's news most effectively?

On a big evening newspaper projection editors (whatever the title) have to make such decisions at great speed. They have to be able to visualise the effect of combinations of type and pictures in various permutations and sizes. There is no time to experiment. They also have to plan their pages before all the copy for them has been received. The copy-taster may have offered, say, a follow-up of the morning story on another around-the-world hot-air balloon attempt, a strong speech on interest rates by a Government minister, a store fire, storms on the coast, and the appearance in court of two men accused of shooting a policeman. How much and which page and with what display? The projection editor also knows that soon a decision will have to be made, in consultation with the editor, on what will be the leading story for the front page. What will it be? The projection editor knows that in ten minutes the court will be hearing the case of the shot policeman but not much copy can be expected for half an hour. However, there are two other interesting items due to start then, according to the day's news schedule. The French President is to speak at a European conference in Brussels. There is a press conference on pay for nurses.

Projection editors have to look ahead and gauge the pressures on precious space even before the copy-taster has received this other news. Will the President say anything new? How much space should be set aside on page one? As they make their judgment, projection editors plan each story on to each page grid on the screen. They have to decide the headline type, the length of the story, and the type it will be set in. Before the page is complete all the copy has to be processed in accordance with the projection editor's prescriptions. It has to go to the text editors, who are the link between the projection editor's imagination and the mechanics of printing.

The text editor will do all or most of these things for every story:

- Write the headline which first attracts the reader's attention, and the subheadings
- Read the story for clarity and meaning and rewrite where necessary
- Shorten the story while retaining essential facts, unity and coherence
- Combine one story with another, or perhaps combine running reports from several news agencies, a handful of correspondents and half a dozen reporters, to produce a single, intelligible report from a series of confused and even contradictory messages
- Add important background facts and provide answers for any implied questions
- Save space where verbosity creeps in (where there is *a capacity for implementation* the text editor prefers to know *what can be done*)
- Correct the grammar
- Check for apparent errors of fact
- Check for legal errors (libel, restricted reporting, contempt of court)
- Check for taste
- Check for house (i.e. office) style

The Revise Editor

Once the text editor has completed these tasks, the copy is often passed to a third executive, the 'revise editor'. Revise editors check the work, ensuring that every detail is correct: simple mistakes can wreck any production scheme and make the whole page late. Revise editors also regard themselves as guinea pigs for the meaning of the language, especially the headline written by the text editor: does it make immediate sense, or has it grown from obscure references to some dream world inhabited by reporter or text editor? American newspapers often dispense with a revise editor and suffer as a consequence in wordiness.

Standards in Editing

All this work has to be done on every newspaper. The text editor is not a mere corrector of the press or a précis writer. There are, it is true, grades of creativity. Speed is valued more than polish on some newspapers. On a busy evening newspaper the text editors will at times find stories arriving far faster than they can edit them. There is little time for polish. They concentrate on the right length, the right news point and the headline, and then get on to the next story. In Britain the text editor on a serious newspaper employing specialist staff writers will be expected to do less than on a popular newspaper. But all British text editors are expected to do more than the American copyreader, who is more of a reader and less of an editor. The skills of condensation are but poorly developed in the United States and Canada. If North American reporters wrote concisely it would matter less, but they do not, and the absence of strict editing leads to wasted space and muffled meaning.

This is not just a matter of saving column-inches; on American newspapers whole columns could be saved every day and used for news, pictures or advertising revenue. The inefficiency and waste are extraordinary.

By contrast, thanks probably to the effect of wartime newsprint rationing fusing with historical development, the British sub-editor is first and foremost expected to be a concise editor; to be described as a tight sub is not a sign of moral turpitude. A good sub-editor takes pride in being able to convert into half a column a report that would take a column if printed as received – and to do so without losing a single relevant fact or straining a meaning. Of course this is skilful work and it has its perils; it runs the risk of distortion when done too hurriedly or unintelligently, and can lead to the savaging of distinctive individual writing which ought really to be used wholly or not at all.

Even the most rudimentary text-editing, however, is better than another all-too-common American practice of shortening agency messages merely by discarding, unread, the last two sheets. In not attempting to edit news dispatches by the word, two assumptions are made. The first is that the portion selected by length for publication is the most important – that the reporter has assembled the most important facts at the beginning of the report. The second assumption is that the portion chosen for publication is incapable of accurate condensation by a specialist in précis. These assumptions are only rarely justified; more often they are ill-founded and even dangerous. Trained reporters will know, of course, that they should write economically, that they should include the most important facts at the beginning of a normal news message, and a news-agency report will have had the benefit of some rough editing at the agency's headquarters. However, several things are overlooked in this reasoning. The news agency, for instance, has the task of supplying news to a vast assortment of newspapers with varying needs and space. The fuller narrative treatment suitable for a big paper interested in the report will be wrong for another paper with less space or less interest in the subject. Secondly, there are many occasions when the best report is obtained by combining key facts from more than one source.

Command of the language is, in fact, the second quality required from a text editor. The first is a sense of news values. Both can be cultivated. Text editors need not be 'writing' journalists. They need not be capable of a single act of imaginative prose. They should be a good judge of writing in others and should develop a style themselves, a clear, muscular and colloquial style. They need not be good reporters themselves, and although it can help to have done some reporting, many a journalist has failed as a reporter but succeeded as a text editor. A young man on the *Manchester Evening News* was found painfully shy for the reporters' room; he transferred to sub-editing. As Sir William Haley he later became editor of *The Times* of London.

News values vary from paper to paper. Text editors should study various kinds of newspaper and their selection and treatment of news between the serious and the human interest. They should re-edit the day's *Times* as if it were the *Sun*. They should be able to adapt themselves, as craftsmen, to the standards of either. A wide general curiosity is vital, preferably backed by a broad education. Anyone who is bored by current people and politics will never make a successful general text editor. Of course a university degree can help, but mainly because of the intellectual discipline that lies behind it. There is no need for non-graduates to feel out of the race, especially if they have any distinctive aptitude for lucidity, any passion for accuracy, any flair for design, any sense of news values, and above all, a willingness to learn.

What Makes a Good Text Editor?

The other qualities required in the text editor are the same as those listed two generations ago by F.J. Mansfield in his *Sub-editing* (London: Pitman, 1939). They make a formidable list, but before anyone flinches it has to be said that all text editors are not expected to possess all these attributes to perfection. To possess some in high degree may be enough for success. Even within specialised text-editing there is room for specialisation; and a good copydesk will blend the different talents of text editors, relying now on the capacity for quick précis by one member and now on another's ability slowly to add sparkle to the dullest text. The qualities collectively are:

- The 'human interest' qualities of sympathy, insight, breadth of view, imagination, sense of humour

- An orderly and well-balanced mind, which implies level judgment, sense of perspective and proportion
- A cool head, ability to work in an atmosphere of hurry and excitement without becoming flurried or incapable of accurate work
- Quickness of thought coupled with accuracy
- Conscientiousness, keenness and ruthlessness, rightly directed
- Judgment, based on well-informed common sense
- A capacity for absorbing fact – and fancy – and expressing them in an acceptable manner
- Adaptability – the power, whatever one's personal predilections, of seeing things from the reader's point of view
- Knowledge of the main principles of the laws of libel, contempt and copyright
- Physical fitness for a trying, sedentary life which takes its toll of nerves, sight and digestion
- The team spirit – a newspaper is one of the most striking products of co-operative enterprise and effort

Text editors should generally come to editing after reporting. Text editors who do not appreciate from their own experience the reporters' aims and difficulties and temptations to err, are invariably the worse for it. A year's reporting, if varied, can be enough.

The ideal way to learn the craft is to sit with senior text editors and see the way they work, and at the same time to tackle gradually more important stories. Too many text editors are flung in at the deep end. They learn to swim but their strokes are atrocious. Text editors should fairly soon discover their own strengths, whether they are happy in writing a straight headline and extricating the hard facts for a terse evening newspaper story when the deadline is near, or at the opposite extreme, in the slow and painstaking task of disentangling a tricky law case. Irredeemably slow text editors will avoid the big city evening papers (well, such papers will avoid them) where speed and accuracy are at a premium all day long. They may be more at home on the popular morning newspaper, where, especially on national newspapers in Britain, rewriting is habitual whenever time allows. In between are the copydesk on the provincial morning newspaper or the serious daily or Sunday or magazine.

Journalists who choose editing as their craft will have less obvious excitement than the reporter: not for them the thrill of detection or the fast plane to Beirut. Their satisfaction lies in the skills of the craft, in communicating. And there are some excitements which reporting cannot match. There are nights of big news, the late-night flash in the Gulf War crisis, when text editors feel they are standing at the very centre of events. There is nothing to touch the fascination of seeing the news develop second by second and projecting a piece of history. Whether journalists see themselves essentially as writers or production people they cannot afford to miss copydesk training if they aspire to executive work. More and more executives in Britain and America are appointed from among those staff members who know the whole process of making a newspaper: how to convert the first idea into a well-founded column of type with display in the page, from the organisation of the research to the editing and projection in print.

No change in the organisation of a newspaper will affect this. Over the years we have seen the development of horizontal team journalism, in which a group of writers pool their investigative and writing talents. But it is a complete misunderstanding of the process to imagine that this system, or any other, does away with the need for copydesk editing skills (still less the need for writing ability). The team editor will normally do this work or another member of the team may have an aptitude for it. But somebody must do it or the journalism and production both suffer. Indeed, one of the difficulties of team journalism, among its attractions, is that the team editor's tasks are so varied that he or she may fail to develop the specialist skills to the highest pitch. This is particularly true of condensation and production work, and when team editors virtually end up editing their own copy. This is never a good practice and is often downright dangerous. Everybody's copy, including the editor's, benefits from a second reading by a fresh critical mind.

Chapter Two

Good English

People think I can teach them style. What stuff it is. Have something to say and say it as clearly as you can. That is the only secret of style.

MATTHEW ARNOLD

English is a battlefield. Purists fight off invading yes-men, dropouts, hobos, killjoys, stooges, highbrows and co-eds. Vulgarians beseech them to trust the people because the people speak real good. Grammarians, shocked by sentences concluding with prepositions, construct syntactical defences up with which we will not put. Officials observe that in connection with recent disturbances there does not appear to have been a resolution of the issue. And journalists race to the colourful scene to report the dramatic new moves.

Everybody recognises that last bit as journalese. The *Shorter Oxford Dictionary* defined it as penny-a-liner's English, the inflation of sentences for the sake of linage profit. But journalists do not deserve a monopoly of odium because they contributed a word for bad English to the language. The penny-a-liner, who has largely disappeared anyway, is a petty corrupter of the language by comparison with Her Majesty's Government and the Pentagon. English has no greater enemy than officialese. Daily the stream of language is polluted by viscous verbiage. Meaning is clouded by vague abstraction, euphemism conceals identity, and words, words, words weigh the mind down.

The Americans are at it on a grander scale. Look what happened to 'poor' people. They became 'needy', then 'deprived', then 'underprivileged' or 'disadvantaged' and latterly they have been members of a 'lower income group', or, to be politically correct, 'economically challenged'. As the cartoonist and writer Jules Feiffer observed, they still don't have a dime but they have acquired a fine vocabulary.

Journalists are daily arbiters in all this. No professor of linguistics has as much influence on the language as the text editor who edits the day's news. Words are our trade. It is not enough to get the news. We must be able to put it across. Meaning must be unmistakable, and it must also be succinct. Readers have not the time and newspapers have not the space for elaborate reiteration. This imposes decisive requirements. In protecting the reader from incomprehension and boredom, the text editor has to insist on language which is specific, emphatic and concise. Every word must be understood by the ordinary reader, every sentence must be clear at one glance, and every story must say something about people. There must never be a doubt about its relevance to our daily life. There must be no abstractions.

This places newspaper English firmly in the prose camp of Dryden, Bunyan, Butler, Shaw, Somerset Maugham, Orwell, Thurber. The style to reject is the mandarin style which is characterised by long sentences with many dependent clauses, by the use of the subjunctive and conditional, by exclamations and interjections, quotations, allusions, metaphors, long images, Latin terminology, subtlety and conceits. 'Its cardinal assumption is that neither the writer nor the reader is in a hurry, that both are in possession of a classical education and a private income,' wrote Cyril Connolly.

Reporters in their gloomier moments will affirm that all text editors, whether British sub-editors or American copyreaders, are butchers. The text editor does indeed have to make many a grave decision to amputate. The details on which the writer has spent hours have abruptly to be cut off because there is no room for them. But the real skill of text-editing does not lie in such drastic treatment. Anybody can lop off a story half-way. Text-editing is interesting only because it offers so much more scope than such simple hack work. Good text editors are surgeons who can save facts and who can make the body of the story more vigorous and healthy. Their instruments are a clear mind and a love of the language. When it is necessary to cut for length they struggle to save details by using the language more economically than the writer. They are specialists in concise writing. When length is not a problem they edit the text for meaning, clarity and accuracy. Grammar, punctuation and spelling they will correct in their stride. The assurance of instant comprehension for the reader is what will take their time.

All types of newspaper, local, regional and national, have to cope with copy which obscures the news, which delays the readers getting the human facts the headline has invited them to obtain. There are many reasons for this. Some copy from contacts and non-staff sources is, to be polite, only semi-professional. There are widely varying standards even among trained staff reporters. Some of the best at ferreting out facts are not pithy writers and never will be. Reporters who can write well are occasionally lured into literary embroidery. Fairly often the reporter, wanted for another assignment, is more hard-pressed for time than the text editor.

The text editor must worry about words, sentences, and the structure of stories. Much of the time is spent on the headline and the first few sentences which lure the reader; often these determine the way the story should be developed. With the constant effort to render events concrete, vivid and human, text editors will develop an allergy to sloppy English. Their fingers will twitch even as their eyes skim the text. There is not much time for reflection. The diagnosis must be immediate and the cure instantaneous.

It is with this environment in mind that the following pages suggest ways in which text editors can improve their reactions. The intention is to analyse the fine skills of using words and sentences, and building these into various kinds of news story; and they attempt to put some of the preaching into practice. Even so they are no more than a compass in the jungle. They offer certain principles or conditions for clear expression, aware that there is no rule for original expression, that the principles may overlap or, infrequently, conflict, and that any chapter on the English word and sentence must necessarily be incomplete. It is not a grammar. Some knowledge of the pitfalls of dangling participles, pronouns and their antecedents, verbs and their subjects, and the sequence of tenses, must be assumed. As William Brewster[1] pointed out long ago, the mere avoidance of grammatical barbarisms will not result in clear writing: 'One might escape illiteracy but not necessarily confusion ... To know what a sentence is saying is important, more important than anything else about it. That is rarely interfered with, directly, by the presence of barbarisms, and not grievously, for the most, by improprieties and solecisms, as they actually occur in writing; these things cause sorrow chiefly to the erudite or to the parvenu of style, whom they offend rather than confuse; the populace cares very little about them.'

Sentences – Limit the Ideas

A sentence is more likely to be clear if it is a short sentence communicating one thought, or a closely connected range of ideas.

There are roughly four kinds of sentence. The *simple* sentence has one subject and one predicate or statement (Eight bandits robbed a train yesterday). The *compound* sentence has two simple sentences joined by a conjunction (Eight bandits robbed a train yesterday and stole £80,000). The *complex* sentence has one principal statement and one or more subordinate statements or clauses which modify the main statement (Eight train bandits, who were foiled by a railway worker, were still being sought last night). Then there is the *compound-complex* sentence where all the statements have one or more modifying statements (Eight bandits with coshes who tried to rob a train yesterday were foiled by a worker who threw stones at them and forced them to drop £80,000).

All those sentences are clear. To attempt to say that newspapers should use only simple sentences is an absurdity. Economy as well as rhythm requires all kinds of sentence to be used. Often it is wasteful to introduce a complete subject and predicate for each idea. The subordinate clause in a complex sentence can state relations more precisely and more economically than can a string of simple sentences or compound sentences joined by *and, but, so,* etc.

And over the years we have learned to cut down loose subsidiary clauses into economical phrases. The real seduction of the simple sentence is that taken by itself it is short and it is confined to carrying one idea. The real trouble with so many compound-complex sentences is that they have to carry too many ideas.

In the example below (left), one sentence is trying to do the work of three. The first thought ends at 'future', and that is where the sentence should end. The text editor should cross out 'and', and pick up two new sentences, as on the right:

The French Government is expected to begin bilateral talks to replace the integrated military structures in the immediate future and will be willing to exchange, say, some infrastructure facilities enjoyed by the US and the United Kingdom for continued sharing in the long range early warning system, for France's *force de frappe* could be destroyed by a sudden missile attack on her airfields.

The French Government is expected to begin bilateral talks to replace the integrated military structures in the immediate future. The French will be willing to exchange, say, some military installations used by the US and the United Kingdom for continued French sharing in the long range early warning system. This is because France's atomic strike force could be destroyed by a missile attack on her airfields.

The second version is immediately clearer. The length of the sentences with too many ideas is not the cause of the disease; but it is often a clear symptom. It is the reason why some writers advise a limit on sentence length. Rudolf Flesch[2] urges an average of 18 words to a sentence. The Elizabethan sentence, he says, ran to 45 words and the Victorian to 29, while ours runs to 20 and less. Web and fax have accentuated this trend to telegraphic communication.

The lesson is that where the ideas in the sentence are complex, they cannot intelligibly be presented in subsidiary clauses separated by a mere comma. The full stop is a great help to sanity. In swift editing – not rewriting – this 55-word sentence can be made comprehensible by being split into two (right):

On east–west relations Dr Kiesinger described the remarkably non-compromising attitude of the East Germans in the reply sent in September after a delay of three months by Herr Stoph, the East German Prime Minister, who attacked the Federal Government's claims to speak for all Germans and proposed a draft treaty between 'the two German states'.

On east–west relations Dr Kiesinger described the remarkably non-compromising attitude of the East Germans in the reply sent in September after a delay of three months. Herr Stoph, the East German Prime Minister, had attacked the Federal Government's claims to speak for all Germans and proposed a draft treaty between 'the two German states'.

A long confusing sentence is often produced by creating a subsidiary clause to carry one or more ideas in advance of the main idea. This defect and others in sentence structure will be examined in more detail in the chapter on introductions, but here is a typical example from a newspaper in the North of England. Look at the difficulties on the way:

Saying that while he accepted medical evidence that asbestosis was associated with the cause of death of a Washington chemical worker, John George Watson, aged 40, of 51 Pattinson Town, the Coroner, Mr A. Henderson, indicated at the inquest at Chester-le-Street last night that the final decision whether the disease caused or contributed to death would rest with the Pneumoconiosis Medical Panel.

Who is 'he'?

Is this the name of the chemical worker, or the 'he' in the first line? We have to read on to learn that Mr Watson is not the Coroner.

What disease? We have to refer back 41 words to the mention of asbestosis.

The opening subsidiary clause here is 21 words long. It does not mean anything to the readers until they have read through to the end of the main clause. While readers are reading the main clause, they have to refer back in their mind to the qualifying subsidiary clause. It is hard in one reading to absorb the meaning of the whole sentence.

The sentence is simply overloaded. The burden of the thought should be redistributed:

> The death of a Washington chemical worker, John George Watson, aged 40, of 51 Pattinson Town, was associated with asbestosis, said the Coroner, Mr A. Henderson, at Chester-le-Street last night. But the final decision whether asbestosis caused or contributed to death would rest with the Pneumoconiosis Medical Panel.

Opening a sentence with a subsidiary clause has special difficulties for the reader when the two ideas do not march in the same direction. News values apart, the text editor should take the sentence carrying the most important thought and give it an immediate identity of its own. Another sentence should deal with the other thought:

At the end of a rousing speech on Labour Government policies which she said were designed to remould the economic life of the country irrespective of the many difficulties involved and the grumbles of those who disliked change, the Minister of Transport, speaking at Aberystwyth yesterday, expressed her bitter disappointment that the Stratford strike had not been settled.

The Minister of Transport yesterday expressed her 'bitter disappointment' that the Stratford rail strike had not been solved.

She said this at the end of a rousing speech at Aberystwyth defending Labour Government economic policies . . .

Sheer wordiness was a fault in this story – but, even if the sentence had been shorter, confusion would have been created by the way the sentence structure linked separate thoughts. As Marc Rose, a *Reader's Digest* editor, once complained to the *New York Times*: 'Born in Waukegan, Ill., I get damn sick of the non-sequiturs'.[3]

Obituary notices are full of non-sequiturs, and it is no use attempting to rewrite them as single sentences, compound or complex:

- A keen golfer, he leaves three children.
- Leaving three children, he was a keen golfer.
- He was a keen golfer and leaves three children.
- He leaves three children and was a keen golfer.
- He was born in Alabama and always arrived punctually at work.

The last example gives the impression that the circumstances of his birth contrived to make him punctual. But there is no such cause and effect. The reader has been led up the garden path. The needlessly linked sentences divert the mind to speculation. There should be two sentences, but even these can be awkward; adjoining sentences need some linking thought, as in the second rewritten example below:

He was born in Alabama. He always arrived punctually at work.

He was born in Alabama. His father came south from New York and opened a drug store with 1,000 dollars he borrowed from a clergyman.

The essence of the matter comes back to limiting the thought a sentence has to carry. This is not something peculiar to newspaper English. There is strictly nothing grammatically wrong with the following sentence but it is incoherent because it is overcrowded with ideas:

The vague and unsettled suspicions which uncertainty had

produced of what Mr. Darcy might have been doing to forward her sister's match which she had feared to encourage, as an exertion of goodness too great to be probable, and at the same time dreaded to be just, from the pain of obligation, were proved beyond their greatest extent to be true.

JANE AUSTEN, *Pride and Prejudice*

It is hard to read this and hard to be sure what Jane Austen is saying. Is it the suspicions or the match itself which 'she had feared to encourage'? It is no solution to rewrite the passage in simple sentences. Complex sentences, provided they are clear, can make assertions about a subject more economically. The simple-sentence version that follows requires 88 words altogether and it barely copes with the thoughts:

She had vague and unsettled suspicions. These suspicions had been produced by uncertainty. She did not know what Mr. Darcy had been doing to forward her sister's match. She feared to encourage these suspicions. She had two reasons. It was very good of Mr. Darcy to help if he was helping. She doubted if anyone could be so good. But she dreaded the idea that he might be so good. She would then have a debt to him. In the event her suspicions were proved to be true.

But a readable, clear and economical version can be produced by splitting the thoughts into four groups and dealing with these in four varied sentences:

She had been filled by vague and unsettled suspicions about what Mr. Darcy might have been doing to forward her sister's match. She had not liked to dwell on these. Such an exertion of goodness seemed improbable, yet she had dreaded the idea that the suspicions might be just for she would then be under obligation to him. Now the suspicions were proved beyond their greatest extent to be true.

Be Active

Bewildering sentences carrying excess weight are obvious. The text editor has to be more alert to detect the deadening effect of a succession of sentences in the passive voice. Vigorous, economical writing requires a preference for sentences in the active voice.

'Police arrested Jones' – that is a sentence in the active voice. The subject (police) is the actor: the receiver of the action (Jones) is the object. We say the verb (arrested) is being used transitively because it requires an object; the verb is said to be used intransitively when it does not need an object. Look what happens to that perfectly good sentence in the active voice with a transitive verb when we write the sentence in the passive voice – when the receiver of the action becomes the subject rather than the object: 'Jones was arrested by police'. We now have five words where three told the story before.

Here is another newspaper example: 'A meeting will be held by directors next week'. That sentence in the passive voice has nine words when the active voice requires only eight: 'The directors will hold a meeting next week'. And better still: 'The directors will meet next week'. Or: 'The directors meet next week'.

Very often a weak sentence can be made emphatic by changing the writer's passive reliance on the 'there is' construction into a sentence employing a transitive verb in the active voice:

There were riots in several cities last night in which several shops were burned.	Rioters burned shops in several cities last night.

The active version on the right has only eight words against the fourteen on the left; and it is so much more direct, too. This is one of the beauties of the English language. Clarity, economy and vigour go hand in hand. Of course there are occasions when the passive voice must be used. Some particular word, usually a proper noun in news reports, must be made the subject of the sentence, and that may legitimately demand the passive voice. For instance: 'A rhinoceros ran over Bill Clinton today'. That is active (and news). But it would be better in the passive voice so that Mr Clinton has precedence over the rhino: 'Bill Clinton was run over by a rhinoceros today'.

With this proviso, sentences in the active voice should be sought by text editors, or rather text editors should seek sentences in the active voice. Ministers and officials and government reports are the worst perpetrators of the passive. Presumably it has something to do with collective responsibility, the notion that all decisions emanate from some central intelligence.

Official reports reek of the passive: it was felt necessary; in the circumstances it was considered inadvisable; the writer might be reminded; it should perhaps be pointed out; it cannot be denied; it will be recognised. In officialese it does not rain; precipitation is experienced. Often the passive is coupled cripplingly with the conditional tense so that, as Robert Graves and Alan Hodge once remarked, the decision is 'translated from the world of practice into a region of unfulfilled hypothesis'.[4] 'The Minister would find it difficult to agree if the facts were to be regarded in the light suggested'. Churchill said 'Give us the tools and we will finish the job'. Officialdom would prefer to phrase it: 'The task would be capable of determination were the appropriate tools to be made available to those concerned'.

These are no exaggerations. Every day in reporting the doings of government and the law newspapers let through a plethora of convoluted passive English. Here are a few more newspaper examples which are revised in the column on the right.

Early this morning the Automatic Telephone and Electric Company's works in Edge Lane were entered. A quantity of platinum valued at £25,000 was stolen from a safe which was burnt open. The watchman, Mr Herbert Clarke, aged 57, who is a widower residing at Albany Road, Liverpool, was coshed and tied up.

Thieves coshed the watchman and stole £25,000 worth of platinum at the automatic Telephone and Electric Co. works in Edge Lane early today. They tied up the watchman, Mr Herbert Clarke, aged 57, and burnt open the safe . . .

A petition requesting a reduced speed limit in Clay Road, between Jefferson and Calkin Road, was presented to the Henrietta Town Board last night.

Thirty two householders petitioned Henrietta Town Board last night for a lower speed limit in Clay Road, between Jefferson and Calkin roads.

The second paragraph (below) of the same report illustrates the earlier point in this section on the need for simple sentences. All too frequently a sentence with one flaw is succeeded by a sentence with a different flaw: compare the involved sentence on the left with the revised version on the right.

The Board immediately turned the petition – signed by 32 home-owners – over to its public safety committee for study and possible referral to the State Traffic Commission. Home-owners are asking that the speed limit be reduced from 50 miles per hour to 35 mph.

The Board passed the petition to its public safety committee for study and possible referral to the State Traffic Commission.

They want the 50 mph limit cut to 30 mph.

Or better still:

Thirty-two householders petitioned the Henrietta Town Board last night for the speed limit of 50 mph to be lowered to 30 mph in Clay Road between Jefferson and Calkin roads. The Board passed the petition to its public safety committee for possible referral to the State Traffic Commission.

Be Positive

Sentences should assert. Newspaper readers above all do not want to be told what is not. They should be told what is. As a general rule, a text editor should strive to express even a negative in a positive form. In each case, the version on the right is preferable:

The project was not successful.	The project failed.
The company says it will not now proceed with the plan.	The company says it has abandoned the plan.
Joe Bloggs, who escaped last week, has still not been caught.	Joe Bloggs . . . is still free.
They did not pay attention to the complaint.	They ignored the complaint.

Sometimes the editing is more difficult. Here is a sentence which attempts to be positive, but has a negative thought intruding. The subsidiary clauses do not help:

> From a military no more than from a political point of view can the successful Vietcong attacks against United States bases in South Vietnam, which killed or wounded 134 Americans, be brushed away in cursory fashion.

This can be revised directly and clearly, though still negatively (below left); it is better still to express the thought positively (right):

The successful Vietcong attacks against United States bases in South Vietnam, which killed or wounded 134 Americans, cannot be brushed away in cursory fashion either politically or militarily.	The successful Vietcong attacks against United States bases in South Vietnam, which killed or wounded 134 Americans, have both political and military significance.

The double negative in particular should be avoided: 'It is unlikely that pensions will not be raised' means 'It is likely that pensions will be raised'. Negative expression is frequent in government and company reports. Here (left) is a sentence of barely comprehensible officialese. What it possibly means (we can never be sure) is on the right:

The figures seem to us to provide no indication that costs and prices ... would not have been lower if competition had not been restricted.	The figures seem to us to provide no indication that competition would have produced higher costs and prices.

Such negative expressions are often a substitute for thought and decision. Newspapers which insist on positive expression run some risk of being accused of distortion; and of course accuracy is paramount, especially in direct quotation. But there are penalties, too, in accepting the needlessly negative expression: penalties in bemusing and hoodwinking the reader and debilitating the language. James Thurber, a passionate advocate of the positive statement, should have the last word:

> If a person is actually ill, the important thing is to find out not how he doesn't feel. He should state his symptoms more specifically – 'I have a gnawing pain here, that comes and goes', or something of the sort. There is always the danger, of course, that one's listeners will cut in with a long description of how *they* feel; this can usually be avoided by screaming.[5]

Avoid Monotony

The injunctions above, to prefer sentences which actively and positively express a single thought, may sound like a recipe for monotony. This would be to underestimate the possibilities of the English language. Setting a limit of around thirty words to the length of sentences does not mean that every sentence must be thirty words. Some can be as short as eight words. If an eight-word sentence is followed by a longer sentence, introduced by a short subsidiary clause, a variation in pace is apparent – as these last two sentences, I hope, suggest. Sentences may also vary in form, between simple and complex-compound; in function, between statements, commands, questions and exclamations; and in style, between loose, periodic and balanced. This is a rough distinction. It is worth acknowledging, however, because a succession of sentences of the same style produces a distinct effect of rhythm.

Loose sentences run on with fact after fact in natural conversational sequence.

> There were the translators in their booths, and the girl secretaries at their tables, and the peak-capped policemen at the doors, and the gallimaufry of the Press seething and grumbling and scribbling and making half-embarrassed jokes in its seats.

That sentence could end and make sense in a number of places. There is no climax. It rolls on. (It is also, incidentally, vivid and effective scene-setting in its observations.)

Periodic sentences, by contrast, retain the climax to the end. The grammatical structure in a true periodic sentence is not complete until the full stop.

> At 60 miles an hour the loudest noise in this new Rolls-Royce comes from the electric clock.

The next sentence could end earlier, but it would also be classified as a periodic sentence:

> Liverpool Street is the finest point of departure in the whole of Southern England because wherever you go from it, whether to Southend or, ultimately, to Outer Mongolia, it cannot fail to be an improvement.

Balanced sentences are works of deliberate symmetry.

> The crisis in Wall Street is a crisis of confidence.

> It will not be done by the law or Government; it cannot be done by Parliament.

Nobody can lay down a formula for varying sentences. It is part of the mystery of language. Sentences must respond to the thoughts being expressed. All that text editors who care about style can do is study the subtleties of rhythm in good authors and to take to ordinary copy a few generalisations which genius, they must understand, can always upset.

The generalisations themselves are based on the idea, again vulnerable to talent, that a prolonged succession of sentences of the same style or the same form is bad. With those cautions, it can be said that a succession of simple sentences is jerky, a succession of loose sentences relaxed or even slovenly, a succession of periodic sentences formal and stiff. The periodic sentence is emphatic but a great many following one another is wearing. The reader is always in suspense, as Mark Twain remarked about the German sentence: 'Whenever the literary German dives into a sentence, that is the last you are going to see of him till he emerges on the other side of the Atlantic with his verb in his mouth'. Or, adapting German grammar: 'Whenever a literary German into a sentence dives, will one no more of him see, till he at the other side of the Atlantic with his verb in his mouth emerges.'

A loose sentence provides relief. Brewster thought a fair proportion of periodic sentences to loose sentences to be even more formal. Readers feel they are being bullied by some arrogant swot. It sounds contrived; hell, it is contrived. But, of course, the balanced or periodic sentence provides bite to a succession of loose sentences. Particularly monotonous is a succession of loose sentences which are compound in form with two co-ordinated clauses linked by a conjunction:

> The firemen climbed their ladders and they rescued all the women. Two doctors came by ambulance and treated all the injured. The ground floor was saved but the top floor collapsed. Firemen warned the crowds while police moved them back. The hotel owner arrived and said he could say nothing.

If in doubt about the rhythm of a piece of writing, try saying it aloud. This passage comes over as a boring singsong.

Chapter Three

Words

Even without improving the structure of a sentence – often there is no time to rewrite – text editors can rescue bad copy by caring for the words. They should prefer the short word to the long, the simple word to the complex, the concrete word to the abstract. They should prefer Anglo-Saxon words to foreign. They should suspect words with prefixes and suffixes, with syllables like *pre, re, de, anti* and *isation, ousness, ation, ality*. Text editors may sometimes dawdle but they should never indulge in procrastination. They should publish an order for the release of buses, but never for the derequisition of transportation. Honorariums per diem and per annum they should forgo, but they should accept money daily and yearly. When they see bloody international conflict, they should make war with their pen. And at times they should be parsimonious, not to say miserly, with words. Nothing is so tiring to the reader as excavating nuggets of meaning from mountains of words. Nothing so distinguishes good writing as vivid economy. In a line of a Shakespearian sonnet, every syllable is suggestive.

To come down to earth there is a joke about a fishmonger which makes the point. It is an old joke, but perhaps we can regard it as sanctified by custom; and say it should be recited as an initiation ceremony for text editors.

The fishmonger had a sign which said:

FRESH FISH SOLD HERE

The fishmonger had a friend who persuaded him to rub out

the word FRESH – because naturally he wouldn't expect to
sell fish that wasn't fresh; to rub out the word HERE –
because naturally he's selling it here, in the shop; to rub out
the word SOLD – because naturally he isn't giving it away.
And finally to rub out the word FISH – because you can smell
it a mile off.

Saving space is one imperative which concentrates the text
editor's mind on saving words. It is not the most important.
Words should be saved because good English is concise. In
Herbert Spencer's dictum, the test of style is 'economy of the
reader's attention', and economy has never been better
defined than by Strunk in his short classic work.[6]

> Vigorous writing is concise. A sentence should contain no
> unnecessary words, a paragraph no unnecessary sentences,
> for the same reason that a drawing should contain no
> unnecessary lines and a machine no unnecessary parts. This
> requires not that the writer make all his sentences short, or
> that he avoid all detail and treat his subjects only in outline,
> but that every word tell.

That is the theme of this chapter, and indeed of this book.
Look after the words and style will look after itself. This does
consist in part of doing what the fishmonger's friend did. Every
word should be scrutinised. If it is not a working word, adding
sense to a sentence, it should be struck out. There are many
occasions when the mere shedding of surplus fat invigorates
the sentence. At other times concise writing requires substituting one word for another word or group of words. It is the
marriage of economy and accuracy which is wanted: the right
words in the right order.

Newspapers are supposed to be jealous of their space. Yet
every day, by slack writing, thousands of words are wasted.
(It is worst on North American and Indian newspapers; it is
somewhat better, but not much, on Australian newspapers;
and best, but a long way from what it might be, in British
newspapers.) This wastage means the loss of many columns
which could be used for news. But the central fact to grasp
about text editors is that they are not engaged simply on a
space-saving exercise. Sentences carrying dross not only take
up more space than they should. They weary eye and mind.

They obscure meaning.

Economy has to be pursued with intelligence. Indiscriminate culling is no virtue. Some writers build monstrous adjectival phrases in an effort to save on prepositions. It is breathless and unclear:

After a *No. 10 Downing Street call, Foreign Secretary Robin Cook* flew last night to Tel Aviv to seek a new *peace plan agreement.*

Did they call him?

Modifiers help economical writing, but strung together like sausages they no longer resemble prose. Some newspapers and magazines even strike out the definite and indefinite articles. It is sometimes done to avoid opening with 'a' or 'the' or beginning several sentences with the same article. The correct answer is to change some of the sentence structure. The definite and indefinite articles are essential to a sentence. They define the subject. Merely omitting them invites brutal ambiguity:

He promised delivery to the chief executive and managing director.

Did he promise it to one man with two titles or to two men?

If concise writing requires more thought than that, it can be helped by fidelity to certain principles. To call them rules would be a disservice to the flexibility of English and the ingenuity of those who write it. The principles can be 'bent' by those who know how. If a shrill note creeps into the advocacy of those principles in the following pages, this note of latitude may be summoned in relief and the dogmatism excused, I hope, as exasperation in the face of the enemy.

Use Specific Words

This means calling a spade a spade and not a factor of production. Abstract words should be chased out in favour of specific, concrete words. Sentences should be full of bricks, beds, houses, cars, cows, men and women. Detail should drive out generality. And everything should be related to human beings. The great escape should be made from 'mere intellectualism, with its universals and essences, to concrete particulars, the smell of human breath, the sound of voices, the stir of living'.[7]

Text editors should always aim to make the words bear directly on the reader. People can recognise themselves in stories about particulars. The abstract is another world. It requires effort of imagination to transport ourselves there. The writer should bring it to us. Economic and political stories abound with abstractions which seem incapable of such translation, but it can be done if the text editors will 'follow it out to the end of the line', in the words of Turner Catledge of the *New York Times*. At the end of the line of every seemingly abstract proposal there is a group and an individual.

A 'domestic accommodation improvement programme' comes out as Government money for people willing to spend more of their own on house repairs. The 'deterioration of the traffic situation' comes out as your partner caught in a traffic jam taking the children to school. An 'improvement in workers' facilities' comes out as a new canteen with sausage and eggs at £1.50; the 'increased incidence of cinemagoing' is more people going to the cinema; an 'inevitable amount of redundancy' is the sack for sixty-six workers.

This advice is on two levels. It is about abstract words and it is about abstract stories. I recognise, of course, that there are times when the general, abstract word is a saver of space, that human knowledge proceeds by the accumulation of detail into the satisfaction of a generality. There are stories which must be carried on in large part in abstractions. But in both instances the abstraction should be enriched by the particular. The abstract word should be given flesh and the abstract story should be spiced with examples. If we are invited to read about inflation we should first be aroused by a reference to prices in the shops; a report on Britain's fashion exports to

Scandinavia might better start with the dresses the Swedish women are wearing. The story may have to be carried on in terms of abstractions like exports, credits and design, but the reader should be borne up by particular examples.

Official departments all over the world are great manufacturers of the abstract. So uniform is the language, so devoid of human life, that there must be an electronic device which expunges any suggestion that people in offices with document files are trying to make decisions about other people. Wherever possible, people are rendered into abstractions or even machinery. Robert Graves and Alan Hodge tell a story of a junior official who once drafted a public announcement beginning, 'The Minister has decided to inaugurate a statistical section'.[8] It was suggested to him that the appointment of one officer scarcely constituted a section. Wisely he agreed. He altered the draft to read: 'The Minister has decided to inaugurate the nucleus of a statistical section'.

There should be a reverse electronic detector in newspaper offices which changes all the abstractions back again into people. Too many of them get into print.

The weakness of the next example (left) in an American local daily is that no readers think of themselves as violators. In the revised version (right) the first three words tell the readers that this might be about them.

Fines up to $50 and imprisonment up to 30 days could be placed against a violator if a mandatory sprinkling ban has to be imposed by the County Water Authority.

Sprinkling your lawn could put you in jail for 30 days or cost you a $50 fine if the Water Authority has to ban it.

And here is another American example:

The Blue Cross insurance director said that data represents the first instance in which utilisation experience of a large prepayment carrier in covering in-patient mental illness has been analysed.

This probably means that the figures give the first chance to see what happens when people are invited to insure heavily against going into mental hospital.

Often it is hard to know what the official language means. A negative decision is wrapped up as a positive:

> The non-compensable evaluation heretofore assigned certain veterans for their service-connected disability is confirmed and continued.

That means that veterans whose physical condition had not changed would not get any money.

Writing with specific words is generally shorter as well as more interesting. A letter-writer to *The Times* once told how he asked a Government department for a book and had been 'authorised to acquire the work in question by purchase through the ordinary trade channels', i.e. buy it.[9] On the left is an example of abstraction in a letter to me; the rewritten version on the right saves 62 words.

We are all aware of the significant need to maintain uppermost in the mind of mankind the stark need of avoiding bloody international conflict. One method by which this can be nurtured is to revive the solemn aspect of the great loss of life which has resulted from such catastrophic struggles, within the theatres of war. The attachment is associated with such an endeavour ... I would appreciate a directive to your staff to review the attachment for the purpose of orienting this information so as to evolve a reasonably newsworthy article through your newspaper toward the end stated above.

Men need reminding of the horrors of war. One way to do it is to honour those who died and I would appreciate it if you could use the attached information for a report on our ideas.

The advice to use specific language is not a trick of journalism. All great writing focuses on the significant details of human life. Compare Herbert Spencer's concoction in the left-hand column with the original language of literature:

In proportion as the manners, customs, and amusements of a nation are cruel and barbarous, the regulations of their penal code will be severe.	In proportion as men delight in battles, bull fights and combats of gladiators, will they punish by hanging, burning and the rack.

Nelson's signal 'England expects that every man will do his duty', lives on. Neither the sentence nor the English fleet would have survived if he had signalled 'It is the national expectation that all serving personnel will complete their tasks to satisfaction'.

Fowler, an acknowledged authority on English usage, would have identified that as periphrasis – putting things in a roundabout way. Other people say pleonasm, which is an awkward Greek word, or diffuseness, verbiage, circumlocution, padding or just plain wordiness. Whatever the disease, it can be checked early on because it so quickly exhibits as a symptom abstract nouns such as

> amenities, activities, operation, purpose, condition, case, character, facilities, circumstances, nature, disposition, proposition, purposes, situation, description, issue, indication, regard, reference, respect, death, connection, instance, eventuality, neighbourhood.

In advanced cases there are strings of such nouns depending on one another and on compound prepositions such as in favour of, the purposes of, in connection with, with reference to, with a view to. Here (right) is Fowler's translation of just such a statement:

The accident was caused through the dangerous *nature* of the spot, the hidden *character* of	The accident happened because the spot was dangerous, the side road hidden and there was no

the side road and the utter
absence of any warning or danger signal.

warning.

Newspapers are full of such irritants as the left-handed
version. An article picked up at random writes about natural
gas with this succession of phrases:

> Strategic question, the central issue, the open question, the
> size of the problem, the circumstances, certain questions, the
> most troublesome issue, the question of storage, the problem,
> the major decision, its immediate problem, far more real an
> issue is the question, further development, the position,
> energy picture, a question of policy, overall development,
> problems of achieving co-ordination . . .

It rounds off with: 'The issue is so far off that for the moment
it remains something of a red herring'.

What follows now is a list of other newspaper examples.
Each time a writer is about to use these abstractions, or a text
editor to pass them, each should ask what the words stand
for. Words stand for ideas, objects and feelings. Vagueness
comes from the failure to marry word to idea. What is 'an
issue', what is 'development', what are 'facilities'?

Accommodation

The theatre has seating
accommodation for 600.

The theatre seats 600.

More people than the hall
could accommodate were
crowded into . . .

An impossibility. Again it
probably means seat.

Activity

They enjoyed recreational
activity.

They liked games.

The king agreed to limited
exploration activity.

The king agreed to limited
exploration.

Basis

He agreed to play on an amateur basis.	He agreed to play as an amateur.
They accepted employment on a part-time basis.	They accepted part-time work.

Capability

The aircraft had a long-range capability.	The aircraft had a long range.

Conditions/Character

The garden was of a tangled character.	The garden was tangled.
The Irish were forced to live in slum conditions.	The Irish were forced to live in slums.
The Argentine delegate said the claims were of a far-reaching character.	The Argentine delegate said the claims were far-reaching.
The survivors were in a desperate condition.	The survivors were desperate.
Warmer conditions will prevail.	It will be warmer.
Adverse climatic conditions.	Bad weather.

Extent

The problem is of a considerable extent.	It's a big problem.

Facilities/Amenities

Shopping facilities/amenities.	Shops.

| Car parking facilities/amenities. | Car park(s). |
| Ablution facilities/amenities. | Wash-basins (rooms). |

Fact that

| In spite of the fact that ... due to the fact that ... because of the fact that ... on account of the fact that. | Although; since; or because. |

Field

| A further vital field in which Government policy is strangling initiative is the export field. | Government policy is also strangling exporters' initiative. |

Those invading barbarians, *issue* and *problem*, often in league with *the question*, run through newspapers everywhere, stealing space and laying waste to living images. This is one of the places where adjectives can be called to duty. The verb, too, can put the invaders to rout.

Issue/problem

| Another *issue* concerning the governors is *the problem* of lateness which has been increasing among the sixth form. | The governors are also worried by increasing lateness among sixth-formers. |
| On the *troublesome issue* of school meals, the council decided to delay a decision until April. | The council put off the troublesome school-meals decision until April. |

Far more real *an issue* in the long term is *the question of* what happens if further gas discoveries are made in the old or new concessions or what happens if they are not. *The position* will become clearer in several years' time when further exploration is done. Then the Gas Council must decide what to do with any further reserves and how fast it should deplete its present resources. More gas and/or faster depletion of existing gas would greatly change the energy picture in Britain. Gas would flow to the bulk markets, displacing coal as well as oil. Price would again become *a question of* policy, as would the possibilities of electricity generation.

What if more gas were found in the next few years? The Gas Council would have to decide on a rate of use, for gas could flow to the bulk market, displacing coal as well as oil. The arguments on price, and about using gas to make electricity, would be re-opened.

Operations

Building operations.

Operations is quite unnecessary. Building/mining is enough.

Participation

The tenants were seeking participation in the making of price policy.

The tenants wanted to help decide the rents.

Position

The Prime Minister said the sanctions position will then be reviewed.

The Prime Minister said sanctions will then be reviewed.

Proposition

Inflationary land costs had made it a completely uneconomic proposition to rebuild.

Rising land prices had made it too costly to rebuild.

Purposes

Land for development purposes.

Land for building.

An instrument for surgical purposes.

A surgical instrument.

A committee for administrative purposes.

A committee to run it.

Question

Over the question of supply, the major decision in the near future will be that of a third terminal.

The major supply decision in the near future will be on building a third terminal.

Situation

The unemployment situation has escalated.

Unemployment is higher.

The teacher supply situation is serious.

Teachers are scarce.

The visit of the Pope to Mexico City has created an ongoing chaos situation.

The Pope's visit has created chaos (what kind?).

An emergency meeting will be called to discuss the situation whereby 900 tins of suspect corned beef were accidentally distributed.

An emergency meeting will discuss how 900 tins of suspect corned beef were accidentally sold.

Use of

The Citizens Committee said the use of buses should be stepped up.

The Citizens Committee said more buses should be used.

The use of 37 gardens has been volunteered by their owners.

Thirty-seven residents have offered gardens.

Here is an extract which combines several examples in one paragraph.

Because of severe drought conditions, the Dansville water supply has reached a critical state. Rolland Link, superintendent of the water department, urged residents in a statement yesterday to conserve water. This could make the difference, he said, as to whether the supply remains adequate enough to serve the people of the community without allocating specific quantities at certain times of the day.

Dansville, hit by drought, is so short of water that it may be cut off for times during the day unless everybody saves more, said Rolland Link, superintendent of the water department yesterday.

You may have noticed several common sources of wordiness. An abstract noun is used with an adjective when a simple adjective will do (of a far-reaching character); and an abstract noun is added to a concrete noun (slum conditions). Another source of wordiness is the change of a live verb into an abstract noun which then requires help from an adjective and a tame verb. Take the live-verb form:

He bowled badly.

That is a sentence with (pronoun) subject, verb and adverb. The adverb 'badly' is pale but it suffices. Compare the construction when the verb 'bowled' is made into the abstract noun 'bowling'. To say the same thing we then need a subject, noun, verb and adjective – and for some reason it is usually a woollier one.

His bowling was poor.

That is weaker – and longer. The text editor should restore purity to such sentences. Verb–adverb combinations are stronger and shorter than noun–verb–adjective combinations. Two verbs are better than verb plus abstract noun.

Here are some examples. Note that when a verb is rendered into a noun a group of abstract indirect words fastens on the corpse:

They will *conduct a survey* of an oasis.	They will survey an oasis.
They voted *for the expulsion of* . . .	They voted to expel . . .
A *parade will be held for the decoration of* the six men.	The six men will be decorated at a parade.
He favoured the *reorganisation of* . . .	He favoured reorganising . . .
Police *paid a visit* to the scene of the crime	Police visited the scene of the crime.
Italy has *expressed a favourable attitude* toward *participating in studies* on the possible development of a Nato multilateral nuclear force, said a communiqué today. The United States has advocated the *creation of* such a force.	Italy favours . . . taking part/joining The United States has advocated this, or . . . advocated creating . . .

Objections have been raised by Macon County teachers.	Macon County teachers have objected.
He will be *responsible for the marshalling* of troops.	He will marshal troops.
They *made an estimation of* the value.	They estimated the value.

In the following example the text editor's antennae should have tingled at the approach of that abstract noun 'creation'. The original sentence is 44 words; the version on the right is only 26 words. Coast rescue is made the subject of the sentence because it identifies the topic at once in a more interesting way than beginning with an administrative body, the Medical Commission on Accident Prevention.

The creation of a national organisation to assist local authorities and voluntary societies and to bring a sense of urgency to the problem of rescue work around the coast of Britain is urged in the first report of the Medical Commission on Accident Prevention.	Coast rescue work urgently needs a national body to help voluntary societies and local authorities, says the first report of the Medical Commission on Accident Prevention.

Write with Nouns and Verbs

Some writers think that style means spraying adjectives and adverbs on sentences. These may give a superficial glitter. They often conceal rusty bodywork. Adjectives and adverbs should not be afterthoughts. They should be permitted only when they add precision and economy to a sentence. Every adjective should be examined to see: is it needed to define the subject or is it there for emphasis?

If something is amusing or sensational there is no need to tell the readers. The facts that amused or shocked should be described and they can apply their own adjectives. After all, as a newspaper style book years ago said, Genesis does not begin 'The amazingly dramatic story of how God made the world in

the remarkably short time of six days . . .' Yet the worst kind of
newspaper writing – said to be colourful – still cannot bear to let
through the naked noun.

> In this *sunbaked* land lying between *strife-torn* Nigeria and
> *unsettled* Sudan, *dissident* Arab tribesmen of the *3,000-strong*
> CLF are badly rattling the *French-backed 6,000-strong* French
> Army.
>   President Pompidou, who inherited the *thorny* problem of
> Chad from de Gaulle therefore faces an *acute* dilemma.
> France's prestige may suffer a *damaging* blow if the rebels win
> a *complete* victory . . .

It is extraordinary how much of this kind of writing is
improved simply by striking out the decoration, where the
adjective is not defining but merely adorning – sunbaked,
strife-torn, unsettled, dissident, thorny, acute, damaging,
complete. The other phrases – 3,000-strong, French-backed,
and 6,000-strong – are economical ways of defining the noun,
but in this sentence they merely add to the monotony of the
style. It would be better to say '. . . the 3,000-strong CLF are
badly rattling the French-backed army of 6,000.'

Sports writers are still the gaudiest. 'This was the Portugal
who crushed Brazil mercilessly from the World Cup, not the
Portugal who so gracefully lost to England'.

That sentence is weakened, not strengthened, by the
unnecessary *mercilessly*. And again: 'After a split second of
eerie silence, the *thunderous* roars told him the *wonderful*
news'. These adjectives do not define the nouns. They are
there for effect. When there is a great deal of this the result is
emasculating.

These are the sequins from one report. It was an exciting
match when you could see it for the adjectives:

> Magnificent; out of this world; their glowing skills and
> unflinching bravery; this man of magic; the thunder of
> exultant, rejoicing thousands; raked relentlessly through a
> shattered defence; an athletic immortal in his own golden age
> flicked in a shot that was a gem, a jewel of gold – no, a Crown

Jewel; the golden dream; subdued and well-thrashed; so gallant and knightly; a disgrace to a noble competition; the red-and-white cauldron of Wembley bubbled joyously; the honest joy gleaming; faltered nervously; 53 tension-haunted minutes; typically outrageous; magnificently, gloriously, wonderfully, riotously.

It recalls Quiller-Couch's advice: 'Read over your compositions and when you meet a passage which you think is particularly fine, strike it out'.

It is not simply that some of the noun–adjective combinations here are cliché. The tedium of the automatic adjectives is too irritating; overemphasis destroys credibility. Text editors should go to bed at night with Strunk's thought that the adjective has not been built that can pull a weak or inaccurate noun out of a tight place. Superlatives should be put through a second sieve for accuracy. The biggest, tallest, fastest, richest so often turns out to be the second biggest, second tallest, second fastest and second richest.

These are some adjectives which are absolute, and modifications should be challenged:

absolute, certain, complete, devoid, empty, entire, essential, external, everlasting, excellent, fatal, final, full, fundamental, harmless, ideal, immaculate, immortal, impossible, incessant, indestructible, infinite, invaluable, invulnerable, main, omnipotent, perfect, principal, pure, simultaneous, ultimate, unanimous, unendurable, unique, unspeakable, untouchable, whole, worthless.

Strike out Meaningless Modifiers

No word should be encumbered with a parasite, consuming space and debasing the language. It is absurd when the word is an absolute. An incident is either unique or it is not. It cannot be 'rather' unique. It is like being 'rather pregnant'. Sellers monopolise a market or they do not. It is meaningless to report them as having 'absolutely' (or partly) monopolised the market. If the copy says the pitch had reached 'a high degree of perfection', the text editor should pass only the fact that the pitch is near-perfect (as in truth it probably isn't perfect). If something is inevitable, it cannot be more or most inevitable. It cannot be nearly inevitable.

The 'lonely hermit' could have been nothing else. To report 'the final outcome' suggests, ridiculously, that there could have been a half-way outcome. It is no satisfaction to those turned away to read that the theatre was 'completely' full.

Many non-absolutes are weakened by qualifiers. Danger is danger, and a good strong word, but often in newspapers you see reports of 'serious' and 'real' danger. Real may be justified if an imaginary danger is contrasted; but whoever heard of an unserious danger? Sir Ernest Gowers, in his admirable book for civil servants,[10] nailed another abuse in the qualifications 'due' and 'undue'. 'The tenants were asked not to be unduly alarmed'. As Gowers says, it differs little from 'there is no cause for alarm for which there is no cause' and that hardly seems worth saying.

Here are some newspaper examples (my italics); comments or rewrites are on the right. Later on in this chapter there is a longer list of redundancies.

At an *annual* value of £1 million *a year*.	Either 'a year' or 'annual' is superfluous.
Some of the remarks made *included* . . .	The remarks included . . .
He agreed to *augment* the *existing* watchman force from five to seven men.	The watchmen must already exist, or they could not be augmented.
Michael Salter, aged 4, was scalded on both legs by *hot* water in his home today.	Hardly with cold.
Johnson discarded *two other possible alternatives* as being impracticable.	If they weren't possible, they would not be alternatives.
He said a driving test was an *essential condition*.	If it's a condition it must be essential: He said a driving test was essential.

| A *growing* gulf seems to be *developing*. | A gulf seems to be developing. |

A further source of wordiness is in descriptions of quantities or measure. Simplicity and directness call for *many, some, few, most, heavy, light, short, long*. What text editors often see on copy is *in the majority of instances, in a number of cases, a large proportion of*. They should never hesitate to change these prolix forms. 'A large percentage of failures' should be changed to 'many failures'. They should also always be ready to question modifying and deprecating phrases. Sir Ernest Gowers detected that writers feel there is something indecent about the unadorned adjectives 'few', 'short', and so on. Adverbial dressing gowns are thrown around these naked adjectives – *unduly, relatively, comparatively*. Yet often there is nothing to compare, and the qualification is meaningless as well as space-consuming. Check: is there a real comparison in the story? If there is not, off with the dressing gown!

Text editors should also suspect *in more or less degree, somewhat, to a certain extent, to a degree, small in size, quite*, and that news accretion *mark*: 'The death roll has topped the 300 mark'. Why 'mark'? It should be reported: 'More than 300 have died'.

Avoid Needless Repetition

The most noticeable needless repetition is repetition of source. Once the report has identified the source of the information there is no need to keep parading it. This is an ailment in American newspapers; it is an epidemic. Only if identity is in doubt need it be repeated.

The United States is ready to sell the Soviet Union 200 bushels of wheat for $380 million in cash, *U.S. Secretary of Agriculture*, Orville Freeman, indicated yesterday. *Freeman* cautioned that no decision had been made. *The agriculture secretary* came to Harrisburg following a meeting with the President on the wheat sale question. Though *Freeman* said no deal had been closed . . .

The constant drip of the source is like Chinese water torture. Nowhere does it seem to have occurred to the text editor that there is such a thing as a pronoun. And again:

Fire early today wrecked the marina in Brooman, causing an estimated £10,000 of damage, *police said. The fire* destroyed the main building and an *undetermined number* of boats, *said police*.

'Police said'. Do we doubt them?

It destroyed the main building and *some* boats.

Some text editors and reporters exhibit in their copy the kind of phobia that makes us go downstairs ten times to check that the light is off. They have a nagging doubt that the reader has not quite got the point – so they keep going on about it. Once is enough for most pieces of information. When the information is merely incidental its repetition is doubly irritating. Here's an example from the *New York Times*:

A disappointment among the data is that while infant mortality has continued to decline, and is almost at the goal, *there remains a great disparity between the rate for whites and for blacks*. The death rate among black infants is about twice that for whites, Dr. Richmond said, and it has been getting that way for decades.

The italicised words in the original story tell us nothing. So it boils down to:

A disappointment is that while infant mortality has continued to decline, almost to the goal, the death rate among black infants is about twice that for whites . . .

Here is a report, from an English provincial daily, of a speech at a factory opening:

A Government grant to promote publicity for the North-East will be announced in Parliament today.

This was revealed by Mr George Chetwynd, Director of the North-East Development Council, after he had opened a new 300,000 particle board plant at the Willington Quay factory of the Tyne Board Company Limited yesterday.

'I cannot disclose the amount of the grant until it has been presented to Parliament', said Mr Chetwynd. 'But it will be a highly satisfactory figure. It will enable us to do a much bigger and better job in the area than we have been able so far.'

The factory which Mr Chetwynd was opening . . .

While Mr Chetwynd declared the plant open in the presence of . . .

Mr Chetwynd, before pushing the button to start the new plant, said he believed this would be a turning point in the future of Tyneside . . .

The new plant opened by Mr Chetwynd will produce . . .

Does anybody want to argue about whether Mr Chetwynd opened that plant?

Why, in the next story, do we have the repetition of 'people'? If it were a story about asthma striking elephants and people, it would be worth making the point. Otherwise it can be left understood after the first reference that the report is about people. Better still, the noun 'people' should be translated into individuals – elderly men, or young children, or women and children. The meaning of the version on the right is clear and it saves 17 words.

The Cuban radio reported today that three more *people* have died from a peculiar type of asthma attack that struck down more than 200 *people* in Havana. Five *people* died of asthma on Wednesday because of a freak atmospheric condition, according to the radio which was monitored in Miami.

Three more people died from a peculiar asthma that has struck down more than 200 in Havana, says Cuban Radio. Five died of asthma on Wednesday night because of freak atmospheric conditions.

Avoid Monologophobia

The world is indebted to Theodore Bernstein of the *New York Times* for this term which has the virtue that it is ugly enough to spring out of the page and hit you. A monologophobe, says Mr Bernstein,[11] is a guy who would rather walk naked in front of Saks Fifth Avenue than be caught using the same word more than once in three lines of type. Some of the writers stricken with monologophobia are the ones who had an aversion (in the preceding section) to the humble pronoun; their remedy is to invent another noun. Here are two examples:

> Palestine's Arabs swore before the United Nations special Palestine committee today to drench the soil of that tiny country 'with the last drop of our blood' in opposing any big power scheme to partition the Holy Land.

> The Minister of Transport, Mrs Barbara Castle, today opened a new motorway extension to Preston. The red-headed non-driver said two more extensions were planned and by 1970 it would be possible to drive the 150 miles without entering a single town. The Minister, who sits for Blackburn, travelled . . .

One country is given three different names: Palestine, that tiny country, and the Holy Land. The insertion of the synonym 'red-headed non-driver' for Mrs Castle leaves readers wondering if they are still reading about the same person. Fowler, who called this 'elegant variation', thought minor novelists and reporters were the real victims 'first terrorised by a misunderstood taboo, next fascinated by a newly discovered ingenuity, and finally addicted to an incurable vice'.[12] The fatal influence is certainly the advice given to young writers never to use the same word twice in a sentence. A monologophobe would edit the Bible so that you would read, 'Let there be light and there was solar illumination'.

The leather sphere seems to have disappeared from the sports pages, but monologophobia strikes in many places. In court reports there is a bewildering alternation of the names of people with their status as 'defendant' or 'plaintiff'. It is better to stick to names throughout:

> The lorry driver said he was going towards Finchley when he saw the deceased suddenly walk into the road.

The most frequent symptom of monologophobia in British newspapers is the aversion to the good verb 'to say'. According to what you read, people don't *say* things any more they:

> point out that, express the opinion, express the view, indicate, observe, state, explain, report, continue, add, declare, comment . . .

People don't *tell* other people things. They inform, notify and communicate. The worst variation is the casual smear when the text editor or writer substitutes 'admit' for 'say'. To 'admit' something in public has different overtones from simply saying it: it implies confession for some wrong. That verb should rarely be used outside court reports. If someone does not deny a point put to him it is better to say 'he agreed that . . .'

The verb 'to claim' is another bad synonym: it implies that we have our doubts. All such variants should be used only when they express meaning more accurately. Let someone 'affirm' a fact only when it has been in doubt. Never let anybody 'declare' what is clearly an informal remark. Emphatically it does not mutilate the language to use 'he said' twice in a report. What does mutilate the language is to say 'he explained' when the man is clearly not explaining anything at all.

Monologophobia is aggravated by the other writing sin of converting a verb into an abstract noun, or transforming a specific noun into an abstract noun. People don't hope; they 'express hope'. They don't believe; they 'indicate belief'. And here is an example from an evening newspaper monologophobe:

> With more staff available for after-care at home, the Swindon
> Maternity Hospital, dealing with an increasing number of
> *admissions*, will be able to send some mothers home earlier.

Are the 'admissions' the same people as the 'mothers'? Why,
yes; no fathers have been patients at Swindon Maternity
Hospital. So the report should have conceded at once that it is
about mothers – a specific and human noun clearly more
interesting than the abstract 'admissions': 'Some mothers will
go home earlier from busy Swindon Maternity Home'.

That is what the report is about. But such reasoning takes
time and patience, and some monologophobes are more
readily cunning in creating bewilderment for the reader.

Monologophobia is related also to over-attribution (see p.
48). Even the pronoun cannot redeem this fault. Part of the
trouble is often inept handling of reported speech. But where
there is only one source it is clear who is speaking and the
text editor should strike out from copy those 'he continued',
'he added', and 'he explained' variations.

> There is no question of any of GEC's 2,000 workers being
> demoted because they fail an aptitude test, said Mr. E.M.
> Cowley, the firm's divisional manager, last night.
>
> Aptitude tests, *he explained*, were part of the firm's normal
> routine. They were to see if people were fitted for promotion,
> not to see if anyone should move down, *he continued*.
>
> 'If there are openings we believe in considering the available
> resources first', *said Mr. Cowley*.

The words in italics could all be deleted without difficulty
here. After 'move down' in the second paragraph, there
would be a colon followed by the quotation.

Watch the Prepositions

There are three troubles: the circumlocutory preposition; the
prepositional verb; and pedantry.

The circumlocutory preposition is a fluffy substitute for the
single preposition which gives the meaning as clearly. The

worst offenders are in the field of, in connection with, in order to, in respect of, so far as . . . is concerned. All sorts of things are found flourishing in the field of: in the field of public relations, in the field of breakfast cereals, in the field of book publishing, in the field of nuts and bolts . . .

'Field' has a very proper association with battle, chivalry and war (hence 'Never in the field of human conflict . . .'), but the word is usually superfluous when used generally. These are newspaper examples, with my amendments and comments on the right:

This and other developments in medical science are at the base of a dialogue now proceeding in the Roman Catholic Church *concerning* its attitude to medical aids *in the field of birth control*.	This and other developments in medicine are at the base of a dialogue in the Roman Catholic Church *on* its attitude to medical aids *in birth control*.
More progress has been made *in the case of* Southern Rhodesia.	More progress has been made *with* Southern Rhodesia.
Arnold Wesker's 'Chips with Everything' is a bitter attack on the class system that leaves much to be desired *as far as satisfactory drama is concerned*.	i.e. dramatically.
The rates vary *in relation* to the value of the building.	The rates vary *with* the value of the building.
In connection with a recruiting exhibition at Scarborough, the famous team of Royal Corps of Signals motor cyclists gave a display.	*As part of* a recruiting exhibition at Scarborough . . .

Prepositional verbs grow like toadstools. Once there was credit in facing a problem. Now problems have to be faced *up to*. The prepositions add nothing to significance. To say one met somebody is plain enough; to say one met *up with* them adds nothing and takes two further words. So it is with win (out); consult (with); stop (off); check (up on); divide (up); test (out).

The prepositions are American parasites. Mostly they can be deleted or replaced by a simple alternative verb. Call is better than stop off at; fit, reach or match will serve better than measure up to. There is strength in a few prepositional verbs such as get on with; go back on; take up with. But most of the modern currency is American dumping which weakens English. It is a poor day when it is no longer considered enough to say honesty pays. Inflation requires honesty to pay *off*; and we are the worse for it.

The third trouble with the preposition is the influence of the pedants. They insist that prepositions must never end a sentence. The preposition, it is said, should always be placed before the word it governs. This is an attempt to impose on English some of the rigour of Latin and it will not do. Shakespeare wrote of the 'heartache and the thousand natural shocks that flesh is heir to'. That is good English. Fowler dealt trenchantly with the pedantry of the preposition but it flourishes in official, legal and police court language. Policemen are apt to say 'the water into which he dived', and lawyers 'The contract into which he entered'.

Pedants would frown on 'The pilot said it depended on what they were guided by'. Trying to tuck that preposition 'by' back where it is supposed to belong produces a sentence everyone ought to frown on: 'The pilot said it depended on by what they were guided'. As Fowler observed, 'too often the lust of sophistication, once blooded, becomes uncontrollable', and you end up with 'The pilot said that depended on the answer to the question as to by what they were guided'.

The best advice is to forget Latin and accept what sounds most comfortable to the educated ear. It sounds better to say the prepositional pedants are people not worth listening to; better than to say these pedants are people to whom it is not worth listening.

Care for Meanings

'When *I* use a word', Humpty-Dumpty told Alice, 'it means just what I choose it to mean, neither more nor less'. The Humpties of the written word present two problems to text editors. Writers give new meanings to old words; and new expressions are being created all the time.

Disinterested is often used in an ambiguous way. Its correct meaning is not bored or uninterested, but impartial or unselfish. But when we read 'The President said he would be disinterested in the conflict', what are we to understand? It should mean the President will stay interested but neutral. To most of us it will. But to some – and perhaps to the writer – it means the President is bored with the conflict and will take no further interest. Here text editors should be sticklers for accuracy. They should not let a good word down. But what shall be their attitude to blurb, kickback, crack down, beat it, to bus, killjoy, cheapskate, gatecrash? It would be a mistake to maintain the pedantry required to protect the old words. The English language has a genius for such vivid new idiom, particularly in American hands. This is an act of creation, the combination of familiar verbs, prepositions, pronouns and conjunctions into rich new images.

It is very different from the act of distortion which destroys disinterested, alibi, immigrant, enervated, chronic and so on. The essential difference is that there is often universal understanding of new idiom and the best of it fills a real need. It comes into being precisely to describe an idea more economically and vividly than the existing vocabulary allows: 'He put it across'; 'He is a killjoy'; 'They do it for kicks'.

It is easy enough for text editors to admit old words on condition that they are travelling in their own name: there are dictionaries to detect impostors. It is harder to verify the passports of new expressions. Webster's dictionary in its 1961 third edition argued that almost anything goes if somebody uses it. But that is too loose. 'Simple illiteracy', as Dwight Macdonald said, 'is no basis for linguistic evolution'.

There are two tests: Does the expression represent a new

idea? Does it do it more briefly or precisely than the old expressions? Much new idiom will for these reasons vanish after a temporary popularity; and text editors should help it on its way. Not all contemporary catchwords are clear signals: some modern ones seem, indeed, only to add to the confusion. Does 'uptight' convey proximity or a state of mind? Does 'cool' refer to the temperature or mean simply 'I like it'? 'A depressed socioeconomic area' says no more than what 'slum' said more briefly; transportation is longer than transport; so is for free instead of free; to author is not better than to write; senior citizen is longer and more pretentious than old man or pensioner; finalisation is a rough usurper for finish or completion; telly is longer than TV. The suffix 'wise' as in bookwise and verbwise should also, wisdomwise, have a short life; but in all these judgments humility is in order. Our language is not the language of Chaucer, and the good words mob, bamboozle, sham, bully, banter and uppish were all originally denounced as vulgar slang by the great Jonathan Swift.

Here are some of the words commonly misused in newspapers. This is a taste of the range of abuse. There are other sources,[13] and the slightest whiff of doubt should send text editors to the dictionary.

Affect: Confused, as verb, with effect. To effect is to bring about, to affect is to change. To say 'it effected a change in his attitude' is correct; so is 'it affected his attitude'. To combine the two – 'It affected a change in his attitude' – is wrong.

Alibi: Means 'otherwise' or elsewhere, but is confused with excuse, which is a wider term. Alibi means being somewhere else when the deed was done.

Alternatives: wrongly used for choices. If there are two choices, they are properly called alternatives. If there are more than two they are choices.

Anticipate: Confused with expect. To expect something is to think it may happen; to anticipate is to prepare for it, to act in advance. To say a fiancée expects marriage is correct; to say she is anticipating it is defamatory.

Anxious: Best preserved as meaning troubled, uneasy. It is a corruption to use it as a synonym for eager or desirous.

Breach: To break through or break a promise or rule. But to breech, with an e, means to put a boy into trousers.

Causal: Perhaps the hardest word to get into a newspaper – everybody thinks it ought to be 'casual': it means relating to a cause, and is often used in philosophical or medical contexts.

Celebrant: Confused with celebrator. A celebrant presides over a religious rite.

Chronic: Confused with acute or severe, medically the opposite. It means long-lasting (from the Greek *chronos* – time). An acute illness comes to a crisis, a chronic one lingers.

Cohort: Confused with henchman. A cohort is a company of warriors, or people banded together. You cannot sensibly say 'Smith came with his cohort Brown'.

Comprise: Confused with composes. Comprise means to contain or include. The whole comprises the parts. The United States comprises 50 states; 50 states do not comprise the United States. Contains, includes or consists of are preferable.

Cozening: Confused with cosseting. To be cosseted is to be petted or pampered. To be cozened, on the other hand, is to be cheated or defrauded.

Credible: Confused with credulous. A credible man is one you can believe; a credulous man, however, is too ready to believe others.

Crescendo: Confused with climax. It indicates a passage of music to be played with increasing volume. Figuratively, it means to rise to a climax. Thus the cliché 'rise to a crescendo' is nonsense.

Decimate: Confused with destroy. By derivation decimation means killing one in ten. Today it is often used figuratively to mean very heavy casualties, but to say 'completely decimated' or 'decimated as much as half the town' simply will not do.

Dependent/dependant: A dependant is a person who is dependent on another for support.

Deprecate: Confused with depreciate. An MP was reported as depreciating sterling as a world currency. That means he had it devalued, which is the job of the Governor of the Bank of England. What the MP did was deprecate sterling as a world currency, i.e. plead against the policy.

Dilemma: Confused with problem. If you have a problem you do not know what to do. There may be many solutions. If you have a dilemma you have a choice of two courses of action, both unfavourable.

Discomfit: Confused with discomfort. To discomfort is to make uneasy; to discomfit is to defeat or rout. Discomfort is either verb or noun; the noun of discomfit is discomfiture.

Disinterested: Confused with uninterested, but instead means impartial, i.e. not having a sectional or vested interest.

Enervate: Confused with energise. It means the opposite. To enervate is to weaken, to energise is to invigorate. The *New York Times* did Mr Arnold Weinstock an injustice: 'Two years later after a power struggle at the top, Mr Weinstock emerged as managing director at the age of 38. He then enervated his company with his now-familiar technique.'

Entomb: Confused with entrap. The entrapped miners may be alive; entombed miners are dead, i.e. in a tomb.

Exotic: Means 'of foreign origin' and only by weak analogy 'glamorous' or 'colourful'.

Explicit: Confused with implicit. It means the opposite. An explicit understanding has been expressed. An implicit understanding has been left implied, not expressly stated.

Flaunt: Confused with flout. 'We must not allow the American constitution to be flaunted in this way . . .' means we must not allow it to be paraded, displayed or shown off. That is the meaning of to flaunt. What the speaker intended to say was that the constitution should not be flouted, i.e. mocked or insulted.

Forego: Confused with forgo. Forego means to go before in time or place – think of the final e in before. To forgo is to give up, or relinquish.

Fulsome: Confused with full. Fulsome means overfull, extravagant, to the point of insincerity. To say 'He gave her fulsome praise' is to make a comment on its merits.

Further: Confused with farther. Keep farther for distances – thus far and no farther – and further for additions (furthermore).

Immigrant: In Britain it has become a euphemism for a coloured person. It should be rescued for what it is – anyone from abroad who has come to settle. It is not the same, either, as alien. An immigrant is a settler, an alien may be a visitor.

Inflammable: Confused with inflammatory. Words may be inflammatory – they may cause metaphorical fire – but they are not inflammable. The paper on which they are written, however, may be combustible, or liable to burn, and therefore inflammable (flammable would be better, but does not have wide currency).

Invaluable: Confused with valueless, which is the opposite. The invaluable stone cannot be priced because it has so much value it is priceless.

Involved: Overworked and misused. Involved is best preserved to mean tangled, complicated. It should not replace verbs like include, entail, implicate, affect, imply, engage. We should say 'the scheme *entails* knocking down ten houses'; 'four hundred workers are *engaged* in the strike' – or 'four hundred are *on strike* or *affected*'; and so-and-so is *implicated* in the crime', and so on.

Judicious: Confused with judicial. Judicial means connected with a court of law, judicious means wise. Not all judicial decisions are judicious.

Lay: Confused with lie. Hens lay eggs, people lay traps and lay down burdens. The dog lies down on the ground; let sleeping dogs lie. People lie down themselves, lie in prison for years and lie in state. Much of the confusion is because the past tense of lie is lay. The correct forms are lie-lay-lain; lay-laid-laid.

Less: Confused with fewer. Less is right for quantities – less coffee, less sugar. It means a less amount of. Fewer is right for comparing numbers – fewer people, fewer houses, less dough means fewer loaves. Nobody would think of saying fewer coffee, fewer sugar, but every day somebody writes less houses.

Licence: the noun is confused with the verb license (not US).

Literally: Confused with metaphorically. This provides umpteen nonsense statements. We were literally flooded with books. He literally went up in smoke. He literally exploded in anger. Literally means exactness to the letter. To say he literally went up in smoke means he was burned, exploded, etc.

Livid: Confused with angry: livid means lead-coloured, but some angry people are very pale.

Loan: Confused with lend. Loan is the noun, lend the verb. The moneylender lends, and so makes you a loan.

Luxuriant: Confused with luxurious. The film star can have a luxurious car which is full of luxury, but not a luxuriant car. That means a car which is producing abundantly, growing profusely. Luxuriant refers to something that grows.

Mitigate: Confused with militate. It is said, incorrectly, that an act will mitigate against a settlement. But mitigate means to appease, to soften. It is militate which is intended – to make war or tell against. Think of military.

None: Means not one or no one and takes a singular verb (just as other distributive expressions like each, each one, everybody, everyone, many a man, nobody).

Oblivious: Confused with ignorant of. Oblivious is from the Latin *oblivium*, meaning forgetfulness. If you are ignorant of something, nobody told you. If you are oblivious, somebody told you but you let it slip into oblivion.

Practice: In English usage, practice is the noun, to practise, practising, practised the verb.

Principle: Confused with principal. The principal is first in rank or importance; principle is a fundamental source or moral conviction. The Principal has principles.

Protagonist: Confused with antagonist and with champion. Literally it means the leading character in a drama; it does not mean advocate or champion. Somebody can be a protagonist without advocating anything. An antagonist is an active opponent.

Quota: It means an allotted number, akin to rationing. To say New York had its full quota of rain means somebody was assigning various amounts of rain to New York.

Recrudescence: Confused with resurgence. 'There was a resurgence of loyalty' is right. To say 'there was a recrudescence of loyalty' is to misuse a good metaphor. Recrudescence means the breaking out of a sore or disease and it should be used, figuratively, for disagreeable events.

Regalia: Regal means of or by kings, and regalia means the insignia of royalty. Royal regalia is therefore tautologous and 'the regalia of a bishop' is contradictory. Freemasons, however, have adopted the term for their insignia.

Replica: Confused with reproduction. A replica is a duplicate or exact copy made by the original artist; anyone can attempt a reproduction.

Stationary: Confused with stationery. Stationary, adjective, is static; stationery, noun, is writing materials.

Synthetic: Is not a synonym for false as in 'a synthetic excuse'. It means 'placed together', from the Greek *syn*, together, and *tithemi*, place. Think of synthetic rubber, made by placing its constituents together, rather than by extraction from a plant.

Titivate: Confused with titillate. To titivate is to adorn or smarten. The seducer may do that to himself, but he will seek to titillate the victim – to excite pleasantly.

Transpired: Wrongly used to mean something merely happened. It comes from the Latin *spirare*, breathe. To transpire is to emit through the lungs or skin and, figuratively, is best used for when some fact, especially a secret, oozes out.

Urbane: Confused with urban. Urban means of a city; urbane means courteous, suave. Not all people in urban areas are urbane.

Viable: Misused as a substitute for feasible or practicable. Viable means capable of independent life – a viable foetus, or seed, or, figuratively, scheme.

Vice: It would be a pity if it became a synonym for sex. There are many vices. It should be used as the opposite of virtue.

Virtually: Incorrectly used to mean nearly all, e.g. virtually all the chocolates were eaten. Virtually usefully means in essence or effect 'as contrasted to formality'. 'He's virtually the manager.' He does not have the title but he manages the business.

While: It means, strictly, during the time that; it is also tolerable as although, but. (While seeing your point, I cannot give you permission.) But it is nonsense to use while as a synonym for *and* or *whereas*. 'Mr Jones is the president while Mr Smith is the secretary', means Jones is president during the time that Smith is secretary. It means they must resign together. Sir Alan Herbert exposes the absurdity: 'The curate read the first lesson while the rector read the second'.

Avoid Clichés

The first million writers (or cave painters) who told us about their 'thorny problems' used metaphor vividly. The prickliness of their position was plain to see. Some time after that the prickliness became less apparent; excessive use of the metaphor blunted it. The adjective had become a passenger. The cliché had been born.

To enjoin writers never to use a cliché is to anticipate a definition and to seek the impossible. Perhaps we can define a cliché as any phrase 'so hackneyed as to be knock-kneed and spavined'.[14] There are a lot of them about. There are no doubt some in this book. It is impossible to ban them, because they serve a natural inclination. At best they are a form of literary shorthand, with the attraction of economy. Is it better to say 'he was bustling and industrious' than 'he was busy as a bee'? What text editors can do with clichés in copy is to ration them, and tolerate only the best. They are worst when they seek to enliven dull patches; but they do nothing of the sort. The imagery is dead. The worst are wasteful, too. 'In deadly earnest' says no more than 'in earnest', 'to all intents and purposes' says no more than 'virtually'. In my list (pp. 87–90) are the commonest newspaper clichés which should all be treated with hostility.

Story Sources of Wordiness

Suggestions for conciser and more human news stories have been set out in terms of words and sentences. Certain kinds of news stories throw up their own wordiness and the way these stories should be edited will be examined now.

Reported speech

Editing speeches and documents requires an adroit combination of direct and indirect reporting. Direct speech ('Accordingly I shall not seek and I will not accept the nomination of my party for another term as your President') has the advantage of accuracy and liveliness. It has the disadvantage of taking a lot more space. Reported speech (Mr Johnson said he will not run again) is the great economiser.

The reporting of official documents and other statements is best done in third-person summary: to rely on direct quotation is to miss the opportunity to render officialese into economic English which touches people's lives. Speeches, too, require third-person reporting, but not as much. The more important the speech, the more space should be given to direct quotation. If only one section of a speech is newsworthy, it is preferable to give that whole section in quotes in original sequence and indicate in third person that other subjects were discussed. It is very frustrating for the reader to have only the third-person summary of a key passage. This is perhaps the worst defect of modern reporting of speeches, a reflection perhaps of shortage of space, lack of seriousness and the failure of the young journalist to master the basic tool of shorthand: cassette recorders are fine but with a long speech it can be maddening trying to find the exact quote you want.

Direct quotes, then, should be preferred – but when it is necessary to use third person for summarising, it is necessary to use it ruthlessly and not render into third person the speaker's verbosity, circumlocutions, cough and all.

Third-person reporting is a skill. It demands both fidelity to the material and a determination to use indirect speech as a knife to cut through to the real content. Fidelity demands that interpretation should be scrupulously accurate. If a speaker makes a statement which is a rebuke, that will be self-evident from the context. If it is not self-evident, then there must be some doubt; but it is dangerous for text editors to resolve the doubt by saying so-and-so rebuked or attacked or criticised. The speaker's words should speak for themselves.

The third-person summary should be true to the meaning and spirit of the material. If the news point is taken from a few minutes or passages at the end, that should be indicated: 'Mr X's comments on incomes came in the last few minutes of a speech mainly defending government policy . . .'

There is no doubt that on occasion clumsy reported speech can do violence to a speaker's tone and ideas. Sometimes the articulate are rendered incoherent and a grand survey is turned into a mish-mash of unrelated thoughts. Here is a piece of reported speech which is extreme but has the virtue of encompassing most of the defects found singly elsewhere:

When the Language Commission was appointed for the purpose of considering the various steps to be taken under Article 344, Mr Subramaniam continued, the Government of Madras had to consider the whole question and give it a lead and submit a memorandum to the Commission. He pointed out that the one point which was considered by them more than once was whether they should seek a Constitutional amendment or they should take the stand that if only the safeguards in Part 17 were properly formulated and worked in the proper spirit it would be possible to meet the various problems arising out of the language problem. They came to the conclusion that it would be possible for them to have all the safeguards worked out under the provisions of the Constitution. As a matter of fact, this matter was again considered when the Language Commission had submitted its report because the Commission had almost ignored most of the major recommendations made by the State Government in their memorandum.

They again came to the conclusion that it might not be necessary to press for a Constitutional amendment if only the other authorities which might be considering the question, namely the Parliamentary Committee, which had to be constituted to consider the recommendations of the Commission, also later the President, who had to pass an order based on the recommendations of the Language Commission, and the Parliamentary Committee, took note of what they would be submitting further. It was only on that basis that the second memorandum was prepared and submitted to the Parliamentary Committee, they said. Mr Subramaniam said fortunately for them, the Parliamentary Committee had taken note of the various points they had made in their Second Memorandum and almost accepted all the recommendations they had made.

There is no place in a newspaper for the speaker's wordiness – 'for the purpose'; 'as a matter of fact'; 'came to the conclusion'; 'recommendations they had made'; 'arising out of'. These are understandable, if unfortunate, in speech; as written words they are glaringly superfluous. Everything in that report is preserved in this third-person version of the speech – which saves about 200 words.

Mr Subramaniam said that when the Language Commission was appointed to consider the steps necessary under Article 344, the Madras Government had to give its views. Madras debated whether it should seek a Constitutional amendment or whether the problems could be met by observing the safeguards of Part 17 in a proper spirit. They decided there were enough safeguards in the existing Constitution.

The Language Commission 'almost ignored' most of the major recommendations of the State Government, said Mr

Subramaniam, but Madras again decided it might not be necessary to press for a Constitutional amendment if only their recommendations would be heeded by the Parliamentary Committee and by the President who had to act on the report of both the Language Commission and the Parliamentary Committee.

Fortunately the Parliamentary Committee had accepted most of the State Government's recommendations.

It is possible, of course, to boil this down even further:

Mr Subramaniam recalled that Madras had decided to put its trust in Part 17. They had stuck to this view even when the Language Commission 'almost ignored' them because they knew they would get a hearing from the Parliamentary Committee on the Language Commission's report. They did and the Parliamentary Committee had accepted almost all the points Madras made.

Here is an example from a South African newspaper. No doubt Dr Donges did say what was reported, but it would have done no violence to his meaning for the text editor to put into print the version on the right:

Dr Donges said he was pleased to say it could not be denied that South Africa had made important progress in the economic sphere.

Dr Donges said South Africa had made important economic progress.

Where a speaker or report changes subject the reporter often strives for continuity by using clumsy transition phrases: 'Turning to the question of . . .', 'Dealing with the subject of . . .' or 'Referring to the . . .'. It is far better to deal briskly with changes of subject, especially lower in a report, with simple phrases: 'On sterling, Mr Hague said . . .' And again, 'Of President Clinton, Tony Blair said . . .' Alternatively, in tighter editing, the text editor can mark separate paragraphs on the copy in this style:

These were the report's other comments:

KOSOVO: 'We must continue to support Nato'.

OVERSEAS AID: The time had not arrived for reductions.

Similarly where text editors are dealing with a complicated bill or White Paper, they should seek to enumerate key points, listing items 1, 2, 3 and so on in separate paragraphs.

A speaker should always be identified early in the story by name and status (Mr J. Bloggs, of the Meat Grinders' Guild) and later by location (speaking at a mass rally at the Albert Hall, London). Where there is more than one speaker, each new speaker should have a new paragraph – beginning with the name. There is no other way. If the name comes anywhere other than in the first line the reader will assume that the previous speaker is still on his feet.

Direct quotation

Good quotes are the lifeblood of the news columns. In ordinary news stories when people are interviewed they do not normally come out with a series of neat, colourful sentences which sum up the whole action. A few of their quotes have to be woven into a story in reported speech. But the good quotes must be treasured; they have the pungency of personal experience. The reporter back from the fire weakened the story by the third-person summary, 'The merchant foresaw the prospect of ruin', which was inferior to (and longer than) what the man actually said: 'This could ruin me'.

The set speech should provide a higher proportion of salvageable quotations than the casual interview, and higher still than the official report. Quotations from speeches should be given to:

● Support statements given in the intro in reported speech
● Capture the subtleties of important or controversial statements, or ones that show a speaker's richness of language

- Report lively exchanges between speaker and heckler, judge and lawyer, and so on
- Change the pace in a long section of third-person reporting

Here is the first category in practice:

> Mr Sidney Silverman, the veteran left-winger, who has been in trouble with his party chiefs more than once, yesterday condemned as undemocratic Mr Wilson's discipline speech to back-benchers.
>
> Mr Silverman, in a letter to the chief whip, said Mr Wilson's doctrine on the submission of Labour back-benchers was 'the most dangerous attack on social democracy in this country in my time'.

The quote there is vital to support the intro: indeed it ought to have been in the intro. But what is rarely necessary is to give the reader in quotes in the body of the story the identical statement that has already been offered in third-person reporting; or vice-versa:

> Canon L. John Collins, Precentor at St. Paul's Cathedral, said in his sermon yesterday: 'I cannot refrain from commenting upon the extraordinary service of thanksgiving which took place in St. Vedast's in the City, on Thursday, attended by the Board of Courtaulds and a hundred or so of their employees'.
>
> He asked what connection the service could have with the Christian gospel which condemned outright the system which made possible the fight between ICI and Courtaulds.
>
> 'One must ask what connection the service can have with the Christian gospel which condemns outright the whole system which makes possible such a fight'.

Once is enough, twice is a feast, three times a felony.

> Mickey Mantle, the New York Yankees' 100,000-dollar-a-year outfielder with the dime store legs said yesterday – the eve of the World Series opener – that he may be forced into a post-session operation on his left leg.

> 'If it doesn't get any better', said Mantle before taking a workout at Yankee Stadium, '*it'll have to be operated on*. It's been getting stronger day by day, but as it stands now, we think *it's going to be operated on*'.

Here is an example which uses both direct quotation and reported speech wastefully:

> Plans call for *the construction of* a one-storey ambulance headquarters building, for which materials and labour will be donated by contractors, Gates Police Chief William Stauber said.
> 'Several sites, I'm happy to say, have been offered free of charge for the headquarters structure and we are now *in the process of determining which would be the best location*'.

Why should Police Chief William Stauber be allowed to gulp mouthfuls of newsprint with 'in the process of determining which would be the best location' etc., when they are simply thinking of where to build the thing?

There are two final cautions. Text editors should not alter quotes and reporters should not invent them. By invention I do not mean the completely fictitious quotation dreamed up by Lunchtime O'Booze, which is rare, but the temptation to attribute to direct quotation what is only an acknowledgment of a question. If the words are in quotes they must be the words the speaker has said personally. That is the point of the marks. If the speaker has merely said 'Yes' to a long colourful question, then the report should only say 'He (or she) agreed that . . .'. It is permissible for reporter or text editor to change the order of sentences to make a statement more coherent, but the sense and individual wording must not be altered.

The commonest fault is to have people saying things more emphatically than they did. The text editor's temptation is to edit the quotations produced by the reporter, which gives a second risk of distortion. Deletion within quotes is justified only if the omission of the words is indicated by dots. It has to be judged carefully. Qualifications should not be dropped.

Alteration of words within quotes is inexcusable. If the quotes do not add anything the answer is not to improve the quotation but to delete it altogether and revert to reported speech or to pick up only the attractive phrase or word in quotes in a combination of reported speech and quotes.

> Prince Philip warned that the selfish approach to conservation would lead to our generation being 'loathed and despised by all who come after us till the end of time'.

That is the limit of tolerance. Once words are enclosed in quotations they should be the words the speaker actually said.

Here is a report as it arrived (left) and as it was edited:

The Town Clerk said: 'The committee reluctantly decided to defer consideration of this request and to ask the owners to meet them to discuss the reasons for, and the implications of, the owner's proposal.'

The Town Clerk said: 'The committee reluctantly decided to ask the owners to meet them to discuss the proposal.'

The meaning has been subtly changed – and the quotation marks are a lie. It is surprising what text editors, in a rash of confidence, will sometimes do. In another report which appeared a bishop referred to 'a financial crisis in the diocese'. The text editor inserted the word 'grave' in the quotes, reasoning that a crisis must be grave, and then carried the word 'grave' into the heading because church and grave seemed apt together. Heresy!

Courts and hospitals

Editing court reports needs especial care. But the legal pitfalls do not justify the way police language is reproduced in the majority of humdrum cases in the lower courts. Nor do legal cautions excuse the false gentility of many newspaper reports:

A milling crowd of students fol-lowed a *police officer* for a dis-tance of a quarter of a mile the night he arrested a fellow stu-dent for *causing an alleged* breach of the peace.

A milling crowd of students fol-lowed a policeman for a quarter of a mile the night he arrested one of them for a breach of the peace.

(Policeman will do to describe a male PC – and why 'an alleged breach' when the case is found proved?)

Magistrates, who fined the stu-dent £5, were told that P.C. Alan Goad arrested him . . .

Three other students, *who were called as witnesses for the defend-ant, said in court* that the group was orderly.

Three other students said . . .

(The context makes it clear they were in court. 'Who were called as witnesses' is almost always verbo-sity.)

When apprehended Dooney had in his possession two radios.

When stopped Dooney had two radios.

Dennis Bloggs was fined £4 when he admitted behaving in a disorderly manner on a Corpora-tion bus and breaking a bus window.

Dennis Bloggs was fined £4 for being disorderly on a Corpora-tion bus and breaking a window.

County police are anxious to know of his whereabouts.

County police want to find him.

The constable telephoned head-quarters and when two officers hurried to the scene they found the youths on the premises of the store.

The constable telephoned head-quarters and two officers found the youths in the store.

John Jones was fined £5 for having inefficient brakes on his van and £2 for having an ineffi-cient speedometer.

'Having' is redundant.

Editing of injuries and hospital conditions is often equally woolly. There should be an office style:

> Alfred Davidson received a sprained neck when his car was in collision with a truck . . .

Did he get it in gift-wrapping?

> Alfred Davidson sprained his neck when his car and a truck collided . . .

That is shorter and more direct, but passive reporting predominates:

Sandy Smith suffered a leg injury.	Sandy Smith hurt his leg.
Lawrence Jones was fatally injured.	Lawrence Jones was killed.
Howard M. Woods, of 53 Hillside Avenue, was *reported in* a 'fair *condition*' last night at Central Hospital. He has a heart ailment. He was admitted *to the hospital* on June 22nd.	Was 'fair' last night . . . That is enough. The quotation marks reveal that it is the description of his condition. He was admitted with a heart ailment on June 22. Where else but to the hospital?
He was allowed home after treatment.	He went home after treatment.

A caution: the quotes on a hospital condition can sometimes look silly:

> Mr J. Smith, city engineer, is 'ill' in hospital with a heart condition.

The text editor knows that this is the hospital's exact assessment of Mr Smith's condition. But with an ordinary ailment, the quotes round 'ill' read oddly to the ordinary reader – and the ordinary reader is our customer.

Finally, some other types of needless repetition:

- Unnecessary doubt: A small Renoir painting was reportedly stolen yesterday. The painting was taken from a wall. 'Was stolen' is enough. Is there reason for doubt? We retell facts, not rumour.
- Useless caution: Why keep saying 'It was learned that . . .'? It is no legal protection if the facts are not right. We could say 'it was learned that . . .' before every fact in the paper.

Chapter Four

Watch this Language

To write simply is as difficult as to be good.
SOMERSET MAUGHAM

The previous two chapters have set down a set of conditions to guide the text editor. Negatively, the series of don'ts means rewriting long sentences, complicated sentences, negative sentences, passive sentences, and a succession of sentences of the same structure. It means avoiding complex words, abstract words, and omitting all needless words. Some of this is summed up in an adaptation of an old nursery rhyme:

> If I had a donkey as wouldn't go
> Do you think I'd wallop him, oh No.
> I'd give him some corn and cry out 'Whoa',
> 'Gee up, Neddy'.

which would appear in too many news columns as:

> If I had an ass that refused to proceed,
> Do you suppose that I should castigate him, no indeed.
> I should present him with some cereals and observe proceed,
> Continue, Edward.

Edward the donkey is a reminder of what text editors are up against. They have to work fast. They have to recognise Edward as Neddy in disguise. They have to be ready with the better word. The three lists that follow are an attempt to help.

They are words that spell waste. All are taken from newspaper reports. Text editors should know the lists thoroughly. They are not exhaustive. Text editors should add to them themselves. If they then cultivate an animus to the offending words, there is a good chance these words will spring out of the copy; text editors will have a substitute already in mind. Busy text editors will have no time to consult a thesaurus or sit and ponder.

The first list gives the bad expressions on the left. They are not all necessarily wrong. Some of them are, but the alternatives on the right are usually crisper and shorter. They're not synonymous but they frequently express the desired meaning. If no alternative is given the word is simply one to avoid. The second list is of redundancies, and the third of common newspaper clichés.

Wasteful Words

Don't say	Prefer
abrasions and contusions	cuts and bruises
absence of	no
accede to	grant/allow
accommodate	hold/seat
accommodation	rooms, seats, etc.
accordingly	so
acquaint	tell
act as	bad substitute for verb 'to be'
a cut on his ear	a cut ear
adequate bus transportation	enough buses
adjacent to	near
adumbrate	outline/sketch
affluent	rich/well-off
ahead of schedule	early
a large proportion of	many
a man by the name of	named
ameliorate	improve
a percentage of	some
approximately	about

Don't say	Prefer
arrangements were in the hands of	arranged by
ascertain	learn
as far as . . . is concerned	as for (but it is better to be direct)
assistance	help/aid
at an early date	soon
attempt	try
at the present time/at present	now
attired in	wore
best of health	well/healthy
beverage	drink
bid (except at auction)	attempt
bifurcation	division/split
called a halt	stopped
carry out the work	do the work
caused injuries to	injured
centre round	centre on/in
cloudburst	heavy rain
commence, commencement	begin, beginning
compared with	than
concerning	about/on
conflagration	fire
conservative (estimate)	low/cautious
consist of	bad substitute for verb 'to be'
constructed of wood	made of wood/wooden
continue to remain	stay
currently	now
customary	usual
decease	death/die
deceased, defendant	prefer the name
demise	death
demonstrate	show
dentures	false teeth

Don't say	**Prefer**
described as	called
despite the fact that	although
discontinue	stop
dispatched	sent
donate, contribute	give
donation	gift
draw the attention of	show/remind/point out
dwell	live
edifice	building
endeavour	try
en route	on the way
evince	show
exceedingly	very
exceeding the speed limit	speeding
expedite	hasten/hurry
expensive	dear
facilitate	ease/help
filled to capacity	full
fissiparous	separatist/breakaway
following (i.e. later in time)	after
freighter	(cargo) ship
from out of the	out of/from
gained entrance to	got in
gathered together	met
give consideration to	consider
give rise to	cause
hails from	comes from
headache (except literally)	problem, difficulty, puzzle
heretofore	before/until now
I am hopeful that	I hope that
hospitalised	went to hospital
illuminated	lit up
implement (verb)	carry out/fulfil/do

Don't say	Prefer
implementation	
impossible of discovery	cannot be found
in addition	also
in addition to	besides, as well as, also
in advance of his meeting with . . .	before meeting . . .
in attendance	present/there
incapacitated	(put out of action)
in conjunction with	and/or
in consequence of	because of
inferno	fire
inform	tell
in isolation	by itself/alone
initiate, institute	begin, start
in many cases/in the case of	often/with (case is an over-worked word)
in order to	to
inquire	ask
in short supply	scarce
in spite of the fact that	despite/although
in succession	running
in the course of	in/during/while
in the direction of	towards
in the event of	in/if
in the field of	in/with
in the majority of instances	mostly
in the vicinity/region/neigh-bourhood of	about/near/around
in view of the fact that	since
is of the opinion	believes
it cannot be denied that	undeniably
lady	woman, unless Lady is a title
larceny	theft, stealing
large volume of complaints	many complaints
leaving much to be desired	unsatisfactory/bad
less expensive	cheaper

Don't say	**Prefer**
amazing level of expertise	amazing expertise
local authority	council
low degree of interest	little interest
made an approach to	approached
made good their escape	escaped
manufacture	make
materialise	happen/come about/appear
maximum	greatest/greatest possible
measure up to	fit, reach, match
meet up with	meet
merchandise	goods
minimum	least/smallest
miraculous	surprising/unexpected
missive	letter
necessitate	force
objective	aim
occasioned by	caused by
of the order of	about
one of the purposes	one purpose
one of the reasons	one reason
on account of the fact that/ owing to the fact that	because
on the part of	by
participate	share/take part (in)
pay tribute to	thank/praise
per	should be followed by another Latin word, e.g. per annum, but prefer, *a* year, *a* head, *a* mile etc.
permanent	lasting
personnel	crew/team/workers
peruse	read
petite	

Don't say	Prefer
placed under arrest	arrested
posh	
possessed	had
predecease	die before
prior to/preparatory to/pre- vious to	before
probe	
proceed	go
proceeded up	went
production	output
progress to	reach
proliferation	spread
prove beneficial	benefit
provided	if
purchase	buy
put in an appearance	appeared
quit	leave
quiz (verb)	question/ask
red faces (except literally)	embarrassed
regarding	about/on
remunerate	pay
rendered assistance to	helped
request the appropriation of	ask for (more) money/funds
residence	home
resides at	lives at
respecting	about/on
result in	end in. Keep results/ resulted in for scores in games
resuscitate	revive
retain his position as	remain
retired for the night	went to bed
shortfall in supplies	shortage
since the particular time	since then

Don't say	Prefer
special ceremonies marking the event were held	ceremonies marked the event
stockpile	stock
submitted his resignation	resigned
subsequently	later
subsequent to	after
succeeded in defeating	defeated
succumbed to his injuries	died
sufficient	enough
sufficient consideration	enough thought
summon (except legal summons)	send for
sustained injuries	was hurt
take action on the issue	act
terminate	end
the remains	the body
this day and age	today/nowadays
to date	so far
took into consideration	considered
took up the cudgels on behalf of	backed, supported
tragedy	
transmit	send
transportation	bus, car, cycle – or transport
the tools they employed	their tools
under active consideration	being considered
under preparation	being prepared
underprivileged	poor/deprived
under the circumstances	in this/that case
utilise	use
valued at	worth
varsity	
venue	
voiced approval	approved

Don't say	Prefer
was a witness of	saw
was of the opinion that	believed/thought/said
was suffering from	had
wend one's way	go
when and if	if
which included	including
whole of	all
will be the speaker at	will speak at
with the exception of	except
with the minimum of delay	as soon as possible
with the result that	so that
worked their way	went
W was in collision with Y	W and Y collided (no blame)

Redundancies

These are expressions which the text editor can strike out without offering a terser substitute. Almost always redundant are the phrases: along the lines of, it should be noted that, it is appreciated that . . . In this list of more than 200 newspaper extracts, the redundancies are set in italic. Deleting them saves space and improves the sentence.

absolute perfection

35 acres *of land*

acute crisis

adequate enough

a distance of

a hearing *to discuss case*

all *of*

all-time record

among the delegates expected *to attend*

an authority *in his own right*

a number of examples

a period of

appear *on the scene*

appear *to be*

appointed *to the post of*

appreciated *in value*

ascend *up*

as compared with

as never before *in the past*

as yet

a team of 12 workers

at some time *to come*

attach *together*

awkward predicament

best *ever*

blends *in*

blue *coloured* car
bold *and audacious*
brand new
broad daylight

chief protagonist
circular *shape*
classified *into classes*
close proximity
collaborate *together*
commented *to the effect* that
commute *to and from*
complete monopoly
completely outplayed
completely untrue
concrete proposals
connect *up/together*
consensus *of opinion*
continue *in existence*
continue *to remain*
co-operate *together*
cost *the sum of*
crisis *situation*

dates *back* from
definite decision
depreciated *in value*
descend *down*
divert *away* from
divide *off/up*
doctorate *degree*
downright lie
drink *up/down*
driver *by occupation*
during *the course of*

early *hours*
eat *up*
eliminate *altogether*

enclosed *herewith*
endorse *on the back*
end product/result
end *up*
entirely absent
entirely new departure
entirely spontaneous
entire state/community/con-
    gregation
equally *as*
essential condition
ever since
exact counterpart

face *up to*
falsely fabricated
few *in number*
final completion/upshot/set-
    tlement
flatly rejected
follow *after*
for *a period of*
forbid *from*
for *the* making *of*
for *the month of*
for *the purpose of*
foundered *and sank*
fresh beginning
frown *on his face*
full complement of
full satisfaction
funeral obsequies
future prospect

gainfully employed
gather *up/together*
general public
good benefit
grateful thanks

have been *engaged in* producing

have *got*

heard *various* requests

he lost his *eye*sight

he was seen *in the morning* on his pre-breakfast walk

he went *in an effort* to determine

hoist *up*

hot water heater

hour of noon

hurry *up*

if *and when*

in a work *situation*

in abeyance *for the time being*

include *among them*

intents and purposes

inter-personal friendship

in *the city of* Manchester

in *the course of* the operation

in *the process of* building

in the interim *period between*

in *the sphere of* politics

intolerable *to be borne*

in two years' *time*

invited guest

involved in a car crash

it is interesting to note that

joined *together*

joint co-operation

join *up*

just recently

last *of all*

lend *out*

less essential

link *together*

little sapling

lonely isolation

made *out* of

major breakthrough

may *possibly*

meet *together*

men *who are* unemployed

merge *together*

more preferable

more superior

mutual co-operation

nearly inevitable

necessary requisite

needless to say

need *necessarily*

never *at any time*

new beginning

new creation

new innovation

new recruits

new record

new renovations

new tradition

nobody *else* but

not *at all*

not *generally* available everywhere

old adage

old veterans

one of the last *remaining*

on the occasion when

on the question of

original source

over *and done with*
overtake a *slower-moving* vehicle

pay *off* the debt
pare *down*
partially harmless
passing pedestrian/car
passing phase
past history
patently obvious
peculiar freak
penetrate *into*
periods *of time*
petrol *filling* station
polish *up*
poor state of disrepair
prejudge *in advance*
presence *on the scene*
pressing for *the imposition of* a 30 mph limit
prominent *and leading*
proposed project
protrude *out*

quite empty
quite perfect

radical transformation
raze *to the ground*
recalled *back*
recommended *back*
reduce *down*
regular monthly meeting
repeat *again*
resigned *his position* as
results *so far achieved*
returned *back*

revert *back*
reward *back*
root cause

saved *from his earnings*
seldom *ever*
self-confessed
separate *apart*
serious danger
seriously incline
settle *up*
short *space of* time
sink *down*
skirt *around*
small *in size*
smile *on his face*
spent his *whole* life
staunch supporter
still persists/continues
strangled *to death*
sufficient enough
summoned *to the scene*
sunny *by day*
surgeon *by occupation*
surrounding circumstances

temporary reprieve
the court was asked to decide *as to* whether *or not*
throughout *the whole length and breadth*
to *consume* drink
topped *the 200 mark*
total contravention
total extinction
totally destroyed
track record (unless it is the running track)

true facts

uncommonly strange
unite *together*
universal panacea
usual customs
utterly indestructible

value judgments
vandals *wilfully* broke
violent explosion
vitally necessary

watchful eye
ways *and means*
whether *or not*
whole *of the* country
widow of *the late*
win *out*
worst *ever*

young infant
young teenager

Stale Expressions

Newspapers used to be rank with cliché. Few in the following list survive in the news pages. They lurk more in sports and features, especially in the form distinguished by an inevitable adjective or adverb (which is one coupled so inevitably with a noun as to have lost any separate life – breathless calm, lively admiration, bewildering variety). Inevitable adjectives and adverbs should be struck out and the noun left to fend for itself. Other stale expressions in the list can generally be felled at a stroke, too. But where other words are needed, beware of substituting an over-contrived simile or metaphor just for the sake of brightness.

acid test
aired their troubles
all walks of life
appear on the scene
armed to the teeth
at pains to explain

beat a hasty retreat
bees in his bonnet
beggars description
bewildering variety

bitter end
blaze (for fire)
blazing inferno
blissful ignorance
bolt from the blue
breakneck speed
breakthrough
breathless silence
bring up to date
brook no delay
brutal reminder

brute force
built in safeguard
burning issue

calm before the storm
chequered career
cheered to the echo
cherished belief
city fathers
clean pair of heels
cold collation
colourful scene
commendably patient
concerted move
conspicuous by its absence
cool as a cucumber
coveted trophy
crack troops
crowded to capacity
crude fact
crying need
curate's egg

dame fashion
daring daylight robbery
dark horse
dashed to the rescue
dastardly deed
dazzling sight
deafening crash
deciding factor
deftly manipulate
dig in their heels
ding-dong struggle
doctors fought
dog in the manger
64,000-dollar question
dotted the landscape

dramatic new move
dreaming spires
drew a line

fair sex
fall between two stools
fall on deaf ears
far cry
fickle fortune
filthy lucre
finishing touches
fit and bronzed
fly in the ointment
foregone conclusion
from time immemorial

gay abandon
gay cavalier
getting into full swing
given the green light
glared daggers
goes without saying
gory details
grim reaper

hardy souls
headache (for problem)
heap coals of fire
heartfelt thanks
heart of gold
high dudgeon
hook, line and sinker
hot pursuit
hub of the universe

inextricably linked
in full swing
inspiring/unsporting display

internecine strife
in the nick of time
in the same boat
in the twinkling of an eye
iron out the difficulty/prob-
   lem

lashed out
last but not least
last-ditch effort
leaps and bounds
leave no stone unturned
leave severely alone
left up in the air
lending a helping hand
like rats in a trap
limped into port
lock, stock and barrel
long arm of the law
long years
loom up
lucky few
luxury flat/yacht

mantle of snow
man worthy of his steel
marked contrast
marked improvement
marshal support
matter of life and death
mercy dash
milady
move into high gear

never a dull moment
news leaked out
nipped in the bud
none the worse for wear

not to be undone
not to put too fine a point on
   it

official capacity
open secret
order out of chaos
over and above

paid the penalty
painted a grim picture
paramount importance
part and parcel
patience of Job
paying the piper
pillar of the Church
pinpoint the cause
place in the sun
pool of blood
poured scorn
powder keg
pretty kettle of fish
pros and cons
proud heritage
psychological moment

raced/rushed to the scene
raining in sheets
rats in a trap
red faces
red-letter day
red rag to a bull
reduced to matchwood
reins of government
remedy the situation
rose to great heights

sadder but wiser

sea of upturned faces
selling like hot cakes
shackles which fetter
sigh of relief
sons of the soil
spearheading the campaign
speculation was rife
spirited debate
spotlessly white
spotlight the need
square peg in a round hole
staff of life
steaming jungle
stick out like a sore thumb
storm of protest
storm-tossed
stuck to his guns
sweeping changes

taking the bull by the horns
taking the situation in his
  stride
terror-stricken
this day and age

through their paces
throwing a party
tiny tots
tongue in cheek
top-level session
tower of strength
true colours
turned turtle

unconscionably long time
up in arms
upset the apple cart

vanish into thin air
voiced approval

wealth of information
weighty matter
whirlwind tour
widespread anxiety
winds of change
wreak havoc
writing on the wall

CHAPTER FIVE

The Structure of a News Story – Intros

'Under the impression your peregrinations in this metropolis have not as yet been extensive and you might have difficulty in penetrating the arcana of the modern Babylon – in short,' said Mr. Micawber, in a burst of confidence, 'you might lose your way.'

CHARLES DICKENS

Hemingway, I read once, wrote the last page of *A Farewell to Arms* sixteen times before he was satisfied. It is the beginnings that give newspaper writers all the trouble. One does not wish to suggest Hemingway was not trying, but sixteen shots at the first sentence or paragraph of a news story is nothing, as is proved every day by the mortality tables of copydesk executives. Any effort to get the beginning right in a newspaper story is worthwhile, because the reader will stop there if the writer fails. What bothers journalists when they sit down to write their first paragraph (called an 'intro' in Britain and a 'lead' in America) is that it seems to them they are being asked to sum up in one paragraph a drama akin to *King Lear* crossed with *My Fair Lady*. If it is not that kind of story, it is the other kind, the fourteenth report of the sanitation and waterways committee, and everyone knows it is easier to follow *Lear* than the mental workings of a county surveyor committing himself or herself to prose. So despite the constant injunctions for intros to be kept short and to the point, reporters will keep coming up with thoughts impossibly complicated for a newspaper, and text editors will have to keep putting them right.

Before we get into this quagmire, let us glimpse the kind of solid ground provided by the late Eugene Doane in the *New York Sun*:

Chicago, Oct 31: James Wilson lighted a cigarette while bathing his feet in benzene. He may live.

Eugene Doane's intro is a rare piece. It manages to tell the whole story from beginning to end. That is splendid, but only the brevity is commended for copying. To sum up such a sequence in two sentences is impossible in most stories. Until somebody like James Wilson does it again and somebody like Doane is around to record it, the wise reporter and text editor should concentrate the hard news intro on effects rather than origins, on what happened rather than how, when or where. They should offer a short sharp sentence conveying a maximum of impact in a minimum of phrase. Of course concentrating tersely on effects can be overdone. James Thurber once rebelled and wrote:

Dead. That's what the man was when he was picked up.

The practical aim for journalists is somewhere between Thurber's cannonball and Doane's epigrammatic essay. An intro as short as 17 words can be inviting:

The first time 53-year-old Sidney Anderson was seen drunk was the last time he was seen alive.

That intro would have been spoiled if an address or a date or a location or the coroner's name had been added. Many offices lay down a maximum number of words for an intro. That sounds primitive, but is necessary and helpful. It forces the writer to essentials. Where longer intros are tolerated, reporters and text editors easily drift into writing the comprehensive unselective intro, with grammatical constructions that are invariably confusing.

There is a typographical objection to long intros, too. They look slabby and uninviting to read. It should be possible to read the intro – and digest its meaning – in a quick scanning. If you have to read an intro with care it is a failure.

A 40-word *maximum* would not be at all unreasonable: about 30 words is better. Editors of the spoken word in broadcasting especially should aim for the shorter intro. Long sentences with subsidiary clauses are a snare for announcers and a strain on the listener.

A limit of 30-40 words is not hard to achieve. The skill is in achieving brevity without depriving an intro of precision. Anybody can write a five-word intro: 'A man was killed yesterday'. That is not news. It is a vacuum. Filling it with just the right amount of detail is where the skill is needed. Too little specific content makes an intro vague; too much is bewildering. The editor has to make sure the intro is precise enough to refer to a unique happening, but the precision must not be prolix. A great deal of harm has been done by the old rule that the intro should try to answer the questions Who? Why? What? Where? When? This is a rule for a news story, but not for an intro. The intro must concentrate on effects, on one news idea. It must contain some identification, but origins, sequence and chronology are all subsidiary to what resulted in the end. The preoccupation with trying to answer all those five questions overloads too many intros, to the detriment of meaning. The obsession with secondary details manifests itself in a number of ways, but two grammatical symptoms are of prime importance. Where intros begin with a long subsidiary clause or a participle, you are in the presence of a muddle.

In the next example the opening clause is set in italic. All this building material has to be carried along in the mind as meaningless junk until the main clause (from 'materials availability') has been read. Only at the end of the long sentence does the reader know what the intro is all about. Meaning is acquired more quickly if the sentence is turned round (right) to begin with the main clause:

With no sign that there is a general improvement in the supply of common bricks, despite big increases in production, or of copper tubes and fittings and sanitary ware, materials availability remains the building industry's most urgent problem, reports the National Federation of Building Trades Employers.

The National Federation of Building Trades Employers reports that materials availability remains the building industry's most urgent problem, with no sign that there is a general improvement in the supply of common bricks, despite big increases in production, or of copper tubes and fittings and sanitary ware.

But better still, of course, the language should be changed as well as the sentence structure: 'materials availability' and 'building industry' are clumsy abstract ways of describing a simple specific:

> Builders are still being held up by a shortage of common bricks, despite big increases in production, and of copper tubes and fittings and sanitary ware, says the National Federation of Building Trades Employers.

A very common form of opening with a subsidiary clause betrays a split mind:

> While Lord Hill was denying last night that the BBC was considering advertising to offset costs, the head of Scottish Television claimed the Government was threatening the future of ITV.

Behind this intro there is a failure of decision. There are two news ideas. The writer has to decide.

> Lord Hill denied last night that the BBC was considering advertising to offset costs.

> The managing director of Scottish Television, Mr _____, claimed last night that the Government was threatening the future of independent television.

Intros beginning with a participle are similarly weak and muddled. The participle is the weakest part of the verb and it is usually the intro to a long subsidiary clause:

Referring to the statement made on Labour plans to force local authorities to introduce comprehensive schools, Alderman _____ _____, Conservative Leader of the Inner London Education Authority, said: . . .

Criticising the Administration, Senator Muskie last night . . .

Saying that on Friday he had agreed terms for the relief airlift, Colonel Ojukwu yesterday . . .

The subsidiary clause at the beginning of a sentence asks too much of the reader. The first part of the sentence means nothing until the reader has read the second part. Readers may give up. If they go on, they have to hold in their mind the jumble of words until they have read a second jumble of words which then give meaning to the whole. Even the writers of subsidiary clauses themselves lose their way and relate the preamble to the wrong subject:

Alarmed by the wave of violence that has swept Singapore during the last six months, the death penalty has been passed on those guilty of kidnapping.

Plump, crew-cut, blinking a little behind black-rimmed spectacles, Allan Sherman was born in Chicago in 1924.

Opening with a subsidiary clause is especially irritating when there is an unidentified pronoun:

With what his colleagues called a 'clarion call' to party unity, Mr . . .

Declaring that it could not be opened until officially approved, Mr . . .

Whose colleagues, what party? What could not be opened – a

public house, a church, an envelope? No reader should ever be asked to cope with such conundrums.

Finally, trouble can also come from long subsidiary clauses in the middle of an intro. What follows is a newspaper example where readers have to carry two subsidiary clauses in their heads before being told what all the fuss is about. This intro can be rewritten in the active voice (1 below).

That delays mentioning the three baby-food manufacturers, which is a pity, but the words baby-food makers will be in the headline. Alternatively (2 below) the intro can lead off with the baby-food manufacturers and the badly intruding second subsidiary clause (*by the scientists who headed the work that led to the banning of cyclamates*) can be compressed and transposed so that it does not interrupt the flow of thought. The use of a dash in punctuation here gives the reader a pause and the story a neat emphasis.

The three baby-food manufacturers, Rumble, Yummy and Toddlertum, who voluntarily withdrew all monosodium glutamate from their products at the weekend were accused today, by the scientists who headed the work that led to the banning of cyclamates, of panicking unnecessarily, and causing public alarm.

(1) Scientists whose work led to the banning of cyclamates accused the three baby-food manufacturers Rumble, Yummy and Toddlertum, of causing needless public alarm by the voluntary withdrawal of monosodium glutamate from their products.

OR

(2) The three baby-food manufacturers Rumble, Yummy and Toddlertum, who voluntarily withdrew all monosodium glutamate from their products at the weekend, were today accused of causing needless public alarm – by the scientists whose research led to the banning of cyclamates.

Let us now examine in detail the obsessions with secondary news ideas, with chronology, and with source, which produce bad intros.

Chronology

In certain feature and news-feature reports (discussed later) a chronological construction is appropriate. This is a clear narrative technique. It is quite different from allowing secondary details to creep into the hard news intro.

> After hearing shooting at the Berlin Wall yesterday an American military policeman raced to the scene and found East German guards trying to drag a refugee back. The American soldier went to a second-storey window overlooking the Wall, threw a tear-gas grenade, to make the East Germans release the refugee, then climbed on top of the Wall and amid a hail of bullets between East and West helped to pull the refugee to the West.

This is dramatic reading but it is nowhere good enough for a hard news intro. The antecedents of the action – which have produced a subsidiary clause at the beginning – are secondary. They come unnaturally in the excitement of telling the news. Anyone who had seen that incident would say: 'I saw a tremendous rescue at the Wall today – an American soldier dragged a refugee across. They were shooting at him all the time.' That is the germ of the hard news intro. 'Yes', your listener will say, 'and what happened to the soldier and the refugee? Were they killed?' 'The refugee was wounded but they told me he'd be all right.'

If you had been telling the story chronologically, that piece of information would have had to wait till the very end of a long recital. Your listener (and the reader) would rightly grow very impatient. In conversation and in news reporting one begins naturally with a quick account of the action – and the result. If we do this here we discard the preamble 'after hearing shooting at the Berlin Wall yesterday'. Indeed we discard the whole first sentence. The first attempt now at a hard news intro can be built from the way one would have told the news orally.

> An American soldier dragged a refugee across the Berlin Wall yesterday. The East Germans were shooting all the time. The refugee was wounded but his life is not in danger.

This tells the story but it is staccato and imprecise. It omits the fact that both sides were shooting during the rescue. It sounds routine: journalists would say it is colourless. Try again:

> An American military policeman braved a hail of bullets to pull a wounded refugee over the Berlin Wall yesterday.

This has compressed the action and tells the result. Even in the second paragraph of the lead we would still avoid going right back in the chronology ('after hearing the shooting').

We would cram in some more action, and begin to substantiate and explain the intro in this second paragraph:

> The soldier, 22-year-old Hans Puhl, threw a tear-gas grenade to make East German guards release the refugee. Then amid fire from the East and counter-fire from the West, he climbed on the Wall to drop a rope to the wounded man, Michel Meyer, aged 21.

You will notice how we have saved till later the explanation of how he climbed on the Wall from a second-storey window – and of course how he came to be on the scene at all. These things happened first, but they are not first in importance and so they have no place in the intro. Only now, in the third paragraph, can chronology take over. The men's names have been given in this second paragraph so that the rest of the story can be told more easily without confusion of the two 'hes' or the elegant variations 'the refugee', 'the soldier'.

In a second example below the obsession with chronology has produced a gargantuan subsidiary clause, introduced by a participle. The intro is rewritten on the right with a simple announcement of the statement's effect.

Replying to Viscount Lambton (C. Berwick-upon-Tweed) who asked if the Minister of Agriculture would relax existing restrictions on the importation of live and dead poultry following upon the introduction of the fowl pest vaccination policy, Mr Christopher Soames said in the House of Commons yesterday: 'I have decided, following the recommendations of the Plant Committee, to allow the importation of poultry breeding stock and hatching eggs where this is likely to be of benefit to the commercial stock in this country.'

Poultry breeding stock and hatching eggs may now be imported more freely. The Minister of Agriculture, Mr Christopher Soames, told Viscount Lambton (C. Berwick-upon-Tweed) yesterday that, following the Plant Committee's advice, imports would be allowed where they were likely to benefit our commercial stock.

A chronologically obsessed intro does not always begin with a tell-tale subsidiary clause or participle. In the next example the intro begins directly enough, but its concern with an over-long sequence delays the real human news. The location details aggravate the failure. 'A field near Chatham Gardens Apartments' does not merely intrude extra words, it delays the action. On the right is the rewritten version – constructed in the same trial and error process as the Berlin Wall intro.

A bulldozer, started up at full speed by vandals and then abandoned, raced one-quarter mile across a field near Chatham Gardens Apartments last night and rammed into a bedroom where two children lay sleeping.

Neither of the children was injured by the six-ton machine which hit a crib containing a

A runaway six-ton bulldozer rammed into a bedroom where two children were asleep last night. It knocked a crib containing a two-year-old across the room.

But the children were unhurt.

The bulldozer was started at full speed by vandals on a field near . . .

two-year-old boy and knocked it several feet across the room.

The vandals, described as teenagers by witnesses, jumped off the out-of-control bulldozer moments before the crash and fled on foot. Damage to the building is expected to run into thousands of dollars.

Patrolmen Edgar Bastian and Dominic Rotolo said the two sleeping children were William Gray, 2, and his sister Marguerite, 10 months. Their parents, Mr and Mrs Richard Gray, were not at home.

You will note where chronological sequence is allowed to take over – after the news lead.

Source Obsession

This disease gives priority to the event, place, organisation or person that yielded the news and too little to the news itself. Here we might usefully distinguish three rough categories of news intro:

- The general news intro retailing a fact for the general reader. This needs a minimum source identification: 'Pensions will go up by £2 a week from January 1'. The source for such a plain fact can follow in the second part of the sentence, or in a second sentence. Too often it intrudes into the first sentence and when there are a lot of such details the intro becomes confusing.
- The general news intro retailing an opinion or quote for the general reader. This needs an early statement of source so that the reader can judge the worth of the statement: 'The Prime Minister said yesterday that he believed unemployment would fall "dramatically" in the

next three months'. All opinion stories must have the source in the first sentence – but the place and occasion of the statement are subsidiary and can follow in the second.

● The specialist news story retailing either fact or opinion for specialist readers, i.e. for local readers, for business readers, or sports readers, and so on. In sports and business sections of national newspapers and in local newspapers prompt identification is required because the names are the essence of the news: 'Joe Bloggs is "certain" to play for England, said the team manager, Kevin Keegan, yesterday.'

The commonest news stories are in the first category, retailing a fact for the general reader. Here for every quotable individual justifiably edging into the first words of an intro, there are ten of this kind, either plain or fancy:

It was announced in the *Church Times* yesterday . . .

At a special meeting of Manchester Corporation Housing Committee this afternoon, it was agreed after a three-hour meeting that . . .

All this before the reader is let into the secret of what the report is all about. Insignificant elements of source in factual general news intros can be deferred to the second paragraph, letting the first sentence tell the news:

All Manchester Council house rents will go up by £1.50 a week. This was decided at . . .

The worst defect of source-obsessed intros in all three categories is focusing on the administrative mechanics behind the news – the committee, the bill, the statement, the hall where the meeting was held, the official who distributed the handout:

North Riding police yesterday issued a statement on the arrangements for the Queen's visit . . .

This makes the issuing of the statement, rather than its content, the important item. There are other examples of how easily the obsession with source makes the administrative mechanics appear to be the news:

> In its voluminous report submitted to the Government earlier this month, the committee on educational integration is understood to have made 213 major recommendations touching upon all aspects of education, including the medium of instruction, education policy and the functioning of universities.
>
> One of the most important recommendations of the committee is that . . .

This is where the intro should begin – with this precise recommendation. The second paragraph will do to tell the reader it is part of a 'voluminous' (i.e. bulky, or 700-page, or 5 kilo) report.

The rewritten version on the right below, bringing the live subject into the news at the earliest moment, saves 3–4 lines of type on a 13-line story:

A bill to authorise the study of the feasibility of keeping the St. Lawrence Seaway open all year round has been approved by the House Public Works Committee.

But the committee yesterday amended the bill, which had been passed by the Senate, to limit the cost of the study to a maximum of 50,000 dollars. The study would include ways of de-icing harbours and channels to permit winter navigation.

Ways are to be sought to keep the St. Lawrence Seaway and Great Lakes open all year round.

The House Public Works Committee yesterday approved a bill to investigate harbour and channel de-icing. But it amended the bill, which passed the Senate, to limit the study to 50,000 dollars.

The next example is an intro from the middle category. The news value of the story depends here on the source, in this case the Law Society, the professional organisation of English solicitors (a description which few text editors handling the agency story bothered to give the reader). The early identification of this authoritative source, however, emphatically does not mean overloading the intro with more than the source, as on the left. The intro should be as on the right:

The Council of the Law Society in a memorandum on motoring offences to the Lord Chancellor, the Home Secretary and the Minister of Transport today recommends the setting up of traffic courts and special corps to relieve the police of non-criminal traffic commitments.

The Law Society wants traffic courts and special corps to relieve the police of non-criminal traffic duties. In a memorandum today to . . .

It would be wrong to delay a source beyond the intro, or to lead with an unidentified pronoun:

Traffic courts and special corps to relieve the police of non-criminal traffic commitments are 'urgently required' says a memorandum on motoring offences today.

They deplore the waste of the police's time on non-criminal traffic offences, says the Law Society today, in calling for traffic courts and a special traffic corps.

No pronoun should ever be used for an intro before the noun is introduced:

He was opposed to capital punishment which he depicted as 'a barbarism that has judicially murdered innocent men', said the leader of the Progressive party, Mr. Snudge.

The leader of the Progressive party, Mr. Snudge, condemned capital punishment yesterday as 'a barbarism that has judicially murdered innocent men'.

Where the source of the statement determines the news value it is best to begin by naming the source at once.

Now, finally, for the third category – the relevance of the

newspaper's audience to the amount of source detail in an intro:

> A father was electrocuted yesterday as he tried to fix the fairy lights on his children's Christmas tree.

That is the essence of the news. It is fine as a general news intro retailing a fact for the general reader of a national newspaper, or London evening. But imagine the accident happened in a town of 80,000 and the story is being edited for the evening paper. Then the intro could profitably say: 'A Luton father was electrocuted yesterday . . .'

Take it a stage further. The accident happened in a small market town and is being edited for the town's weekly newspaper. It now becomes a story for a specialised audience. It would now be right to let the intro say: 'Mr . . . of . . . was electrocuted on . . .'

Text editors must ask themselves this: How many readers will be induced to read the story primarily by the inclusion in the intro of the name of the man, or place? Is it significant to the readers of this newspaper? On local or provincial papers text editors should err on the side of including the name in the intro. When the area referred to is cheek by jowl with the publishing centre of the paper it looks needlessly vague to write:

> The future of a town's ambitious swimming pool scheme hangs in the balance after a shock victory last night by opponents of the plan.

Readers of that in a Bristol area paper could have been told without fear straight away that it was nearby Keynsham's scheme. The following intro would have been all right in a national newspaper:

> A managing director under fire from housewives who claim his factory chimney wrecks their washing has asked a local councillor to help track down complaints.

But that intro appeared in a Darlington paper and about a Darlington factory. The second paragraph went on:

> Mr D. J. Grant, head of Darlington Chemical and Insulating Co., has asked Coun. Clifford Hutchinson to join him in ending the washday menace of the Faverdale area of the town.
> Last week residents complained that grit from the chemical works chimney is burning holes in their washing.

For the local paper this second paragraph, plus recognisable names and places, would have been better as the intro; indeed the first paragraph could be deleted altogether.

There is a further inducement for the regional newspaper to be more specific (but without falling back on subsidiary clauses). It is that disguising the identity of the place leads to the proliferation of vague intros hinged insecurely on the indefinite article:

> A council chairman has resigned because of a row over prayers . . .

> A doctor has accused a local authority of carelessness . . .

Overloading

Details of sequence and source have been identified as two impediments to the intro. The third is trying to make one sentence carry too many details or ideas. That is a fault in a sentence anywhere. In an intro it is fatal. Yet it is a common failing even among sophisticated reporters. Entranced by all they have discovered, reporters are tempted to thread all the most colourful beads on to the same thin thread of a sentence, and it just breaks.

> Mr Joe Bloggs, the handsome grey-haired missing textile company founder, aged 48, who had a passion for fast sports cars, and was often seen with Princess Hilda, the wool heiress, before disappearing from the Dover Express on July 2, will be

charged with misappropriating £325,068 in the High Court on September 1.

Hell, yes, but what size hat does he wear?

That fictional example of Reporters' Baroque is 52 words, at least 20 too long for the basic news. If text editors work to a word limit they have to strike out the excess detail for insertion lower in the story. This is the real justification for limiting the number of words in an intro. As well as discouraging subsidiary clause openings, it forces the editor to squeeze the real news into the intro. A guillotine concentrates the mind wonderfully.

One simple sentence to an intro, one idea to a sentence. In the example below, the 44-word first intro on the left needs two breaths. The version on the right restricts itself to the single news idea – that a policeman's sense to keep talking saved the lives of a family. Once that single idea has been conveyed in the intro, substantiation can follow:

A policeman kept up a running telephone conversation with a despondent mother of five who said she was going to turn on the gas in her home and end the lives of herself and her children last night, then quickly dispatched a police car.

Police Constable Peter Folino said the woman called twice and said she had turned on the gas on the second call. Then she hung up. Because of Folino's quick action, police arrived in minutes and turned off the gas before the mother or children suffered any ill effects.

She was being questioned early today.

Police Constable Peter Folino kept talking last night – and saved the lives of a mother and five children.

The despondent woman phoned the police to say she was going to gas herself and her children.

Folino talked and quickly sent the police who turned off the gas before the family was hurt.

He said the woman had called twice. On the second call she said she had turned the gas on, then hung up.

She was being questioned today.

The second version saves three lines on a story originally

totalling 17 lines: a worthwhile saving for the ten minutes that it should take to write off the more direct version. Only when the intro has established the news point – the happy ending – does the story go back to the beginning of the event and develop chronologically.

The news gets lost again here, and the intro should be split, as on the right, into two sentences:

A noisy meeting of 3,000 workers voted in Birmingham today to instruct their shop stewards to get the BMC management and the ETU together to settle within 24 hours the pay dispute which has halted all car production and thrown more than 21,000 workers idle in the Midlands.

A noisy meeting of 3,000 workers voted in Birmingham today for peace moves in the BMC pay dispute which has halted car production and thrown more than 21,000 idle in the Midlands.

They instructed their shop stewards to get the BMC management and the ETU to settle within 24 hours.

Most overloaded intros can be lightened in quick subbing. The facts deleted are then interpolated in the next paragraph or lower. This transposition of a phrase or two can make all the difference to the immediate intelligibility of an intro. The italicised section here does not need to be in the intro:

A former French parachutist who was serving a life sentence in the island fortress of St Martin de Re *for complicity in the murder of a police officer in the Algiers insurrection of 1962*, has escaped by means which recall the flight of Edmond Dantes from Chateau d'If in 'The Count of Monte Cristo'.

He is believed to have left the prison, which is about a mile off La Rochelle, on the Atlantic Coast, in the trunk of another prisoner pardoned by President de Gaulle and released on Friday evening with two others.

The man, Clause Tenne, was reported present when the morning roll call was taken, though officials are not sure now whether it was he, in fact, who replied 'present'.

The first intro is 55 words long. The literary reference is fine, but the reader loses some of the flavour by the way the editor has left in so much superfluous detail. The italic section should be transposed to the third paragraph or even lower as a separate background statement:

> Tenne was imprisoned for complicity in the murder of a police officer in the Algiers insurrection of 1962.

Editors can, again, save this overloaded intro:

> It is a sobering thought that, ten years after the Committee on Grass Utilisation, *under Sir Sydney Carne*, reported that improved methods in production and use of grass *were not coming into wide use as rapidly as they should*, speakers at a conference *on grass conservation* at Bristol last week should have used even stronger words *to describe the existing situation*.

That really needs rewriting, but quickly editing the intro as it stands the words in italic can be deleted altogether or easily transposed to a later sentence to leave:

> It is a sobering thought that, ten years after the Committee on Grass Utilisation called for better methods of grass production and use, speakers at a conference at Bristol last week should have used even stronger words.

In the discussion so far I have stressed the need to shed the intro of extraneous detail, whether of sequence, source or subsidiary news point. But clearly the words that remain in an intro must pull their weight. It is easier to keep the intro short if it does not carry identifying detail; but some specific identifying detail is needed in all news intros. The test is whether the detail applies to a single news point, how far it identifies the news subject and how far it merely adds to the decoration. If the detail is an integral identifying part of a single news point, it is unlikely to be an example of sequence or source obsession or overloading. The intros on the left below show the perils of denuding. They are anaemic compared with the intros with detail on the right. The anaemic intro is a less common error, but it demonstrates the limits of word-shedding and economical generality.

An agricultural show cancelled some events yesterday because of the spread of cattle disease.

All livestock classes at the Royal Smithfield Show were cancelled yesterday because of the spread of foot-and-mouth disease.

An air crash in which British holidaymakers died last month may have been caused by poison gases leaking into the pilots' cabin.

The pilot of the DC4 chartered airliner which plunged into a mountain near Perpignan last month, killing 83 British holiday-makers, was probably seriously affected by carbon monoxide poisoning.

Three Aids to Better Intros

We have now examined three main causes of bad intros: chronology, source obsession and overloading. Before we look at some specialist problems of the intro, here are two suggestions for finding a route through any labyrinth.

The telegram

Where does the avalanche of words touch real life? What effect is the news buried in it going to have on people's lives and happiness? Decide that, then imagine telling the news by telegram. Well, since nobody sends telegrams much these days, imagine you are at a public pay phone with three minutes or less to get the point across. Obviously we do not want an intro in breathless telegraphese, but the mental trick often helps to elicit the real meaning of the story: editors of text for print and broadcasting will find they dispense with the incidentals, the venue and the background and the tempting details. It is just the same as imagining having to tell somebody urgently what the story is all about. It is gratifying how this simple trick helps to shed literary complications and reveal the hard nugget of news.

For instance, in the following story, exactly as received, the text editor would not dream of *talking* about 'consequential increase'.

> If British Railways decide to forgo an application to the Transport Tribunal for fares increase in the period for which London Transport have agreed not to make fares increases, any consequential increase in British Railways' revenue deficit will rank for grant, Mr Tom Fraser, Minister of Transport, said in a written answer.

The text editor should think of the telegram being sent to a rather aged relative who wouldn't know a subsidiary clause if it hit him.

> BRITISH RAIL WILL PEG FARES.

Or expanded:

> BRITISH RAILWAYS INVITED BY TRANSPORT MINISTER FRASER TO PEG FARES FOR SAME PERIOD AS LONDON TRANSPORT STOP GOVERNMENT WILL PAY ANY DEFICIT.

This telegram should then be filled out:

> British Railways were invited to peg their fares yesterday by the Minister of Transport, Mr Fraser. He said that if they agreed to keep their fares down in the period already agreed by London Transport, the Government would meet any deficit.

If the text editor looks at the following intro on an accident story and applies the telegram technique, the clouds disappear. Nobody would tell a friend, 'Minor head lacerations were suffered by Peter Muratore'.

> Minor head lacerations were suffered by Peter Muratore, 36, of 287 Hartsdale Road, Irondequoit, about 2.45 a.m. yesterday when he fell asleep while driving north in River Boulevard, at the University of Rochester campus, and crashed into a parked car, police said. He was treated at Strong Memorial Hospital

and released. The parked car was owned by Mrs Shirley Graham, Greenville, S.C.

PETER MURATORE, 36, 287 HARTSDALE ROAD, IRONDE-QUOIT, FELL ASLEEP DRIVING NORTH IN RIVER BOULE-VARD STOP CRASHED INTO PARKED CAR UNIVERSITY ROCHESTER CAMPUS 2.45 A.M. MINOR HEAD CUTS TREA-TED STRONG MEMORIAL HOSPITAL STOP PARKED CAR OWNED BY MRS SHIRLEY GRAHAM.

And we end up with this intro:

Peter Muratore, 36, of 287 Hartsdale Road, Irondequoit, fell asleep while driving north in River Boulevard and crashed into a parked car at the University of Rochester campus at 2.45 a.m. yesterday.

He was treated for minor head cuts at Strong Memorial Hospital. The parked car was owned by Mrs Shirley Graham, Greenville, S.C.

It is absurd, in any event, to start with such a low-key word as 'minor'. Always look for the positive statement for the intro, and, subject to accuracy, save the qualifying and nullifying statements for a subsidiary position.

The important you

Intros should make the personal relevance of the story a lead point whenever possible. On the left is a New York report which focuses on garage union members. But the real point of impact of the story is on thousands of drivers who will have to park their own cars. Note that the rewrite is about half as long, because we have avoided repeating the same information.

City parking garage attendants last night authorized a strike that could lead to a walkout early next month – a potential disruption to the lives of tens of thousands of motorists.

Tens of thousands of drivers will have to find and reclaim their own parked cars if attendants in 1,500 privately owned city garages walk out on March 5.

They authorized their union,

With less than two weeks to go before their contract with private garage owners expires, union leaders said it's increasingly likely their members will walk off the job on March 5.

Fred Alston, business manager for Teamsters Local 272, said many of his 5,000 members haven't had a raise in eight years and that owners so far have offered them only an extra 5 cents an hour.

'Since 1991 the guys haven't gotten an increase, and they're offering 5 cents?' said Alston. 'It's a slap in the face.'

A strike by the union would cause headaches for drivers in Brooklyn, Queens, Manhattan and the Bronx. It would force motorists who rent spaces in nearly 1,500 privately owned garages to fetch their own cars or rely on replacement crews, Alston said.

Joel Stahl, of the Metropolitan Parking Association, which represents most of city garage owners, said he couldn't address Alston's charges because negotiations are under way.

Teamsters Local 272, to strike then if a new contract is not signed. Fred Alston, the Local's business manager, said many of his 5,000 members had not had a raise in eight years and that owners had offered only an extra five cents an hour. 'It's a slap in the face.'

Garages could try to bring in replacement crews. Joel Stahl, of the Metropolitan Parking Association, representing most of the owners, would only say negotiations are under way.

The key word

In trying that technique of putting the copy aside and composing a mental telegram or swift e-mail, the text editor will often find that a single word or phrase is the vital signal. With the accident to Mr Muratore it was 'fell asleep'. This key word concept is one of the secrets of successful headlines. It can also help with intros. Here is an example. The Middle East Command in Aden announced one Saturday that two named soldiers were missing presumed dead after a clash with rebel Yemen tribesmen. The next day the Army commander called a press conference and announced that the men who had died in the fighting were later beheaded and their heads were exhibited on sticks in the Yemeni capital of Taiz.

Now, the news here comes down to a single word: BEHEADED. The intro has simply to say that two soldiers presumed killed in fighting *were beheaded*. But look at how one morning paper handled the story:

> The heads of two British soldiers killed last Thursday were exhibited on sticks in Taiz, twin capital of the Yemen, according to 'reliable information' given to a Press conference in Aden yesterday by Major-General John Cubbon, GOC Middle-East Land Forces.

The text editor allowed the second event – the exhibition of the heads – to overtake the real news which, at this stage, was the actual beheading. Until readers have realised that there has been a beheading they are not ready for the information about heads on sticks in Taiz. Another intro was:

> A British officer and a soldier, killed in an ambush by the 'Red Wolves' of the Yemen, were beheaded by the Arabs.
> Then their heads were put on show sticks at Taiz, twin capital of the Yemen, it was revealed yesterday.

The criticism of this intro is that it takes too long to reach the key act and key word, the beheading. This next version was cluttered:

> Two British soldiers, killed in bitter fighting, were beheaded by screaming tribesmen who carried the heads as trophies across the frontier to Yemen.
> Then, according to reports reaching here today, the heads were stuck on spikes and exhibited in the main square of Taiz, twin capital of the Yemen.

This one benefited by its directness:

> Two British soldiers have been killed and decapitated by the Yemeni.

One paper did not use the key word, as we see it, but it squeezed in two strong news points intelligibly:

> Two British soldiers killed in fighting with tribesmen had their heads cut off and exhibited on sticks in Taiz, the Yemen capital.

Special Intro Problems

Intros beginning with quotes and intros based on reported speech need critical attention. They are apt to produce problems of identification and meaning and to be replete with officialese.

Quotes

Some offices ban quote intros because of typographical complications. There is more against them than that. Readers have to do too much work. They have to find out who is speaking and they may prefer to move on. Only for the most startling quote will the average reader feel like making the effort. Few baits of quotation are good enough in this over-fished pond. Often, as here, they merely delay the real news point (left), which is given in the version on the right:

'I have had no row with Mrs Castle but I am very sad at leaving', said London's Mr Traffic, Sir Alexander Samuels, last night after resigning as honorary chief adviser to Mrs Barbara Castle, the Minister of Transport.	London's Mr Traffic, Sir Alexander Samuels, has resigned as honorary chief adviser on road traffic to Mrs Barbara Castle, the Minister of Transport. He said last night: 'I have had no row with Mrs Castle but I am very sad at leaving.'

Quotes are almost always better *in support of* an opening

statement. The right choice was made here:

> Mr. Ian Smith, the Rhodesian Prime Minister, today accused the United Nations of incredible deceit and hypocrisy over its efforts to smash Rhodesia's self-proclaimed independence.
> 'I venture to predict', he said in a New Year television address, 'that there is more justice where the demon Satan reigns than where the United Nations wallows in its sanctimonious hypocrisy.'

The next example shows how an intro grounded on the third person can be more pithy and lively.

> Vice-President Humphrey, speaking today on the 21st anniversary of Sir Winston Churchill's 'Iron Curtain' speech at Fulton, Missouri, predicted that the Iron Curtain could be replaced by the 'Open Door'.

This is comprehensible, attractive and accurate. The third-person intro enables the text editor to contrast the Iron Curtain and the Open Door as the Vice-President did, even though Mr Humphrey did not do so in the style of a newspaper intro. To have begun with a quotation would have involved this:

> 'It is my belief that we stand today upon the threshold of a new era in our relations with the peoples of Europe, a period of new engagement', said Vice-President Humphrey yesterday.
> 'Exactly 21 years ago today Winston Churchill spoke the well-remembered words "from Stettin in the Baltic to Trieste in the Adriatic, an iron curtain has descended across the Continent" . . . The Curtain has become increasingly permeable in some places . . . I do not believe that a realistic settlement of European problems can be achieved without the participation of the United States and Russia. The goals of Western European unity and of Atlantic partnership are not in opposition to the goal of the Open Door. They are the key to that door.'

Three paragraphs are now needed to convey the point of

Vice-President Humphrey's address. Quotes in stories like this are best used to substantiate the intro, not to replace it.

Should quote intros be banned altogether? It would be a mistake. There are times where the third-person intro is duller or where the problems of identification are not acute:

> The last words the legendary Cuban guerrilla leader, Che Guevara, spoke just before he died were to identify himself and admit that he had failed.

That meets the usual criteria for an intro, but here is a livelier version, using a direct quote:

> 'I am Che Guevara, I have failed', were the last words of the legendary Cuban guerrilla leader, spoken to Bolivian soldiers just before he died of his wounds early yesterday.

And again:

> The Governor-General of Canada, General Georges Vanier, made a plea for unity yesterday.

It is safe but it is not as good as the direct quote:

> 'I pray God that we all go forward hand in hand. We cannot run the risk of this great country falling into pieces.' These words were part of a plea for unity . . .

Tenses

Sol Chandler once observed of Australian newspapers, addicted to the past tense and conditional, that it would not surprise him to see any paper's splash on a great event start with: 'Australia had declared war on China, the Prime Minister told the Federal Parliament in Canberra yesterday'.

The past tense (left) is slower and can be confusing (does this passage mean the President once believed in a volunteer force but has now changed his mind? No, it does not). The dramatic present (right) should be used for intros and main text:

An all-volunteer armed force was the ideal, said the President in a message to Congress.

An all-volunteer armed force is the ideal, said the President in a message to Congress.

Verbosity

Text editors should always be on the alert when they see intros written by rail officials, clerks of works or court officers. They are not adept at the job.

> A British Rail official said yesterday that the main-line cancellations were an economy move because a sufficient number of passengers were not now using the through train.

This meant that *too few people are using* the through train.

Reported statements from officials, if merely rendered direct into third person, are a common source of muddled intros (and muddled copy). I did say something about third-person reporting earlier (pp. 64–71), but the point for now is that the intro does not have to put into indirect speech every single word the man uttered. The freedom third-person reporting gives is to put the news into simpler words – always provided they convey the sense accurately. It is absurd, in these instances, to seek refuge in direct quotes:

Penn Yan – 'The adverse publicity against the village of Penn Yan during the past several weeks in regard to the gross pollution of Seneca Lake was based on misleading information issued by uninformed sources', Municipal Plant Superintendent Leland A. Welker said yesterday . . .

Penn Yan – Tests showed Penn Yan village is not to blame for the gross pollution of Seneca Lake, said Municipal Plant Superintendent Leland A. Welker yesterday. Mr Welker said the adverse publicity was 'based on misleading information by uninformed sources' . . .

That intro (left) was written by Municipal Sewage Plant Superintendent Leland A. Welker. Municipal sewage plant superintendents need supervision on intro-writing. The reporter or text editor has to do the work, and they will not –

I hope – allow 'in regard to'. It should have been rewritten as on the right.

Portmanteau intros

I have urged text editors to concentrate in every intro on the single essential news point. There are a few occasions when they have to fall back on a portmanteau intro:

> The President made a major statement yesterday on problems in the Far East, Germany and the Near East.

Most portmanteau intros are as dull as this. But every one, even the occasional lively portmanteau intro, carries a real trap for unwary editors:

> Bribery, violence, anarchy and ignorance are dramatically exposed in a report to be published tomorrow by the Institute of Race Relations.

It would be hard to contrive a more arresting portmanteau intro. Tell me more, says the reader. But in the long story which followed there was no single word of violence. Text editors should always check that the story delivers the goods promised in the intro; with portmanteau intros they should check every promise.

Questions

No news intro should start with a question, whether in quotes or reported speech, and still less in any other form. Intros are for telling the reader, not for interrogation.

Abbreviations

It is unrealistic not to recognise that certain abbreviations have passed so much into the language that may be safely used in the intro: TV and UN and NATO internationally; BBC in Britain; and GOP and CBS in the United States. These are a few examples. There are others. Even so, it is good working practice to avoid abbreviations in intros. Just as in text, they should be spelled out when used first time; and text editors should never assume that the initials which are familiar to them will be familiar to the reader. Excessive use of abbreviations is in any event unsightly.

Delayed intros

The discussion has so far concentrated on the straightforward news story where the technique is to bring in at once the human results of the activity. There are times when the point of the intro can be delayed with effect. This is when delaying the news point momentarily can add punch or suspense or emphasise a contrast.

There are any number of gradations of delay in a story. I am referring here only to intros. Some stories are deliberately written so that the punch comes in the last line. Court stories in the popular papers especially are written so that the routine hard news point is concealed in a vignette. This is a technique affecting the whole construction of the story and we will examine it later. For the moment we remain concerned with the general news intro.

The delayed intro in general news can be as short as waiting to the end of the first sentence. Instead of saying 'Peter Bloggs was recaptured yesterday', it could be:

> Borstal escapee Peter Bloggs went for a swim yesterday – and came face to face with an off-duty policeman in swimming trunks.

The delayed intro is a device for all types of newspaper, including the serious:

> The application form described Oliver Greenhalgh as a rodent operative. Questions on qualifications and experience were ignored. After a payment of £11 a certificate was issued stating that Mr. Greenhalgh had been accepted as a fellow of the English Association of Estate Agents and Valuers.
> Oliver Greenhalgh is a cat.

The same paper also used a delayed intro to effect in reporting on General de Gaulle's tour of Poland. It would have been possible to report the news in the traditional first sentence – that General de Gaulle was rebuffed by the First Secretary of the Polish Communist Party. But the paper gave the intro an element of suspense with the final words coming like the pounding of a fist on the table:

> General de Gaulle now has the answer for which he has been waiting since he arrived in Warsaw. It came today, from Mr. Gomulka, the First Secretary of the Polish Communist Party and the 'strong man' of Poland, after his address to the solemn session of the Polish Parliament, the Sejm. The answer was hard, uncompromising, and just barely courteous.

Text editors should consider using a delayed intro occasionally on a suitable hard news story when the normal construction would read like the intro in every other paper. There was a good opportunity to exploit contrast when Britain's submarine, the *Repulse*, was launched and ended up on a mudbank. Instead of simply saying 'Britain's submarine went on a mudbank at the launching yesterday', the text editor might have contrived a delayed intro:

> Shipyard workers cheered. A bottle of home-made elderberry wine, released by Lady Joan Zucherman, broke over the bows. HMS *Repulse* slid proudly, perfectly down the slipway at Barrow. And two minutes later £55 million-worth of Polaris submarine was aground on a mudbank.

To sum up this chapter on intros here is a horrific talisman of 79 words, subsidiary clauses and all:

> In his address to the annual meeting of North Riding Dental Practitioners, held at the Golden Fleece Hotel, Thirsk, the chairman, Mr. C.W.L. Heaton, expressed his concern that there were still many practitioners in the area who did not appreciate the importance of their attendance at meetings as complacency of this nature did not give much encouragement to those who were striving to secure a betterment factor in forthcoming negotiations between the Minister of Health and the dental profession.

CHAPTER SIX

The Structure of a News Story – The News Lead

The structure of a news story depends both on length and content. The story told in three or four paragraphs is simply an intro followed by further details. As the length increases, however, those further details multiply and their introduction and treatment must be handled carefully. Much will depend on the nature of the story, whether it is basically one of action or one of statement and opinion. Chronology is a guide to the construction of the action story: it is no guide to the construction of the complex statement–opinion story.

Action Stories

Let us return to the story of the Berlin Wall rescue (pp. 97–8). The original intro was:

> After hearing shooting at the Berlin Wall yesterday an American military policeman raced to the scene and found East German guards trying to drag a refugee back. The American soldier went to a second-storey window overlooking the Wall, threw a tear-gas grenade, to make the East Germans release the refugee, then climbed on top of the Wall and amid a hail of bullets between East and West helped to pull the refugee to the West.

We rewrote that intro:

> An American military policeman braved a hail of bullets to pull a wounded refugee over the Berlin Wall yesterday.

The intro now distils the essence of the news. It is a simple direct sentence not overloaded with detail. But it has not indicated all the most important news points in a long and detailed story. This now has to be done in other sentences and paragraphs which together make a news lead. Each succeeding sentence should be as simple and direct as the intro. It should give a news point and, if possible, add detail the generalised intro has omitted.

> The refugee was hit five times – but he will live. The soldier, 22-year-old Hans Puhl, threw a tear-gas grenade to make East German guards release the refugee. Then amid fire from the East and counter-fire from the West, he climbed on the Wall to drop a rope to the wounded man, Michel Meyer, aged 21.

The most dramatic items of the news story have now been presented in a succinct news lead. Some of the identifying details (such as names) excluded from the intro have been added – but without delaying the development of the key points. The news lead has concentrated on results. It has omitted both other detail and explanation. The story now has to explain how the refugee, Meyer, got into his predicament; how the soldier, Puhl, climbed on the high wall, how he came to be on the scene at all, how the firing started. How should we do all this? In action stories, as I have said, chronology is the master. Once the most dramatic items have been presented – and only then – we go back to the beginnings and build a sequential narrative. In doing this, we check that every point in the news lead is substantiated – for instance that there was a 'hail' of bullets and not merely a couple of shots. The logical narrative is simple enough. The skill is in the way we amplify what we have already told the reader and knit together the two sides of the story.

The paragraph after the news lead should read something like this:

> Meyer had swum the River Spree to reach the Wall at dawn. East Border guards opened fire and he was hit five times in the arm and legs. Hans Puhl, born in Bremerhaven but taken to

the US when he was 14, was on duty at the Checkpoint Charlie crossing point when he heard the shooting about 100 yards away.

We have gone back to the beginning of the action, both for Meyer and Puhl. We have explained how Meyer and Puhl got where they did and have given an anticipatory explanation of Puhl's fluent German. Everything now follows the way it happened, told as much as possible in the words of the actors:

Puhl, rifle in hand, climbed to a second-storey window overlooking the Wall and saw Meyer being held by two uniformed East Germans who started to drag him away.

'I pointed my rifle at them and shouted in German: "Let the boy go",' Puhl said. 'When they ignored me I threw a tear-gas bomb. It landed only a yard from them and they let go of Meyer.

'Two civilians lifted me up and I leaned against the top of the Wall with my hands resting on it. I held my pistol loaded but cocked. I saw Meyer lying there and told him in German: "Stay there while we cut the wire (barbed wire on top of the Wall)".'

Three East German guards in a trench 100 yards away began firing at Puhl, an easy target in his white MP's hat: 'Shots hit the top of the Wall and debris was flying all round me'.

Two West Berliners cut through the barbed wire fencing topping the seven-foot Wall and firemen helped to drag the fence down. Then they threw a rope down to Meyer. All the while bullets were flying in both directions over the Wall, hitting houses on the West Berlin side and damaging furniture in the flats. Meyer fastened a loop of the rope under his arms and was pulled up. On top of the Wall he collapsed and was dragged across by his clothes.

A woman eyewitness in a house by the Wall said: 'It was a terrible scene. The boy never uttered a sound. I could see he was hit and he never screamed. It was eerie'.

This ends the action. Note that quotes are introduced to provide variety and directness; how little use is made of the continuation word 'then' – too many 'thens' make it sound like a police report; and that we have now substantiated the lead without using the same words: 'bullets were flying in both directions' is better than repeating the intro phrase 'hail of bullets'.

So much for the action. We can now add non-action background and assessment, which has no part in the chronology (and which could all be cut under pressure of space).

> Puhl said he had been entitled to fire at the East German guards as he was allowed to shoot in defence, but he had not done so.
>
> Yesterday's incident occurred within half a mile of a memorial at the Wall to Peter Fechter, the 18-year-old East German boy left to bleed to death at the foot of the Wall in 1962. 'The action by our MP evens the score for Peter Fechter', said one American officer.
>
> It was the longest battle since the Wall went up and the most serious in that it was the first time a US soldier had gone into action to save a refugee.

This then should be the normal construction in action stories:

1. Intro and/or news lead: the most dramatic incident(s), the human result(s) of the activity
2. Development in chronological narrative
3. Background and assessment if any

Here is the story of an award for a pit rescue, with my comments on the right:

Colliery overman Mr John Hodgson, aged 50, of Silksworth, turned himself into a human pit prop when a fall of stones threatened to crush a trapped man at Silksworth mine. For his gallantry he was last night awarded

Intro: the most dramatic presentation – and the conclusion in two sentences: first the rescue, then the medal, and his reaction.

the British Empire Medal – and was amazed by it.

It was a night shift at the Silksworth Mine on January 12, says the *London Gazette* citation. Three men were working on withdrawing waste edge supports. There was a sudden fall of stone from the roof and one of them was trapped. He was pinned in a sitting position behind a conveyor belt drum box, under a fallen roofbar and partly buried by rock.

'Overman Hodgson quickly arrived on the scene and immediately took charge of the operations. Realising that great slabs of stone which were hanging over the trapped man would fall if orthodox methods of support were tried, he directed two men to steady them on each side while he himself, sprawled across the drum box, supported the centre.

'Hodgson instructed the others to jump to safety and then he released his hold and scrambled back over the conveyor belt in a working height of only 4ft 6in.

'The whole roof above the place where the man had been trapped immediately collapsed, filling the space where the men had been working to rescue him.'

Mr Hodgson's two colleagues, Mr Walter Appleby, of 50 Potts Street, Sunderland, and Mr

The action has ended. Supplementary details can now be added.

Harry Cooper, of 32 Ashdown Road, Sunderland, were both awarded the Queen's Medal for Brave Conduct.

Mr Hodgson, a miner for 30 years, was amazed to hear of his award last night. He recalled being questioned by a mines inspector, but added: 'They seemed to be harping on about it and I thought there might be an inquiry'.

The man trapped by the fall, Mr Ernest King (52), of Holborn Road, Hilton Lane, said last night: 'I have had other lucky escapes since I started at Silksworth in 1937 but I have never been trapped like this.

'It's a queer feeling just lying there with tons of stones likely to fall'.

Backing up intro again.

It would not matter to the construction if these paragraphs were higher, say before the mention of the Queen's Medal. The essential is to tell the action chronologically, substantiating the intro before bothering about other details.

A Good News Narrative

Barry Bearak, of the *New York Times*, was in Macedonia in the spring of 1999 to report on the refugees from Kosovo. He gives us a brilliant example of the story-telling technique. The italics are mine and my comments are on the right.

BLACE, Macedonia, April 29 – When they came upon the minefield in the rugged mountains near the border, the 64 Kosovo Albanian refugees were warned to stay in single file and not stray from the narrow path or stumble on a branch or rock in the *predawn gloom*.

First, the structure. He opens the story not at the beginning of the action but at mid-point. There are other action points where the story might open, but this opening is suspenseful without being aggravating in keeping the suspense for too long.

Twenty people *trod* through the *mud* without a problem, and that is perhaps what made the *tired old farmer*, Osman Jezerci, less wary.

Characterisation of farmer makes his fate sadder.

'Osman, don't go so far over there,' someone called out to him.

Mr. Jezerci looked over his shoulder, possibly to see who was speaking. And that is when he *drifted* a few more feet to the left, those near him said. The *explosion lifted his body off his legs*. The man beside him died, too. So did a young woman, Selvete Kukaj.

Italicised words in these opening paragraphs are good verbs and nouns, evoking the atmosphere. A less good observer would just have reported that the farmer 'died' or 'was killed'.

Within an hour of the blast on Wednesday, two others died from their wounds. These two – a 12-year-old girl named Zyjnete Avdiu and an 18-year-old woman, Miradije Kukaj – were buried here today in a solemn ceremony attended *by a large crowd of people who did not know them.*

Arresting thought that they were buried by 'people who did not know them'.

This has become the habit in Blace, a Macedonian border village of 100 homes. In the last five weeks, since NATO began bombing and throngs of Kosovo Albanians started fleeing, people from here have laid 12 strangers to rest in their cemetery.

The opening news lead having been completed, we flash back to the origins of the journey, i.e. what occurred in the first place to get them into a minefield.

Liman Jashari, the village hohxa, or holy man, said the ritual Muslim prayers in Arabic and then switched to Albanian to soothe the mourners at the funeral.

'Before us, we see two bodies,' he said. 'It is fate that they died close to our homes before proceeding to heaven. We must remember that *everything that comes before us is the will of God.*'

He surely believed this, though it did not stop him from weeping as the bodies were taken from coffins and laid into the earth. The two young women wore white sheets as they were lowered into the ground. Their heads were placed on pillows of sod.

Each day, Macedonia awakens to a new tale of refugee misery as if this part of the world were keen to outdo itself with affliction. The day before, a 10-year-old boy, near death with a bullet wound and two open leg fractures, had been brought across the border in a wheelbarrow. Then came the horror of *a minefield on a moonlit night.*

'Fear made us leave our homes, fear of the Serbs,' said Ibrahim Avdiu, 39, Zyjnete's father. 'My whole life has been turned upside down with fear.'

As with most stories told by the ethnic Albanian refugees, Mr. Avdiu's starts with being ordered by Serbs to leave Kosovo. His family's home was in Kacenik, a small city only 10 miles from Macedonia. Fighting has been fierce there between Serbian forces and the rebels of

A less skilled reporter would have left it at 'the hohxa said ritual prayers' but Bearak noted the simple eloquence of what he said.

'Each day, Macedonia awakens . . .' is not only a neat way to join the second part of the story, it also gives a sense of time, of a village beginning to stir. The 'moonlit night' is a link, though the criticism might be made that 'moonlit' is not quite right as an identifier since the night was not so described earlier on.

Link passage. To have had this any earlier would have delayed the emotional pull of the funeral and the necessary scene-setting.

the secessionist Kosovo Liberation Army. Some put the death toll at more than 100 in the last month.

Mr. Avdiu, a day laborer, took his wife and four children to the nearby village of Llanishte. From there, they could see some goings-on through binoculars. Bulldozers, he said, were pushing bodies into mass graves. He and hundreds of others plotted their escapes.

People set out for the border in various groups. The journey, while short, was hard. The welcome cover of darkness was accompanied by the unwelcome distress of frost. Gullies had to be crossed, rocks had to be climbed. Very early on Wednesday, Mr. Avdiu led a horse through the heavily wooded terrain. Clutching the saddle was his invalid mother-in-law.

The group had accepted guidance from six members of the Kosovo Liberation Army. These were the men who cautioned them about the minefield and pointed the way up the narrow path.

When the mine exploded, the blast shook the ground and turned dirt and stones into projectiles. People were wailing, unsure whether to run or stand still. They wiped their faces with their hands and smelled their fingers, *trying to determine if the wetness was sweat or blood.*

Observation of reaction. From this point the story can be carried forward chronologically.

Arsim Kukaj, 20, was the only son in a family with five daughters. Two of his sisters had been walking at his side, trying to protect the sole male heir by standing in the sight line of any snipers the family might encounter.

'My sisters were afraid I would be shot, but instead of getting in the way of a bullet they died because of the shrapnel,' he said, bereft, unable to say much more.

'Ibrahim Avdiu's wife and sister were injured. As he tended to them, he said, he could hear 12-year-old Zyjnete, his oldest child, crying out, *"Daddy, I'm dying."*

Mr. Avdiu's younger brother, Izet Asutiqi, scooped the girl up and draped her over his back. He began running. 'I did not know where I was going, but I just started down a road and hoped it would lead somewhere,' he said.

He carried her for two hours, though she was dead long before that, he said. His shoulders and back ached from the weight. Finally, he put her on the ground and looked for landmarks to remember. He continued down the road.

In Blace, Mr. Asutiqi staggered into a small grocery. He drew a map on the ground with a stick. Villagers then risked Macedonian border guards and Serbian

"Daddy, I'm dying . . ." would have made a moving moment for an intro to the story, but it would have required more recapitulation to explain how we got to this point.

troops to search for the body across the border. They carried both dead girls up and down the trails in shifts. They did not chance more time to locate the other dead.

This morning, the hoxha did the ritual cleaning of the bodies. The girls' bloody clothes were replaced by the white sheets. The village men prayed in the mosque and then passed the coffins hand to hand down a road and then up a hill to the cemetery. Three mules grazed among the tombstones as the mourners went past in the early afternoon.

Once in the ground, the bodies were covered with *wood planks and then dirt*. With six men at work with spades, *it took less than two minutes to fill the graves*.

Except for the dead, only men attended the ceremony, as is the custom. But as the funeral ended, one of Miradije Kukaj's older sisters wandered in a daze toward the mound. She collapsed and kissed the dirt, laying her cheek against the grave *as if listening for a pulse*. When men lifted her up, she searched about for flowers, but found only a single violet blossom. *It was wilted and she threw it down in despair and bawled*.

'Don't cry,' people said, attempting comfort. *'Crying will not awaken your sister.'*

Note the quality of observation. Concrete nouns, active voice verbs.

A poetic passage – listening for a pulse, a single violet blossom. And then the brutal realism of the despair.

As the villagers of Blace returned to their homes, several pointed to smoke not too far off in the mountains. The Serbs had set fire to the village of Gorance, the hoxha said, just as they had set a place called Rozhance ablaze the day before.

More refugees would soon be coming through the mountains.

The story does not just taper off. It takes us back to the opening scene and reminds us that this is just one day in a series of horrible days.

Now let us imagine Bearak's story rendered into ordinary straight news. My rewrite is adequate for that purpose – but it is nothing like as engrossing as Bearak's narrative.

Blace, Macedonia, April 29. Five Kosovo Albanians in a party of 64 were killed when they stepped on mines in mountains near the border.

Three died at once, a farmer named Osman Jezerci, an unnamed man, and a young woman, Selvete Kukaj.

Within an hour of the blast, two more died – a 12-year-old girl named Zyjnete Avdiu, and an 18-year-old woman Miradije Kukaj.

They were buried today in Blace, Macedonia, in a solemn ceremony attended by a large crowd of people who did not know them.

This has become the habit in this Macedonian border village of 100 homes. In the past five weeks, since NATO began bombing and throngs of Kosovo Albanians started fleeing, people from here have laid 12 strangers to rest in their ceremony . . .

Statement–Opinion Stories

News values determine the structure of statement–opinion stories. The beginnings of speeches or documents or interrelated series of verbal exchanges do not begin the news story unless they provide the most important news. Importance, not chronology, is the art of this treatment. The action story requires the most dramatic points in the news lead, with some detail; the statement–opinion story requires the most important points in the news lead, with some detail. The art of the news lead, in both types of story, is in picking out all the highlights with just the right amount of detail. That means enough detail to excite but not to confuse.

This is a subtle matter. What we shall call the *generalised* news lead indicates the highlights of the story without giving the details. The absence of detail keeps the lead reasonably short; the strength of the generalised lead lies in being comprehensive and intelligible. Its weakness is vagueness. The specific news lead gives details at once. Its strength is precision. Its weakness is that if it is to remain brief it cannot indicate all the highlights of the story; and if it tries to do that it can become too long and hard to take in quickly.

Ideally, in the longer stories there should be a news lead which in three or four sentences/paragraphs summarises every news point with some of the detailed identification. It is not enough, in 100 words of news lead, to give the news points in a wholly generalised way. By the time readers have read three or four paragraphs they should have begun to find the generalised news points clothed in precise detail. All the points in the headlines should have been covered by this time.

Let us examine a statement–opinion story as it was treated in a number of different newspapers, and consider the ideal blending of the general and the particular in the news lead and deployment of the secondary news points. The story was that the Minister of Technology, at that time Mr Tony Benn, had attacked the American Westinghouse Corporation for trying to tempt away a team of British atomic scientists. The scientists had been working on two advanced atomic power reactors and in an appeal to the scientists to stay, Mr Benn disclosed that Westinghouse had previously made a 'completely inadequate' offer for a licence to manufacture the reactor.

There are both precise and generalised ways this story can

be told in an intro and news lead. Given roughly 100 words the challenge is to construct a news lead which deals with these points:

1. Mr Benn has written an unprecedented open letter appealing to certain British atomic scientists to stay in Britain.
2. He has attacked a US company for trying to tempt them away as a team.
3. This company's bid to manufacture the reactor under licence had previously been rejected because the bid was 'completely inadequate'.
4. This is not, therefore, just another 'brain drain' story. The company was offering salaries three to five times the scientists' present salaries, much more than the normal differential between US and British salaries.
5. Even so, this was an attempt to catch up 'on the cheap' on Britain's world lead in fast-breeder reactors, a lead gained by 20 years of investment by the British people at a cost of hundreds of millions of pounds.
6. Twenty-four Dounreay scientists had replied to the Westinghouse advertisement.

These facts, in an intro and news lead, can be expressed in either a generalised or specific way. The short generalised expression is on the left, the longer specific version on the right.

The Government	Mr Tony Benn, Minister of Technology.
An American offer	An offer by the Westinghouse Corporation.
Atomic scientists	Atomic energy scientists and engineers at Dounreay, Scotland, and Risley, Lancashire.

Atomic plants	Fast-breeder reactor at Dounreay and design establishment at Risley.
Tempting salaries	Salaries three to five times the present salaries. Westinghouse understood to offer £3,000 to £7,000 for a scientific officer, rising to £15,000 to £35,000 for the best senior staff. Salaries at Dounreay range from £1,100 to £5,000 a year.
An attempt to gain British knowledge	Westinghouse had previously offered to buy a licence for the fast-breeder but offered terms 'completely inadequate in respect of commercial value'.
An American bid to gain British scientists	Westinghouse advertised and 24 Dounreay scientists have answered the advertisement.

Before reading further, text editors might try writing a news lead of around 100 words. This will consist of an intro sentence, followed by two or three supporting paragraphs. The news lead must cover all the news points intelligibly and give as much information as possible.

How the Dailies Handled the Story

A good example of a wholly generalised intro appeared thus:

1. The Government last night issued an unprecedented appeal to Britain's leading atomic scientists not to join the brain drain to America.

This intro is vague. It gives no details on the single news point chosen. It does not give any idea of the other news point that a minister is attacking an American corporation for a particular act of poaching. The story advantage of a generalised intro has therefore been wasted. At the other extreme, this one was specific:

2. Mr Benn, Minister of Technology, has written to atomic scientists working at Dounreay, Caithness, and Risley, Lancashire, warning them of an American plot to discover the secrets of Britain's latest reactor, the fast-breeder reactor at Dounreay, by persuading the senior scientists working on the project to join the Brain Drain.

This intro has tried to indicate the two news points of the appeal to scientists and the attack on an American company but it loses the reader in the particulars. It is 50 words long. It is also going further than strict accuracy would permit in the word 'plot': this was not used by the minister.

No other daily attempted to indicate these two news points in one sentence. Three of the other dailies chose to concentrate the intro sentence on the news point of the minister's appeal to scientists; two concentrated on his attack on the American company. Here are the intros, with comments:

Intros angled on the minister's appeal

3. The Minister of Technology, Mr. Tony Benn, last night took the unprecedented step of writing an open letter to atomic engineers and scientists who have been offered jobs by an American company.

More specific than version 1, but it fails to indicate the line of Benn's letter or the reason for it.

4. Mr. Tony Benn, Minister of Technology, made a dramatic appeal last night to Britain's top nuclear scientists to refuse a tempting offer to join an American firm.

Again more specific than version 1. It spells out Benn's appeal to the scientists to refuse and it indicates the news point of high salaries.

5. Mr. Tony Benn, the Minister of Technology, last night appealed to Atomic Energy Authority scientists and engineers to resist recruiting efforts by the Westinghouse Electric Corporation of the United States.

A specific intro – but by concentrating on a single news point it remains intelligible. It is precise – without going too deeply into the woods. Nothing would have been gained in this context by generalised references to 'atomic scientists' or 'an American company'.

Intros angled on the minister's attack

6. Technology Minister Mr. Tony Benn lashed out last night at an American company's bid to recruit top nuclear scientists.

Fairly generalised intro but it omits the reason for the Minister's attack – the attempt to get nuclear technology 'on the cheap'.

7. Mr. Tony Benn yesterday made an unprecedented attack on a major United States corporation for trying to get British nuclear technology on the cheap.

Generalised (unlike the intro above it fails to specify Benn's position in the Government). This intro gives the reason for the attack, but does not indicate that the US corporation is trying to recruit British scientists.

The most successful intro was version 5. It is an example of the specific intro at its best – concentrating on a single news point, it is able to be precise without becoming long or confused. None of the generalised intros really succeeds as well because none exploits the opportunity given by the generalised style for indicating more than one highlight of the story. Is it possible in one sentence to cover both the news points of the minister's attack on the corporation and his appeal to scientists? It is. For instance:

Mr Tony Benn, Minister of Technology, appealed to British atomic scientists yesterday not to join an American company which was, he said, trying to gain British nuclear technology on the cheap.

This suffices but it is not wholly satisfactory. It is short enough, but running the two news points together reduces their force, especially as one has to be relegated to a subsidiary clause.

We are in fact dealing with a story which has so many news points and details that a news lead is inescapable. An intro sentence alone cannot cope with the news points and supporting details. We now examine how the British dailies and one American paper coped with the news lead:

Version A's news lead was:

Mr Benn, Minister of Technology, has written to atomic scientists working at Dounreay, Caithness, and Risley, Lancashire, warning them of an American plot to discover the secrets of Britain's latest reactor, the fast-breeder reactor at Dounreay, by persuading the senior scientists working on the project to join the Brain Drain.

Twenty-four atomic scientists from Dounreay, where salaries range from £1,000 to £5,000 a year, are understood to have replied to an advertisement by the Westinghouse electrical company of America, offering jobs in the United States.

Westinghouse offers are understood to be between £3,000 to £7,000 for a scientific officer, rising to £15,000 to £35,000 for the best senior staff.

This is 109 words. It is precise (overlooking the misuse of 'between' in the last paragraph). But it omits the important news point about the inadequate bid for a licence. This is a failing, and the reason for that is that the paper spends too many words substantiating the American company's persuasion. The second and third paragraphs are almost wholly devoted to salary details. These should have been dealt with succinctly in a general way ('salaries three to five times' as great) so that there was space in the news lead to bring other important points to the top.

Indeed, this fault continues because the paper went on to

give details of the Westinghouse advertisement for scientists before telling the reader about the earlier bid for a licence. This news lead, therefore, is too detailed, to the exclusion of news points.

The version B news lead was:

> Technology Minister Mr. Tony Benn lashed out last night at an American company's bid to recruit top British nuclear scientists.
>
> Mr. Benn accused the American Westinghouse Company of trying to cash in on British know-how 'on the cheap'.
>
> And he asked research scientists and engineers in the two major Atomic Energy Authority plants – Dounreay (Scotland) and Risley (Lancashire), to reject the U.S. offers immediately.
>
> The minister's appeal follows Westinghouse pledges of salaries for Britons who join their nuclear power station design plants in Pittsburgh. The money: Up to five times what the men are earning.

This is 95 words. Again it fails by omitting the central news point about the 'inadequate' bid for a licence. The phrase 'trying to cash in on British know-how on the cheap' is less readily understood – the only comparison given here is in the salaries, and they are not 'on the cheap'. To appreciate the row the reader needs to know about the licence bid, about the attempt to recruit scientists as a team, and the fact that Dounreay has the world's most advanced fast-breeder reactor. If the text editor had added the words 'at salaries three to five times as high' at the end of that first paragraph the whole fourth paragraph could have been used for omitted news points. It is the use of concise phrases like this which enables the text editor to make the news lead really do its work.

Now the version C news lead:

> The Government last night issued an unprecedented appeal to Britain's leading atom scientists not to join the brain drain to America.
>
> It accused Westinghouse Electrical Company of trying to filch the scientists and their know-how.
>
> Westinghouse has been advertising for scientists who have

been developing the new fast-breeder reactor system, on which Britain leads the world.

The American firm recently made a 'totally inadequate' offer for a licence, Minister of Technology Mr. Tony Benn, said last night in an open letter to scientists at the atomic energy centres at Dounreay in the far North of Scotland, and Risley in Lancashire.

This is 101 words. The paper has recovered from the vague start. The third and fourth paragraphs are concise presentations of news points with details. The licence is there, the 'inadequate' offer, the open letter, Dounreay and Risley, the fast-breeder reactor system, the British lead. Only one news point is missing: the salaries.

The fault with this news lead lies in those first two paragraphs. It was not really accurate to refer to 'the brain drain' since the minister stressed this was not a brain drain story. That first sentence could have said:

> The Government last night issued an unprecedented appeal to Britain's leading atom scientists not to let themselves be tempted to America by the Westinghouse Corporation.

This would have freed the second paragraph for a news point. The phrases 'not to join the brain drain to America' and 'trying to filch the scientists and their know-how' waste words on generalities.

The version D news lead was:

> The Minister of Technology, Mr. Tony Benn, last night took the unprecedented step of writing an open letter to atomic engineers and scientists who have been offered jobs by an American company.
>
> The men work at the Atomic Energy Authority plant in Dounreay, Scotland, where the most advanced power reactor in the world is being built.
>
> America has nothing to compare with Britain's achievement.
>
> Twenty-four Dounreay scientists answered a job advertisement by the American Westinghouse company and some are

believed to have been offered posts at up to five times their
present salaries.

This is 93 words. The news points omitted are the licence bid
and indeed the whole concept of the minister's letter as an
attack on the American company. Again the concise way of
making the salaries point would have saved space. This could
have been done at the end of the first sentence . . . 'at salaries
up to five times higher'. The licence point could then have
been brought up from the fifth paragraph (where it appeared)
into the fourth paragraph. In the existing fourth paragraph
the text editor is led into wasteful repetition: 'The American
Westinghouse company' . . . 'Dounreay scientists'. There is
repetition in the idea of Britain's lead. The second paragraph
at the end says 'the most advanced power reactor in the
world'. Then the third paragraph says 'America has nothing
to compare with Britain's achievement.' There is no space to
spare for this in a pithy news lead.

Look next at the version E news lead:

Mr Benn, Minister of Technology, made a dramatic appeal last
night to Britain's top nuclear scientists to refuse a tempting
offer to join an American firm.

He accused the firm – Westinghouse – of trying to get
Britain's nuclear power know-how on the cheap.

The appeal was made in an open letter from Mr. Benn to
Atomic Energy Authority engineers and scientists at Risley,
Lancashire, and at Dounreay, Scotland.

The world's most advanced commercial prototype 'fast
breeder' power reactor, able to generate electricity cheaper
than any other method, is being built at Dounreay. And most
of the AEA design work for fast reactors is carried out at
Risley.

This is 106 words. The point about the licence is omitted. The
salaries above the normal US differential are covered –
adequately enough for the news lead – with the 'tempting
offer' phrase. All the main news points would have been
included if only the licence reference had been added to the

second paragraph. This would have squeezed the details about Risley out of the news lead, but that would not have mattered. This version made intelligent use of general and precise references until the particularisation was overdone with the details of Dounreay and Risley.

The Version F news lead was:

> Mr. Benn, the Minister of Technology, last night appealed to Atomic Energy Authority scientists and engineers to resist recruiting efforts by the Westinghouse Electric Corporation of the United States.
>
> He accused the Americans of trying to get nuclear energy knowledge on the cheap by offering inflated salaries to attract men away from Dounreay and Risley. He said that Westinghouse had applied to buy the licence for the AEA design of the fast-breeder reactor some time ago, but had offered unacceptable terms.
>
> In an open letter to the AEA men, Mr Benn says the AEA is now building at Dounreay the most advanced commercial prototype power reactor in the world – the fast breeder.

This is 113 words – and every one carries its weight. There is no wasteful repetition. There is very little generality – just enough to enable news points to be squeezed in. 'Inflated salaries' will do for the pay. 'Unacceptable terms' suffices for the minister's reference to the licence, though 'completely inadequate terms' would have given extra precision for one more word.

Finally for the British papers the version G news lead:

> Mr. Tony Benn yesterday made an unprecedented attack on a major United States corporation for trying to get British nuclear technology on the cheap.
>
> The Minister of Technology was appealing to nuclear scientists at the Dounreay fast-breeder reactor in Caithness, 24 of whom are thought to have answered an advertisement from the Westinghouse Corporation which would offer them between three and five times their present salaries.
>
> Mr Benn wrote that the Dounreay reactor was the climax of 20 years of investment by the British people and that an offer

made earlier by Westinghouse was 'completely inadequate in respect of the commercial value of what we have to offer'.

This is 109 words. It vies with version F as the best news lead. Version G's generalised intro is sharp. It has the point about 24 men replying to the advertisement and the detail on salary comparisons. Version F, however, gains where it is more precise. Version G omits the key word 'licence' in the third paragraph. It does not really explain that the American company wanted to build the British design on licence. The reference to the Dounreay reactor being the climax of 20 years' British investment almost meets the point about Britain's lead in design – but not quite. Version F again is specific here. The news lead in version F is in admittedly quieter vein than some of the others. There are no adjectives. But the language is simple, well chosen, and lets the news make its own impact.

An American Example

This is a story of strong Anglo-American interest. Let's see how the international edition of one US daily handled it. The news lead was:

> The Westinghouse Electric Corporation of America found itself in the middle of a furore today about the brain drain of scientific talent from Britain. A headline in the *Daily Telegraph* said 'US plot to win British scientists'.
>
> Westinghouse itself in a statement issued in New York and London did not deny it hoped to attract skilled technicians in nuclear research. It said it acted in a 'straightforward manner' in advertising in the British press to fill jobs in the US.
>
> A Labourite MP said he would demand an explanation from Minister of Technology, Mr Benn, who provoked the furore by accusing Westinghouse of trying to obtain nuclear know-how on the cheap.

This is 111 words. There are many things wrong with this as a news lead for American (or British) readers; and indeed the whole story is weak. For American readers the stress on the American company is right for the intro. It is in the further paragraphs that the story fails. The biggest flaw is that the news lead stumbles over itself to give the company's reply before the reader knows what is Mr Benn's central charge. That comes in paragraph 3; paragraph 2 has been devoted entirely to the disclaimer (in the development of the story this is taken up again in paragraph 5). It is far too slow to delay until paragraph 3 that the controversy has been provoked by the British Government. The *Telegraph* headline is colourful and worth quoting but it cannot displace the substance of the story, which is that the Minister of Technology has made an attack.

The rest of the US newspaper story was:

> He said, in an open letter to scientists at the Dounreay experimental establishment in Scotland, that Westinghouse's offer of employment was not really another example of the familiar brain drain. He said it was instead because of Westinghouse trying to purchase the knowledge and experience a whole team of scientists had gained by hiring away a few key persons.
>
> In reply Westinghouse said many of the scientists involved had education and experience that could be utilised in the company's fast growing nuclear power activities. Labourite, Mr Hector Hughes, said he would ask Mr Benn to tell Parliament how many scientists have gone to the US in the last six months.

Anyone editing this story on an American paper ought not to have been satisfied with it. Why, the text editor might ask, should a big American corporation want British scientists? (Not until the last paragraph is the reader even told that it has something to do with nuclear power for domestic purposes.) Of course the story completely fails to deal with the Westinghouse licence bid. It fails again by being too generalised. We have 'nuclear research; nuclear know-how; nuclear power' but not once do we have the specific fact that

Dounreay is a fast-breeder reactor and a crisp explanation of what that is.

The American news lead has other faults. The salary comparison is omitted – at least as interesting to American readers as British. And a good deal of space has been wasted by the kind of loose wording assailed in earlier chapters. Some of it in italics here: '*in the middle of* a furore'; 'scientific *talent*'; 'Westinghouse *itself*'; 'in a statement *issued* in'; 'Westinghouse's offer *of employment*'; '*in reply*'; 'the scientists *involved*'.

So much for the news lead. How should the rest of the story have been developed? There are two immediate necessities: the content of the minister's letter, so that the remarks can be seen in context and so that the news lead can be substantiated. And, secondly, any reply from the US company. What else? Comments from the atomic scientists involved; comparisons of salaries; discussion of the fast-breeder reactor, and an independent assessment of Britain's position. Having constructed the news lead, the text editor may have to weave these other elements into a composite story from several reporters, the news agencies, the scientific correspondent, and so on.

There is no set formula for the development of such a news story, only guidelines. The first is: Substantiate the news lead. The second: Never run ahead of the reader's knowledge. The third: Remember it is your newspaper's job to report the news impartially. Let us see how these guidelines might have helped us with the atomic scientists story.

Substantiating the news lead means, if possible, running the minister's letter in full. What if there is not the space to do both this and give Westinghouse comment plus an explanation of what a fast-breeder reactor is? The other two principles must claim some space and the minister's letter will have to be cut – or any wordier sections rendered carefully into more concise reported speech.

If we are to take the reader with us into the story, the second principle means that the explanation of a fast-breeder reactor must come fairly high up in the story – before we have used lots of words about fast-breeder reactors on the false assumption that the reader knows already. This explanation need not be long.

One of the British papers did it neatly within parentheses: 'The fast breeder system (by which the nuclear power station makes its own fuel at the same time as it makes its own electricity) is the climax of 20 years of investment by the British people in civil nuclear technology, said the Minister'.

Note the way the explanation is not allowed to delay the development of the story. The same sentence takes the story a stage further. A viable construction here, then, would be:

1. News lead on selected key points, 3-4 paragraphs
2. Paragraph giving Westinghouse denial (which was brief)
3. Quick explanation in passing of 'fast-breeder reactor' and on into
4. The minister's letter
5. Comments from atomic scientists
6. Scientific assessment of Britain's position; comparative salaries

Arguably the brief Westinghouse comment could have followed at the end of or adjacent to the story – with a separate headline for prominence. But this treatment requires a certain length. Where denial or comment is brief and the story itself is long, it is unfair to tack the denial at the end, almost as an afterthought. Even if there is a separate denial story a skilled editor should be able to indicate the fact in the main narrative without delaying its progress:

> The Minister's charge – strongly denied last night by the company – was that . . .

The suggested structure for this story makes one assumption: that as section 4 one would choose to publish the minister's letter in full and certainly in sequence. With a relatively short letter like this no text editor should do otherwise. For the intro it is right to take a striking quote or passage from anywhere in the letter, but later that quote must be given in its proper context (just as intro quotes from speeches should always later be given in context). There is no point in transposing paragraphs at this stage; it is a form of inaccuracy or deception. If parts of the letter are being omitted this should be indicated by sequential dots, or by explanatory phrases for each quotation such as 'The Minister went on . . . He appealed . . . The Minister ended . . . ' This is only necessary as a signal to the reader when parts are being omitted. When a document is being quoted in full, it should be allowed to run without such interruptions.

Speeches and Reports

The way speeches and documents may be summarised in third-person reporting has already been discussed (in Chapter 3). Here we are concerned only with the construction of such stories.

They should not begin with the beginnings of the speech or the document unless these beginnings provide the most important news point. They rarely do. News leads on official reports are more likely to be based on points from the conclusions; intros on speeches more often pick up a point from the end than from the beginning. It is common political practice to serve the plums for dessert.

The structure of a speech report should be:

1. Intro stating most important news point, with or without supporting direct quotation in a sentence or phrase
2. Any further points summarised in third person with or without incidental quotation
3. Substantiation of the news lead (1 and 2 above) with direct quotations. This is the only place where third-person reporting needs to be substantiated by production of the direct quotation on which it is based. Any phrases quoted in the intro must also be put in proper context
4. Development of the speech, preferably of the most important section in direct quotation
5. Third-person summary of other main points, with or

> without direct quotes, each to be more briefly treated
> than the main points

Judging importance in speeches and statements is, of course, something the text editor can do only with experience and knowledge – knowledge of the subject of the speech, the political context, the news background. There are some general guides. Preference for the intro should be given to those parts of the speech which promise or imply action. Opinion and logical argument are not normally as newsworthy as announcements or promises or hints of action. 'Action' is the Prime Minister announcing a proposed new law or the president of a golf club promising to resist a new road across the course. Both are news developments. Something has happened or may happen. There is an attitude which will have repercussions. Text editors must not hesitate to rewrite a reporter's intro entirely if they think an 'action' news point is too far down in the speech. They must be ready to do to the report what the reporter has done to the speaker. They must be ready to bring the news point to the top. This was an intro:

> Mr Nikita Khrushchev, the Soviet Prime Minister, is of the view that the provocative flight of the American reconnaissance plane was only a probe and not a preparation for war.

But the real news was in the third paragraph of the reporter's copy:

> Mr Khrushchev warned that if the United States wanted to unleash a war 'we shall be compelled to fire rockets which will explode bombs on the aggressor's territory in the very first minute'.

This was the news. It was positive; it implied action. There is a rough test, too, for newsworthiness of the opinion sections of a speech. It is not enough to say that controversial opinions are news. They may be; or they may be stale. A better indicator of the news value of opinion is the test of contrariness. How much would it surprise you if the speaker were saying the opposite?

If it would surprise you a great deal, there is no news value in his present affirmation. There is a speech, say, by Iraq's Saddam Hussein at a time in 1999 when he is occasionally being bombed by US planes. He denounces United States imperialism. As Mandy Rice Davies said in another context, 'Well, he would wouldn't he?' The denunciation is not news. If he had praised the United States one would be stunned. So would the readers. Therefore these latest unsurprising opinions are not worth prominence.

A Protestant politician in Northern Ireland says the Roman Catholics are to blame for violence in Ulster. It would surprise everyone a great deal if he had said the Protestants were to blame. There is therefore little or no news value in these latest opinions. They are controversial – but they are also predictable. The test of contrariness is obvious, but it is surprising how often it can help when addressed to an apparently important, but really worthless, statement. It is the pin for a balloon filled only with hot air.

Running Statement–Opinion Stories

The text editor on a daily newspaper will often have to pull together a series of stories from several sources, arriving at different times, and produce one coherent narrative. The construction is similar to that of the single statement–opinion story, but the text editor must link the separate sections smoothly and interpolate background. This is real subbing. The lazy way is simply to add each separate element of the story as it arrives with no attempt at reassessing priorities. This is a classic example:

> The Supreme National Defence Council of Greece met urgently tonight under the chairmanship of King Constantine after renewed Turkish threats of an impending invasion in Cyprus. The meeting, the second in 24 hours, continued until the early hours of the morning.
>
> A Greek Government statement late tonight said that, if

Turkey attacked Cyprus – ostensibly to protect the Turkish Cypriot minority – 'no one would be in a position to avert the automatic exacerbation of the situation on the island, and of justifiable but catastrophic reprisals against the Turkish minority by uncontrollable Greek Cypriots'.

Mr Pipinelis, the Greek Foreign Minister, said at a press conference that Greece was determined to accept no settlement of the Cyprus dispute which would be 'incompatible with the national interest and Greek dignity'. He said that the Greek reply to last Friday's Turkish Note had been delivered to Ankara. It made suggestions for a settlement of the crisis.

The Turkish Note – which demanded among other things the withdrawal of the Greek troops stationed in Cyprus – was not an ultimatum, he added.

ATHENS, Nov. 22 – The Greek Armed Forces were brought to an advanced state of readiness. Military airfields were blacked out throughout Greece and pilots were briefed. Heavy troop movements were reported in north-east Greece, near the Greece–Turkey border. Military movements were also reported on the Turkish side of the border.

ANKARA – The Turkish Cabinet met to consider what one Minister described as Greece's 'rejection' of Friday's Note.

In Istanbul earlier in the day 80,000 demonstrators, organized by students, marched through the streets demanding war.

NEW YORK – U Thant, the United Nations Secretary-General, said he was sending a special representative to Cyprus, Greece and Turkey, to ask the Governments to exercise the utmost restraint and to try to reduce tension.

Mr. Cyrus Vance, a former Pentagon official, left for Ankara as President Johnson's special representative. He will fly on to Athens.

NICOSIA – Turkish reconnaissance aircraft were sighted over Cyprus for the second successive day. One newspaper reported a resignation offer by General Grivas, the commander of the Cyprus armed forces.

LONDON – The situation was described during the day as

'most dangerous'. It was believed that there was a real danger of a Turkish invasion of Cyprus.

Readers lurch through this story with no clear idea where they are going or what is going on. It is left to the last paragraph for at least someone's guidance that the crisis really is considered dangerous. What the text editor has to do is give the reader a God's eye view of the crisis; to relate the events in one capital to the events in another; and to introduce assessment and background and action where they help the reader's understanding and carry the story forward. The same events were presented in this way (author's numerals) in another daily:

1. As 80,000 Turks marched through Istanbul yesterday calling for war with Greece, U Thant, the United Nations Secretary-General, issued an appeal for peace.

2. He announced that he would send a personal representative to Nicosia, Athens and Ankara, to discuss the situation with the three governments.

3. At the same time a concerted diplomatic initiative by the American, British and Canadian governments got under way. The three countries are to make representations to Greece, Turkey and Cyprus, calling for urgent action to prevent deterioration in the situation.

4. Behind this is a formula evolved by the Canadian Government earlier this month. Mr. Pearson, the Canadian Prime Minister, who is now in London, had long talks yesterday with Mr. Wilson and the Commonwealth Secretary, Mr. Thomson, on the Cyprus situation.

5. Mr. Pearson thinks that the British and Canadian governments, by virtue of their troop contributions, supported by American diplomatic power, should be able to insist on far-reaching changes in the present contorted domestic political situation in Cyprus itself. An essential element in this is the personal trust which President Makarios feels for Mr. Pearson.

6. If the UN force were temporarily increased in size and given wider powers, so Mr. Pearson argues, then the Greek and Turkish national forces stationed on the island could be

reduced from their present inflated levels of more than 8,000 and 1,000 respectively.

7. It is recognised in London that the danger of Turkish military intervention in Cyprus has definitely grown in the past 48 hours. In Cyprus itself tension mounted yesterday as Turkish reconnaissance planes were sighted over the island for the second successive day.

8. According to diplomatic quarters, there has been a full preliminary deployment of Turkish land, sea and air forces, while the Turkish Government has authorised the President to use far-reaching emergency powers. In the summer of 1964 the two Turkish Houses of Parliament gave the President authority to order military action in, or in the neighbourhood of, Cyprus. The President has now been authorised to order similar action 'in other areas' – meaning against the Greek mainland or Greek islands.

9. Turkey's militant mood was indicated by yesterday's march in Istanbul while other big demonstrations are planned for today throughout the country in support of the Turkish Government's demands that the number of Greek troops in Cyprus should be drastically reduced, that General Grivas should be dismissed, and that guarantees for the safety of the Turkish-Cypriot minority should be given.

10. In particular, Turkey will continue to insist that there should be no repetition of last week's attacks on members of the Turkish minority by Greek militia and Greek-Cypriot forces. The Turkish suspicion is that these attacks were inspired by General Grivas, in his desire to have a military showdown which could lead to the union of Cyprus with Greece.

11. The British Government is making contingency plans for the possible withdrawal, in the event of large-scale fighting, of British forces on the island to the British sovereign bases. British civilians would, it is assumed, be collected there too. There are about one thousand British troops on the island, and Britain's is the biggest contingent in the UN peacekeeping force. With its Canadian, Danish, Swedish and Irish contingents, the UN force amounts to about 4,500 men in all.

It is worth studying this treatment for its strengths and

weaknesses. This is a running story. The crisis was a Turkish threat to invade Cyprus, the Mediterranean island close to Turkey. Behind this threat was a complaint of the Turkish minority on the island that they had been intimidated by the Greek community. A reader knowing none of this should still have been able to understand the story and relate the latest developments to this new knowledge.

First the structure of this story, then the criticisms.

Paragraphs 1, 2, 3 are the news lead, summarising developments in Turkey, the United Nations, the United States, Canada and Britain. Paragraph 1 is the intro proper. It succeeds in setting the scene for war and the efforts for peace.

The action of the Turks marching through Istanbul adds urgency to the U Thant talks and takes the reader forward, the diplomatic developments beginning in paragraph 2. The scene is changed neatly in paragraph 3 with the transitional phrase 'At the same time . . .'

Paragraphs 4, 5 and 6 elaborate the diplomatic activity and introduce background on the Greek and Turkish national forces on Cyprus. 'Behind this . . .' clearly introduces this phase of the story which is told in three paragraphs.

Paragraph 7 introduces new points – the military activity and the London assessment, and mentions the background threat of a Turkish invasion of Cyprus. It does this smoothly in a way which will tell new readers what the fuss is all about without delaying the story too much for the informed reader:

7. It is recognised in London that the danger of Turkish military intervention in Cyprus has definitely grown in the past 48 hours.

Imagine for a moment how much weaker paragraph 7 would have been if the text editor had left in the muffling word 'situation':

7. It is recognised in London that the situation has definitely grown more dangerous in the past 48 hours . . .

Paragraph 8 substantiates paragraph 7 on the dangers. It leads easily to paragraph 9 with the phrase 'Turkey's militant mood', and there is an inferential reference to the lead intro. Paragraph 10 begins with the signal phrase that detail is to be presented: 'In particular'. It also provides the very necessary background to the genesis of the crisis, the serious omission in the other daily paper's treatment, given earlier.

Paragraph 11 rounds off the story with the specifically British involvement – first the news about the contingency plans, then the background to make them intelligible.

This is altogether a more coherent and meaningful way to handle a story from several sources. Unlike the other treatment, it does not assume that the reader has kept in close touch with the story from its beginning. The running news story is not very different from a feature series. The reader needs to be reminded, incidentally, of the story so far.

But even this structure is not ideal. How would you improve it?

There is one thing wrong with the news lead: it does not have the key background words 'Turkish invasion of Cyprus'. The opportunity is missed twice with retreat into the vague tag 'the situation'. The second criticism of the editing of this story is that it descends to detail and background too quickly, thus delaying important active news. It is not until the seventh paragraph that the military activity is mentioned and the tension on Cyprus itself. This is part of the latest news and worth a place in the news lead. The existing news lead spends too much time detailing the diplomatic activity. *Indicating* that there is intense diplomatic activity is proper for the news lead – but *elaborating* it before other important hard news is wrong.

The solution to all those weaknesses lies in paragraph 7. It is in the wrong place. Transpose it to paragraph 3. This brings in the military news and it does something else: it brings in the key concept of a threatened Turkish invasion of Cyprus. This makes other small textual changes necessary in the subbing. The old paragraph 3 would become paragraph 4. It would be necessary to reword it to refer back to U Thant's activity:

4. America, Britain and Canada supported U Thant's peace moves with a concerted diplomatic initiative . . .

Paragraph 8 would also be affected since it was linked to the old paragraph 7. The text editor has now to write a link phrase to indicate that a new section begins at the end of the diplomatic background.

8. The urgency of the diplomatic moves was reinforced by reports of a full preliminary deployment of Turkish land, sea and air forces. The Turkish Government has authorised the President . . .

Here now is the full revised version:

As 80,000 Turks marched through Istanbul yesterday calling for war with Greece, U Thant, the United Nations Secretary-General, issued an appeal for peace.

He announced that he would send a personal representative to Nicosia, Athens and Ankara, to discuss the situation with the three governments.

It is recognised in London that the danger of Turkish military intervention in Cyprus has definitely grown in the past 48 hours. In Cyprus itself tension mounted yesterday as Turkish reconnaissance planes were sighted over the island for the second successive day.

America, Britain and Canada supported U Thant's peace move with a concerted diplomatic initiative. They are to make representations to Greece, Turkey and Cyprus, calling for urgent action to prevent deterioration in the situation.

Behind this is a formula evolved by the Canadian Government earlier this month. Mr. Pearson, the Canadian Prime Minister, who is now in London, had long talks yesterday with Mr. Wilson and the Commonwealth Secretary, Mr. Thomson, on the Cyprus situation.

Mr. Pearson thinks that the British and Canadian Governments, by virtue of their troop contributions, supported by

American diplomatic power, should be able to insist on far-reaching changes in the present contorted domestic political situation in Cyprus itself. An essential element in this is the personal trust which President Makarios feels for Mr. Pearson.

If the UN force were temporarily increased in size and given wider powers, so Mr. Pearson argues, then the Greek and Turkish national forces stationed on the island could be reduced from their present inflated levels of more than 8,000 and 1,000 respectively.

The urgency of the diplomatic moves was reinforced by reports of a full preliminary deployment of Turkish land, sea and air forces. The Turkish Government has authorised the President to use far-reaching emergency powers. In the summer of 1964 the two Turkish Houses of Parliament gave the President authority to order military action in, or in the neighbourhood of, Cyprus. The President has now been authorised to order similar action 'in other areas' – meaning against the Greek mainland or Greek islands.

Turkey's militant mood was indicated by yesterday's march in Istanbul while other big demonstrations are planned for today throughout the country in support of the Turkish Government's demands that the number of Greek troops in Cyprus should be drastically reduced, that General Grivas should be dismissed, and that guarantees for the safety of the Turkish Cypriot minority should be given.

In particular, Turkey will continue to insist that there should be no repetition of last week's attacks on members of the Turkish minority by Greek militia and Greek-Cypriot forces. The Turkish suspicion is that these attacks were inspired by General Grivas, in his desire to have a military showdown which could lead to the union of Cyprus with Greece.

The British Government is making contingency plans for the possible withdrawal, in the event of large-scale fighting, of British forces on the island to the British sovereign bases. British civilians would, it is assumed, be collected there too. There are about one thousand British troops on the island, and Britain's is the biggest contingent in the UN peacekeeping force. With its Canadian, Danish, Swedish and Irish contingents, the UN force amounts to about 4,500 men in all.

It would be a good exercise for text editors to imagine they have to cut this story. They should now have all the various elements clearly in their mind. Should all the sections stay and the detailing be reduced? Or should some sections be cut altogether, retaining the other details? In a large international story like this it seems a pity to cut any of the sections: but if this means detail has to be cut it must not be detail which gives the story meaning. Safe detailed cuts (to the full revised version): the second sentence of paragraph 8, and the last two sentences of the final paragraph of the story. The Turkish Government's demands could be confined to the particular demands in paragraph 10, which would save the latter half of paragraph 9. If further cuts were needed the whole of the last paragraph could go. If a really drastic cut were called for, the first four paragraphs would stand – when paragraph 7 of the original story has been transposed. This illustrates again how important it was to move that paragraph higher.

Let us now see how to pull together a series of separate reports on the diplomatic and military moves during a war between India and Pakistan. On a typical day there are agency messages from Moscow, New Delhi, Karachi, Washington and London.

The military reports do not seem to take the war much further, but there is intense diplomatic activity. The two elements which strike text editors as most newsworthy – and they will have kept themselves well informed on developments – are a warning by Russia to China not to interfere and a possible trip to Moscow by the UN Secretary-General. America also warns China to keep out of the war. The text editor needs to write off a news lead from the messages:

1. Both Russia and the United States warned China to keep out of the Indo-Pakistan war last night. Russia's warning came at the end of a day of intense diplomatic activity and a report that

Note how crisply news points are compressed into this intro lead – Russia's warning; America's warning; diplomatic activity; U Thant's trip and its purpose.

U Thant was on his way
to Moscow to seek Rus-
sia's help in arranging a
cease-fire.

2. On the battlefront mean-
while India and Pakistan
held grimly to their lines
in the week-old war,
with no sign of a break-
through by either side.

The news lead continues with
an assessment of agency
reports from both fronts. The
fighting details can now be
left until very much later.

3. The Soviet Govern-
ment's warning to China
was in a statement
issued by the Tass news
agency. It again called
on India and Pakistan to
stop fighting and on
other nations for
restraint and responsi-
bility.

The first four words indicate
that development of the lead
is about to take place. It is
substantiation, not repetition.

4. China was not named
directly but the lan-
guage pointed unmistak-
ably to Peking: China
has sided violently with
Pakistan and con-
demned Russia's earlier
appeals for restraint.

A key paragraph of back-
ground and interpretation
written in by the text editor.
Running the Russian statement before the interpretation, or worse still without it,
would confuse readers. They
would be puzzled by the
absence of a specific reference to China.

5. 'The whole world and all
states', said the state-
ment, 'should warn
those who facilitate the
fanning of the conflict
by their policy that they
thereby assume grave
responsibility for such a
policy and for such
actions.

Agency copy. Direct quotes
are essential to substantiate
the intro and give the tone of
the Russian message. At this
point the text editor has
picked up original agency
copy from Moscow and edited
that.

6. 'No Government has any right to add fuel to the flames. There are forces which seek to profit by worsened Indo-Pakistan relations. By their incendiary statements they push them towards further aggravation of the military conflict – and can cause present developments to escalate into an even bigger conflagration. Many states find themselves drawn into conflict one by one.

    'This is a dangerous prospect. As shown by the experience of history, this may have the gravest consequences, not only for the peoples of the region where the conflict began, but also far beyond it.'

    Still direct editing on Moscow agency copy.

7. The statement renewed the offer of Russia's good offices in ending the war. After a cease-fire India and Pakistani forces should return to the Kashmir dividing line of the 1949 armistice.

    A summary of the rest of the statement written by the text editor.

8. In Washington yesterday, America's warning was given by US Secretary of State, Mr Dean Rusk: 'Our own advice

    The first two words written on to agency copy alert the reader that a new phase of the story is about to be dealt with. The phrase 'America's

to Peking', he said, 'would be to stay out and let the Security Council settle it'. Mr Rusk said the Soviet attitude had been helpful so far.

9. [The Chinese have cited Russian appeals for restraint as evidence that Moscow 'revisionists' are working hand in hand with American imperialists.]

10. U Thant's possible trip to Moscow was reported by 'informed sources' quoted by Reuters in Delhi. They said he was expected to fly to Moscow tomorrow. U Thant was in New Delhi yesterday and talked to Indian Foreign Minister Swaran Singh. A second meeting with the Prime Minister, Mr Shastri, was postponed until today.

11. In a big tank battle for the Pakistani town of Sialkot, near the Kashmir border, India claimed her troops had made some advances but Pakistan said the Indians had been beaten back.
   On the central front near Lahore, similar claims and counter-claims were made. On

warning . . .' refers inferentially to the intro and proceeds to substantiate it.

Another piece of background information interpolated by the text editor to emphasise the unusual nature of the US–USSR diplomatic agreement and of China's belligerent isolation.

Again the inferential reference back to the intro and then its elaboration. Editing on agency copy.

The story is rounded off with the war reports, the text editor's distillation of a flood of copy.

Caution and compression are the watchwords on a dull day. Claim and counter-claim are related in each instance. It is vital to retain the sources and the contradictions in stories

the southernmost front Pakistan claimed to have occupied a major part of Indian territory.

India said her troops had thrust further into Pakistani Kashmir.

Pakistani planes reported setting two Indian air bases on fire, raided military installations at three other towns and for the first time struck at Jammu airport inside Kashmir.

like this. They should not be deleted for space or smoothness. One may be editing out the truth.

The way this story has been constructed should make quick cuts very simple. If hard cutting is needed, the last three paragraphs could go, leaving the reader to survive on the intro indication that the war is at a stalemate. The Soviet statement could be run shorter by deleting paragraph 7, and one element of background could be discarded – the square brackets of Section 9. Paragraph 4 would be retained. If further cuts still were needed the statement could be reduced to paragraph 5.

Even while editing a story to a required length, a text editor may be told that further cuts are needed. This happens often on afternoon newspapers and in editing broadcast news. Having envisaged a clear structure for the story, it is not difficult swiftly to identify the sections that can safely be excised.

CHAPTER SEVEN

Background

Background for Intelligibility

Disraeli once remarked that there were only two people in the world who really understood the situation in Schleswig Holstein. One of them was dead. He was the other and he had forgotten. It is the text editor's responsibility to make sure that when Schleswig Holstein etc. gets into the paper or on the air everyone can understand what the latest twist in the story means. So the text editor of the statement–opinion story has these two tasks: get the structure right and give enough background to make the story meaningful to the new reader. But shouldn't it be the reporters' job to give the background? Yes, but specialist reporters frequently fail to do so precisely because they know so much. They forget that while they have been immersed in one subject, readers have been mending the roads, auditing accounts, making the beds or singing grand opera. Their minds are not well prepared for alien complexities and subtleties.

Many text editors make the similar mistake of regarding the reader as a professional digester of everything the news organisation has ever published on the subject. American newspapers, and broadcasters, have been somewhat better at appreciating that the reader may have lived a day, a week even, without the evening news or the morning paper. This does not mean that on the 50th day of the 1999 Kosovo war, the text editor has to retell the entire history of Yugoslavia, or that every brouhaha in Europe requires a recapitulation of the history of the European Union. But polling suggests we assume far too much awareness even of landmark events.

In the developing story of a few days' duration, or a foreign story, it is wiser to assume that the reader is a suburban Rip Van Winkle who has slept through all the stages now so familiar to the text editor who has been in the thick of them. The skill is in editing for such readers without weighing them down with a recital of everything that has been going on. Every developing story has to be constructed so that the vital background information is conveyed but conveyed without unduly delaying the new events, and without irritating readers who are up to date.

There is one caution before we see if this can be done: developing court stories are special. The nature of the case must briefly be given, but previous statements by witnesses can be recalled only if they are vital to an understanding of the present proceedings. A background paragraph quoting what a previous witness said (or the same witness said earlier) might be construed as comment. It may well be transparent that the man is not saying what he said when you edited his previous statement. But under British law it is wise to leave that discovery to the judge and jury.

Background should be given succinctly, in passing. There is no need to recapitulate every single one of the previous facts – just sufficient to make the new developments meaningful. Reporters who have absorbed the idea that background is important sometimes get carried away and present the reader with an unnecessary wodge of yesterday's news. Here are two bad examples from newspapers. The original story is in the left-hand column and my rewritten version on the right.

County Durham club chief, Mr Bob Blythe, yesterday picked up the gauntlet thrown down publicly, he said, by Mr Stan Hall, long-serving secretary of the working men's club movement who has resigned.

It was last week that 43-year-old Mr Hall, who ends his 20-year service with the county

County Durham chief Mr Bob Blythe yesterday rebutted the charges of the former secretary, Mr Stan Hall, that the Northern Federation Brewery Ltd was dictating to the county's 322 clubs.

Mr Blythe, a brewery director as well as president of the county branch of the working

Club and Institute Union at the end of next month, said that among his reasons for resigning was that the Northern Federation Brewery Ltd. was 'dictating' to the county's 322 clubs.

He also said there had been a clash of personalities between him, Mr Blythe, president of the County branch CIU, and Mr John Ward, the Vice-President.

Mr Blythe and Mr Ward are also two of the nine members on the board of directors of the Federation, the brewery which supplies most clubs in the North with beer and has advanced mortgages for new premises of up to £4.5m.

Last week Mr Hall said: 'In spite of the fact that I was clearly employed as secretary of the Durham branch, control was, in fact, exercised by members of the Federation Brewery. Clubs are shareholders and prominent clubmen serve on the board'.

Mr Blythe yesterday said he regretted that Mr Hall had said anything about his resignation and was anxious to point out that 'there is no feud existing between the branch executive and the board of directors of the Northern Clubs Federation Brewery'.

men's clubs, said there was 'no feud' between the clubs and the brewery which supplies most clubs and has advanced mortgages for new premises up to £4.5m.

Mr Blythe said he regretted etc. . . .

The first and last paragraphs are the news: all the rest is background. Some of that background may be required in the story – but later. To begin with, only enough is required to make the latest developments meaningful to a new reader. Other background should be introduced as the narrative progresses.

In the next instance the news is delayed with background in the second, third and fourth sentences. Note the vagueness of what the row is about – 'the lorry parking row' does not tell us that the County Council has approved a plan local people dislike. The rewrite on the right clarifies and also introduces the 'monstrously noisy' quote.

Blanktown urban council, vocally supported last night by some of the citizens, is determined not to let the lorry parking row die down.

Last month the county council voted to take no action on Blanktown's demand that planning permission for the park should be revoked. Blanktown had complained that the County Council should never have passed the plans because the lorry park is built in a once quiet residential area and had brought many complaints locally.

Blanktown has so far organised a petition and had two angry public meetings and last night the anger had not abated. Mr James Johnson who lives two houses away from the lorry park said it was 'monstrously noisy' . . .

[More speeches with a last paragraph:]

The meeting decided to invite the MP to a protest demonstra-

Blanktown urban council, vocally supported last night by an angry meeting of citizens, will go on fighting to stop a 'monstrously noisy' lorry park approved by the County Council for a once quiet residential area.

The County Council's refusal to revoke planning permission will be contested by Blanktown protesting to the Minister of Housing, inviting Blanktown's MP to a protest demonstration; and asking townspeople to write to the County Council.

[Pick up report of the meeting.]

tion; to press the County Council and send it full details of
complaints; and formally to
complain to the Ministry of
Housing.

If you are in doubt about where and how to introduce the
background, remember that we learn by relating new facts to
what we already know. In an ordinary running news story a
good general guide is (a) give the informed reader a signal in
the intro – a passing reference to the news context, and (b)
give the fuller background, in one paragraph, at paragraph 3.

Sir Basil Blackwell, the book-seller and publisher, told a jury at the Central Criminal Court yesterday that it was nonsense to say that the controversial American novel, *Last Exit to Brooklyn*, was in the tradition of Zola, Dickens and Galsworthy.	'Controversial' gives us a clue about the dispute.
Sir Basil, who is 78, was appearing for the Crown to rebut literary authorities called by the defence. He said he considered the literary merit of *Last Exit to Brooklyn* to be slight.	Takes the story forward by explaining why Sir Basil was there and that he considered the book's literary merit slight.
Calder and Boyars Ltd have pleaded Not Guilty to two charges under the Obscene Publications Act, 1959, which allege that they had in their possession copies of the book for publication for gain and that they published an obscene article, namely *Last Exit to Brooklyn*, written by Hubert Selby, jnr.	The full background – but restricted to one paragraph – runs little risk of delaying the new events too much.
In reply to Mr John Mathew, for the Crown, Sir Basil said: 'Dickens was a great artist. He	Picks up the news events again.

certainly portrayed wicked and
evil men but he made them
live.'

You can often indicate the background with a key word in a passing phrase. A report referred to the possibility that the Russians might release an American pilot named Powers. The text editor assumed everybody knew who Powers was. But it is better to tell ten readers, glancingly, what they know than to omit telling one reader the only fact which enables understanding of the story at all. Here the text editor could have played safe by saying: 'Captain Powers, the pilot of the U2 spy plane shot down over Russia . . .' The key reminder is U2 spy plane. Similarly, in this extract the key words are 'border dispute':

> Violence flared when about 5,000 people, protesting against the recommendations of a Government commission on an 11-year-old border dispute between Maharashtra and Mysore states, tried to prevent Mr Y. B. Chavan, the Home Minister, from attending the meeting.

Background is easier than interpretations; on interpretation you run the risk of introducing too much opinion or bias. The report on a stage in a teaching dispute is essential interpretation:

> After three months during which the National Union of Teachers have been imposing sanctions in more than 1,200 schools, it is clear that its dispute with the local education authorities has reached a climax.

This usefully seizes the reader to say: Look we know you have lost track of all the troubles of the last three months, but you really ought to read this latest development.

Interpretation drifts too far when a text editor writes in:

> The Turks *have caused the trouble* by pressing for a drastic revision of the balance of power in Cyprus.

In a bitterly contested dispute, it is enough to say:

> The Turks are pressing for a drastic revision of the balance of
> power in Cyprus.

If there is one thing American newspaper journalists have
learned better than their colleagues elsewhere it is the
importance of explaining as they go along. Consider the way
Anthony Lewis of the *New York Times* cleverly etches the
background for US readers in his report from Britain. The
italics are mine to show the phrase written in as background
to the events:

> LONDON, Nov. 29 (NYT) – In a major shift of power within
> the Labour Government and a move toward new policies, Roy
> Jenkins today became Britain's Chancellor of the Exchequer.
>   He replaced James Callaghan whose three year struggle to
> maintain the value of the pound ended 11 days ago in
> devaluation. Mr Callaghan resigned and shifted to Mr Jen-
> kins's former post as Home Secretary, *in charge of police and
> other internal affairs.*

British text editors would not write in copy for British readers
the phrase 'in charge of police and other internal affairs'. But
they would write in what the US newspaper might leave out
when presented with copy referring to say, Mr Sargent
Shriver as director of the Office of Economic Opportunity.
They would write in the phrase 'which administers America's
anti-poverty programme'.

In domestic stories the biggest failure to provide background or interpretation is in dealing with labour disputes. It
may seem that the dispute has dragged on long enough for
everybody to know what it is about; but do not believe it. Fair
reporting, to both sides, requires that some explanation
should be written into every story. And only day-by-day
recapitulation saves readers from being lost in the eddies of
negotiation and compromise. The background can be a
phrase:

> The drivers, *working to rule because they refuse to have guards riding in freight trains,* are hoping the Trades Union Congress will intervene.

It may be a paragraph:

> The dispute stems from a battle between the Associated Society of Locomotive Engineers and Firemen (ASLEF) and the National Union of Railwaymen (NUR), to which guards belong. The ASLEF drivers fear they will commit industrial suicide if they allow guards to ride in the engine cab now that the freight guards' brake van has been abolished.

It may seem that the longer the dispute goes on, the more the text editor can rely on a phrase. This is wrong. The newspaper may manage on phrases for a few days, but from time to time a fuller explanation should be written in. This is in the public interest in the wider sense – to enable readers not merely to follow the story but to form their own judgment on rights and wrongs as the labour dispute produces effects on everyday life.

In a complicated dispute lasting several weeks it is a good idea to spend time preparing a concise explanation which can be carried daily in a panel or footnote. Where one or other side in the dispute wants to say nothing, it is as well to record this fact so that your paper is not accused of reporting only one side.

We can now examine how professional text editors tackled a common problem in a second-day story. Having set the standards, let us see how the daily papers managed on the second day of that story in Chapter 6 about the atomic scientists being tempted to America's Westinghouse Electric Corporation. The development announced was that the Minister of Technology, Mr Benn, was flying to the Atomic Energy plant at Risley in Lancashire and would meet some of the scientists who had been invited to the United States.

In editing this story we may have to remind the reader of Mr Benn's vehement protest at the alleged poaching by Westinghouse. We have to do that quite soon in the story so that the significance of Mr Benn's trip is clear: the details of the trip should not begin before Mr Benn's visit has been set in its new context. There is no justification for assuming every reader will recall the news context. We do not need to elaborate it. A concise signal will do.

You might yourself at this point write in one paragraph how you would relay the background. The essential points you want to remind the reader about are: (a) Mr Benn is meeting scientists who have been invited by Westinghouse to the United States; (b) Mr Benn yesterday condemned the invitation; (c) Mr Benn accused the American company of trying to gain British nuclear knowledge 'on the cheap' after under-bidding for the rights to it under a proper licensing agreement. To get all three background points in quickly and concisely without delaying the new story requires careful attention to every word.

Version A conveyed two of the background points – but rather too late in the story:

> Mr. Benn, Minister of Technology, has asked to meet a delegation of four senior Dounreay nuclear scientists at Risley, Lancashire, tomorrow.
>
> Two of the team of four, representing the scientific staff at the Dounreay research establishment, Caithness, are Mr. Arthur Parry, deputy director of the establishment, and Mr. Roy Matthews, head of administration.
>
> They will fly to Manchester in an aircraft chartered by the Ministry.
>
> Mr. Benn's visit to Risley, one of the two centres of fast-breeder research, is a routine one. But it is understood that it has been brought forward because of the Ministry's concern over the Westinghouse Electric Corporation's attempt to attract nuclear scientists to the United States.

A great improvement is made if the text editor transposes paragraph 4 to be paragraph 2. The existing paragraph 2 links into the new arrangement with a small change of phrasing: ('Two of the team of four Mr. Benn will meet are Mr. Arthur Parry, deputy director of the establishment, and Mr. Roy

Matthews, head of administration, who will represent the scientific staff at the Dounreay research establishment, Caithness'). The omission in the background paragraph (4) is Mr. Benn's letter. His strong personal feelings could at least have been indicated if the text editor had changed 'Ministry's concern' to 'Minister's concern'. The paper had a much better background paragraph in a story inside the paper:

> Mr. Benn's letter, disclosed on Wednesday, appealed to scientists not to accept the offer and accused Westinghouse of trying to get hold of our information 'on the cheap' after their attempt to secure a proper licensing agreement had failed.

Version B gave a clue to the news context in the intro and the background in paragraph 3. Like version A this page-one background fails to indicate Mr Benn's personal involvement and does not mention his attack on Westinghouse:

> Technology Minister Mr. Benn will meet 250 scientists at the atomic energy centre at Risley, Lancs, to discuss the brain drain.
>
> Ten scientists from the Dounreay fast breeder reactor station in Caithness will also be at the meeting.
>
> Mr. Benn's visit was scheduled for after Christmas but has been brought forward, his Ministry said last night, 'in view of the news that Westinghouse are inviting our scientists to apply for posts in the United States'.

The paper slips up here by relying on the Ministry spokesman for the background briefing in paragraph 3. The good thing about this treatment was the attempt to indicate the background in a phrase in the intro sentence, which could then be elaborated a little later.

Version C had the same technique, but did it much better because the intro reference gave the reader a clue at once to Mr Benn's passionate involvement '. . . in his campaign to plug the threatened brain drain to America':

> The Minister of Technology, Mr. Tony Benn, has called a

meeting with atom scientists today, in his campaign to plug the threatened brain drain to America.

Mr. Benn will fly to the Atomic Energy Authority Centre at Risley, Lancs, to address 250 scientists and engineers, including a party being flown from Dounreay atomic station in Scotland.

The visit is one of a series Mr. Benn is making to atom stations, but he has brought it forward following reports that 24 Dounreay men have answered advertisements for jobs with the American Westinghouse company.

On Wednesday Mr. Benn published an open letter to scientists at Risley and Dounreay accusing Westinghouse of trying to get British scientific knowledge 'on the cheap'.

The trouble with this paper's development of the background in paragraphs 3 and 4 is that it spends just a bit too much time on yesterday's news: the background is not succinct enough. The text editor would have improved the pace here if in paragraph 4, for instance, the words 'published an open letter to scientists at Risley and Dounreay' had been cut and simply left it at 'On Wednesday Mr Benn accused . . .'

Version D gains full marks for bringing in the background as soon as the second paragraph, but the paragraph is much too vague:

Mr. Benn, Minister of Technology, is flying north today to visit the headquarters of the Atomic Energy Authority at Risley, Lancs. Arrangements for the visit have been made at short notice.

Yesterday it was disclosed that he has written to atomic scientists working at Dounreay, Caithness and Risley, warning them of an American plot to discover the secrets of Britain's latest reactor by recruiting senior scientists.

The reader might well wonder what 'American plot'? The text editor should have written in a phrase such as: '. . . warning them of an attempt by America's Westinghouse Corporation . . .'

The paper, in another story, gave a better demonstration of putting the news in context. This was the story of the

Westinghouse denial: the denial is the news and in a brief story like this the background should not be too obtrusive. Note particularly how the background is run into the story with the second paragraph phrase 'the company's present recruiting efforts':

> Complaints by Mr. Benn, Minister of Technology, that the Westinghouse Electric Corporation was trying to obtain 'on the cheap' the secrets of the Dounreay fast-breeder reactor were firmly denied today by the company.
>
> A Westinghouse spokesman in Pittsburgh said Mr. Benn's interpretation of the company's present recruiting efforts in Britain was 'completely false'. He also said the British Atomic Energy Authority had been demanding a 'completely prohibitive' price for the licensing of information on the Dounreay fast-breeder reactor.
>
> The company refused to say what it had offered Britain in the unsuccessful negotiations to work out a licensing agreement. But it was learned from a reliable source that the parties were '10 million dollars apart' at the end of the talks.

None of these editing attempts was perfect – but they all made an attempt in perhaps hectic circumstances. I have made these criticisms, in more relaxed circumstances, to try to define the aim and standards all good text editors set themselves. Provided it is accurate, it is far better to make a hurried and imperfect attempt at putting the news in context than not doing it at all. Curiously, the paper which did so well on the first day of the Benn story did particularly badly on the second day – simply by not bothering at all with background. The italics are mine and so are the comments on the right:

Mr. Tony Benn, Minister of Technology, has asked to meet a delegation of four senior Dounreay scientists at Risley today to discuss *the Westinghouse offer*.

Two of the delegation will be Mr. Arthur Parry, deputy director at Dounreay, and Mr. Roy

What Westinghouse offer? There is not a clue here that it was an offer to recruit individual scientists. Conceivably it might have been an offer from Westinghouse to the British Government. Nowhere in the story is this ambiguity directly resolved.

Matthews, head of administration there. They will fly to Ringway, Manchester, in a plane supplied by the Ministry of Technology.

Late last night, Mr. Matthews said: 'Quite frankly, we don't know precisely what's on the agenda for discussion. All we have been told is that Mr. Benn has asked to meet us in Risley tomorrow. But it is a fair assumption that the main topic will be about *the Westinghouse offer*.'

The reader, as well as Mr. Matthews, is still in the dark.

The other members of the delegation are Mr. Kenneth Butler, chairman of the Dounreay branch of the Institute of Professional Civil Servants and Mr. Geoffrey James, the branch councillor of the Institute's Dounreay branch.

Properly 'Institution'.

Last night a spokesman for the local branch of the institute said that the two officials would point out to the Minister that the reason *why top scientists were wanting to leave Dounreay* was that they did not have the full confidence in their future with the Atomic Energy Authority there.

Forget for a moment the clumsy 'were wanting to'. The way this is put suggests that the initiative 'to leave Dounreay' has come from the scientists. The whole story is growing more confusing because of the failure of the text editor to recap on the Westinghouse advertisement and Mr Benn's attack.

A deputation from the IPCS which saw Mr. Benn yesterday, told him that there had been prolonged uncertainty over the AEA's research programme. *Dr Dickson Mabon's* statement about a rundown at Dounreay had never been satisfactorily explained, there had been a

And who is he?

severe cutdown at the *world-famous Culham laboratory* and only yesterday staff at *Winfrith* had been warned of a 3.5 per cent cut involving 70 people.

There had been an 'extraordinary downgrading of the chairman of the AEA which was in marked contrast with Steel Board salaries and what was being rumoured for the new chairman of British Rail.

Mr Roy Matthews, director of the Dounreay Atomic Station, from which at least a dozen scientists are thought to have been interviewed by the US Westinghouse Corporation, said there was no comparison between Dounreay facilities and Westinghouse, whose fast breeder reactor was only on paper. Westinghouse would be building a prototype when Britain's first commercial fast reactor came into use in the seventies.

But there are mixed feelings among the Dounreay scientists. While Mr. Jim Mockett, assistant manager of the reactor, said a recent American visitor from the Enrico Fermi atom station near Chicago was envious of Dounreay facilities, Mr. M. Tucker, a young scientist, said there were a lot of other young men who would like to cross the Atlantic.

'Some of us have been discussing *this advert* and we came to

Is it really?

Where's that?

For the first time we are told that Westinghouse is an American firm. Even now we are given only a woolly idea that part of the story is about Britain's lead in the fast-breeder reactor and Westinghouse's attempt to catch up.

Which advert?

the conclusion we would need about four times our present salary before it would be worth going,' he said.

Westinghouse's nuclear reactor division, based at Pittsburg, has not yet issued any statement following *the row*. A spokesman for the firm in London could not say how many men had been interviewed nor confirm or deny reports of offers as high as seven times their present salaries.

What row? Not a clue that it is an attack by the minister on Westinghouse. Indeed the paper seems to have two rows going, since most of the story has been about scientists' criticisms of Government atomic policy.

'But talking in terms of *enticement and underhand activities is absolutely rubbish*', said the spokesman. 'Westinghouse are stretched on the ordinary nuclear power programme – 14 projects this year. They have now a fast breeder reactor to produce. They are advertising in the States for men. They know scientists are here, so they placed the advertisement.'

The plot thickens. Who is 'talking in terms of enticement and underhand activities'? There is nothing at all to link this with the minister. The rest of the paragraph seems irrelevant unless the reader knows of Mr Benn's charge that it was an attempt by Westinghouse to gain nuclear secrets on the cheap.

There are 300 professional people at Dounreay, and the establishment has been reduced in the past year by under 8 per cent, said the spokesman. He did not think the rate of contraction was greatly accelerated during the past year than previously.

He thought morale at the plant was 'reasonably good'. No higher than that? He replied: 'In the early days, when the place was building up, one got a kick out of the freedom and creative activity. We have now gone on to more or less routine work. But on the development side there is still zeal.'

In the Commons yesterday, Conservative MPs pressed for information about what the Government was doing to halt the brain drain. Mr. Peter Shore told Mr. Cranley Onslow (Con. Woking) that no money had been spent by the Department of Economic Affairs in analysing or attempting to reverse the brain drain. 'I would not myself have placed so great a weight on the fiscal system as you do', said Mr. Shore.

Mr Benn's own attempts to halt the brain drain have still not been mentioned: even at this stage Mr Benn's visit to Risley is not projected as an attempt to persuade the scientists to stay in Britain.

Several days after Mr Benn's original letter a Sunday paper took the story further. It provides a useful illustration of the way to give the background while taking the story forward in a piece of informed reporting. Note how in every sentence the background reference is used as a link to new information, thus informing the new reader without wasting the time of the reader who remembers the events earlier in the week:

> The attack last week by Mr Benn, Minister of Technology, on the American Westinghouse Electric Corporation was far more than a melodramatic appeal to British nuclear scientists to stay at home.
>
> His impassioned open letter to scientists at Dounreay, Risley, and other centres of fast reactor technology, came only two days after the Prime Minister announced a seven-point plan for a European technological community. The charges in Mr Benn's letter were calculated to appeal to strong Common Market feeling against technological domination by America.
>
> The letter can also be regarded as an unusual piece of British salesmanship to the Common Market. It refers specifically to the value of Britain's fast reactor technology to the whole of Europe.

By revealing officially for the first time that Westinghouse had tried to acquire a licence for British fast reactor know-how, the Minister proved that the American company was interested more in specific information than in making good their shortage in manpower.

Background for Interest

Text editors should write in background mainly for intelligibility but also for interest. A few extra words of detail add bite to a story. Rather than letting copy pass with a reference to 'Lockerbie', or 'the Lockerbie disaster' the text editor writes in 'the Lockerbie plane crash when 270 died after a bomb exploded in mid-air'.

When a member of a legislature resigns, the winning margin of votes at the last election should be written in so that the political fortunes of the seat can be assessed. If there is a bad train or plane crash, the previous worst, and any similarities should be recalled. Sometimes the text editor with a good library can create a whole story by relating information already known to a new development – for instance, the agency flash which brought the news in 1961 that Russia had decided to resume testing nuclear weapons and would test a series of giant nuclear bombs with a claimed yield equivalent to 20, 30, 50 and 100 million tons of TNT.

Here the lines of development include the background on disarmament talks, and the interpretation of 100 million tons of TNT into proportions the reader can grasp. The text editor sends for sets of clippings and can build up a story on the bald announcement. First the diplomatic side:

This ends the three-year-old truce on the testing of hydrogen bombs. The last known Soviet nuclear tests occurred on November 1 and November 3, 1958, within days of the start on October 31 of that year of the nuclear test-ban conference in Geneva.

The last United States test took place during October, 1958. The US declared that it would continue its suspension of nuclear testing on a voluntary basis, provided that no further tests were conducted after those in the early days of November, 1958.

The test-ban talks between Britain, the United States and Russia have been deadlocked for the past five months. During the talks the only known nuclear tester has been France.

The text editor could build the scientific background into a separate story:

The 100-megaton (100-million-ton) bomb, if it is ever tested, would cause barely imaginable devastation. The bomb the Americans dropped on Hiroshima in 1945 was equal to only 20,000 tons (20 kilotons) of TNT – and it wiped out 80,000 people in one explosion. The 100-megaton bomb is 5,000 times as powerful. Even the smaller of the bombs announced, the 20-megaton, can cause third-degree burns 45 miles away.

It is not long since bombs were weighed in pounds. When the last war began a 1,000 lb bomb was enough to create terror among a civilian population. Four years later came the 'blockbuster', which was *ten tons* of TNT, and then in March 1945 the Royal Air Force's 22-ton Grand Slam, the heaviest conventional bomb ever used operationally.

If the Russians go ahead with their tests they are bound to throw up radioactive debris which will drift over the world creating new fears of pollution.

As it happens, the biggest bomb tested to date at that time was probably one of 57 megatons in the USSR on 30 October 1961 – according to the *Guinness Book of Records*, which is one of the easy sources for text editors when a bare agency message needs fleshing out in a hurry.

The chance for this kind of creative editing comes more often than you may think: a recurrence of floods (check and write in what action was promised last time); a runaway lorry on a hill (check previous accidents and protests); a take-over bid (check all the ramifications). Perhaps the most familiar opportunity is the death of a well-known person. On a busy evening paper, especially, there will be no time to invite an accomplished obituary. The text editor will call at once for the library clippings and add as much as possible in the time available. It is usually best for text editors to do this, rather than pass the task to a reporter, because the text editor can more easily weave into the story any further new agency information such as tributes, the circumstances of death, or a note on the political implications, and so on. Check the library clippings with *Who's Who*, if you can.

Another opportunity is the compendium story – when a series of similar events are pulled into one story. In an icy weekend there were five separate drownings on frozen ponds in different places. It was good copy-tasting and editing to pull them together into one story with a common intro:

Five boys were drowned on frozen ponds over the weekend.

That is the general intro. If one accident is outstanding it can be made the intro, with a second general paragraph bringing in the other items.

At all times translate foreign figures into domestic – dollars into pounds (or vice versa) – and give both. Relate everything to the ordinary lives of the readers. Tell them what a 'pasteurised' egg is as well as a fast-breeder reactor; don't leave them guessing what an invisible export is – or where they could find Aldabra. (It's in the Seychelles.) If you have to hesitate yourself before you write in an explanation, consider how much easier you are making things for the reader. Never let anything pass which you yourself would not be able to explain without the help of the library.

Story-telling

The discussion so far has been on straight news stories of two types: action and statement and statement–opinion stories. The opening advocated in both is the same, to reveal at once the most dramatic or important human results of the activity. I would make one exception – the occasion when the news point is deliberately delayed for a sentence. That delay can add pith and contrast. It offers variety. And the news point is still high up in the story.

Delaying the point by a sentence or two is still essentially hard news treatment of a story. Delaying beyond that – perhaps to the end of the report – is a technique, not of news reporting, but of story-telling. The technique is common in feature writing: 'How I escaped from the dreaded Wonga tribesmen', says the headline and the story begins with the day the writer caught the boat train. The story begins at the beginning and goes step by step to its stirring conclusion. The emphasis is not on what happened but on how it happened. The technique is clearly distinct from the hard news treatment of an action story.

For most hard news stories story-telling is too slow a technique. It is exasperating to the reader who wants to find out what happened. But story-telling has its uses even in news columns. There is a certain monotony when every story on every page opens with the same hard news urgency. Story-telling provides a change of pace. It is most useful of all in popular newspapers which package news as entertainment, and for weekly news magazines and newspapers who are behind the dailies with the hard news, but who have extra detail to relate. But story-telling must be used frugally. It must never be the most prevalent structure.

Let us look at the two forms of treatment. First the straight news report. It meets all our tests of being direct, active and human:

> Several American marines were hurt yesterday when they walked into a minefield outside their camp.
>
> They were following a 14-year-old Vietnamese boy who later admitted that he had laid the minefield himself. He said he had been tortured by the Vietcong to do it.
>
> The Marines said he was a 'cute little guy' who hung around the camp gate asking questions. They had talked to him and answered his questions – on explosives.

One popular tabloid treated this as an exercise in story-telling:

American Marines at a camp in Vietnam thought that the friendly 14-year-old Vietnamese boy was a 'cute little guy'.

He would hang around the camp gates asking questions.

The Marines told him what he wanted to know . . . about explosives.

Then one day the boy led a number of the Marines into a minefield outside the camp – a minefield he had laid himself.

Some of the Marines were hurt. The boy, caught later, said he had been tortured by the Communist Vietcong into doing it.

The first version would have been quite acceptable to many newspapers. But anyone editing on a paper which tries to make a popular appeal will often be impelled to use the story-telling technique.

The following story has the customary hard news intro – when the hard news is really not there to justify the report's position as a news story:

Margate Corporation will today receive a rear-door flap for a dust cart – which had been 21 days on its way by railway.

British Rail said: 'With a continued heavy flow of traffic it is regretted that the consignment in question, having been off-loaded into Platform 2, has not yet been sent on its way, but it will be delivered tomorrow.'

Passengers on the 5.41 p.m. from King's Cross to Welwyn Garden City were puzzled by the large crate addressed to Margate Corporation standing on a platform for more than a fortnight. So one of them wrote to the Town Clerk, Margate, and the Stationmaster at King's Cross.

The only element of interest in this story is that curious passengers saved Margate's rear-door flap. The story could be given a livelier beginning in the hard news style:

Commuters on the 5.41 p.m. King's Cross to Welwyn Garden City helped to equip a Margate Corporation dust cart yester-day.

Puzzled by the large crate for Margate standing untouched on their platform 2 for more than a fortnight they wrote to Margate Corporation and King's Cross stationmaster.

The crate contained . . .

One paper made the most of the news item by adopting the story-telling technique:

> The enormous, gunmetal-grey crate on Platform 2 at King's Cross, addressed to Margate Corporation, intrigued the commuters on the 5.41 p.m. to Welwyn Garden City. Every night they examined it and wondered what could be inside.
>
> Until today . . . more than a fortnight later . . . they could stand the suspense no longer.
>
> And their spokesman, solicitor Mr. W.J. Shaw, wrote to the Town Clerk at Margate and the Stationmaster at King's Cross.
>
> 'It seems amazing that British Rail can leave consignments, which may be urgent, lying around on a station for weeks,' said Mr. Shaw at his Holborn office this afternoon.
>
> What IS in the 6ft × 4ft crate which weighs 1cwt 56lb?
>
> A rear-door flap for one of Margate's dust carts.
>
> It was despatched from the Letchworth engineering firm of Shelvoke and Drewery on August 27.
>
> Said a spokesman for British Rail: 'With a continued heavy flow of traffic it is regretted that the consignment in question, having been off-loaded into Platform 2, has not yet been sent on its way.'
>
> This afternoon the dust-cart flap is on its way to Margate and should arrive tomorrow.
>
> It will have taken 21 days.

The story-telling structure is ideal for routine court reports. The court reports in some serious newspapers may be published for the significance of the legal judgment, and in local papers, for the familiar names of those involved. For many newspapers, however, it is neither of these news points which attracts. The court reports are published for the human drama they provide. Names and legal sequels are the small print in the credits column of a theatrical programme. Of course text editors must take great care to tell only the story supported by the judgment and by what the witnesses said in court. If there is a doubt it should be resolved in favour of the straightforward report. It is better to bore a thousand readers than to defame one.

Here is a straightforward court report:

> Four factory workers were fined a total of £14 for using intimidating behaviour against a fellow worker at West Bromwich magistrates court yesterday.
>
> They were . . . They were accused of intimidating 32-year-old Lester Seville, a tool setter of Blackthorne Road, Walsall, who had not joined a strike, now 13 weeks old, at the factory, Newmans Tubes Ltd, Wednesbury.
>
> Charges of using threatening behaviour were dismissed.
>
> Mr Seville told the court the four men were pickets who stopped him one night when he left the factory to try and persuade him to join the strike. 'I was frightened because of their attitude', he said. They were quite prepared to use 'a little bit of pressure.'
>
> Mr George Jones, defending, said the men merely wanted to hold a quiet conversation with Seville.

Using the story-telling technique, the text editor would select the point where the action began and build the story from there.

> Four pickets lay in wait one night for a fellow worker – to try to persuade him to join a strike.
>
> And they were quite prepared to use 'a little bit of pressure', according to the worker, 32-year-old Lester Seville.
>
> 'I was frightened because of their attitude,' he told magistrates at West Bromwich, Staffordshire, yesterday.
>
> It happened during a strike, now 13 weeks old, at Newmans Tubes Ltd, Wednesbury.
>
> Mr George Jones, defending four men before the court, said that they merely wanted to hold a quiet conversation with Mr Seville, a tool setter, of Blackthorne Road, Walsall.
>
> At no time did they use any force or threats.
>
> The four accused . . . were fined a total of £14 for using intimidating behaviour.
>
> Charges of using threatening behaviour were dismissed.

The source of news reports may be delayed even more. It is not until the sixth paragraph here that the reader is told that the following is a court report. (The headline: 'Golfer takes a swing at the Sergeant.') Paragraph 6 is worth your attention. It is the link between the yarn and its source.

Golfer Sidney McCallum lost his temper, took a swing . . . and broke a policeman's jaw.

It happened between the eighth and ninth holes on the Richmond Park golf course, Surrey.

McCallum, a 42-year-old cable jointer, of Petersfield Rise, Putney, London SW – 'a fairly quick golfer' – was playing the course behind Sergeant Francis Bott.

And McCallum told the sergeant 'Get a move on, you're slowing us up'.

Sgt Bott said: 'We can't go any quicker because of those chaps in front.'

Then, Mr K. Hargreave, prosecuting, told the South Western magistrates court yesterday, the sergeant received 'a very hard blow.'

He was taken to hospital with a broken jaw, concussion and amnesia. He has lost six weeks' work but is expected to return on December 1.

McCallum later told police that Sgt. Bott had tried to throw him: 'I was out for a game of golf not a punch-up. I stepped back and hit him once.'

The magistrate, Sir John Cameron, told McCallum: 'Fortunately violence on the golf course is not very prevalent. I am not going to take as serious a view as if this had occurred on a football ground.'

He conditionally discharged McCallum for a year for causing bodily harm, but ordered him to pay £10 costs.

And so, too, with the reporting of wills. If one is working on a local paper, the news will be how much has been left and to whom. There is no substitute for the details here, presented directly as 'Mr X left . . . and his bequests were . . .' If the person involved is not well known or the sum not large, the popular national or big evening paper will generally expect the story to be edited so that the point is near the end rather than the beginning. They will not want:

> Mrs Wells of Barton-on-Sea left a bottle of sherry and a bottle of gin in her will, announced yesterday, to a Gas Board official because he was so cheerful when installing her central heating.

The executives will ask for a rewrite which makes the news into a tale:

> Every time the man from the Gas Board called at Mrs Amy Wells's home, she changed her mind about the radiators she was having installed.
> But the gasman kept on smiling.
> And though he did not know it then, his smile had won him a friend.
> Mr Lawrence Price, district sales manager of the Southern Gas Board, who supervised the installation of the radiators two years ago, heard last night that Mrs Wells, of Barton-on-Sea, Hampshire, had remembered him in her £11,655 will.
> Mrs Wells, who was 82 when she died, left him a bottle of gin and a bottle of sherry – 'for keeping on smiling every time I changed my mind.'

Exercises in Choice of Style

The narrative or story-telling style of news reports has validity on a number of occasions which can be identified:

1. When a narrative can be used as an adjunct to a main news story, rather like zooming from a general scene to a detail
2. When a story is so familiar from other media that the readers/viewers know the result, but would now be intrigued by detail and drama
3. Second, third and fourth days of developing stories; for instance, once the news of the massacre of schoolchildren in Littleton, Colorado, had been recorded on days one and two, there was ample scope for picking up individual

stories and telling them in narrative style. What happened hour by hour, for instance, to the SWAT team (Special Weapons Attack Team). A day in the life of one of the teachers. And so on. The varying styles might usefully be demonstrated by looking at a number of published reports that appeared in the American press

On the left is a straight news story of a student disappointed by a beauty treatment. As a crime story it is small beer. But told as a little human story it would have more appeal. The version on the right is the rewritten narrative style of the story. It is more interesting and it saves 24 per cent of the space.

Authorities yesterday shut down the illicit medical practice of a Queens woman – dubbed Madame Olga – who allegedly disfigured a college student by giving her illegal injections designed to prevent wrinkles, prosecutors said.

Olga (Madame Olga) Ramirez, 34, was charged with practising medicine without a license, assault, reckless endangerment and possession of hypodermic needles, Queens District Attorney Richard Brown said.

'I am very upset,' said Izadeli Montalvo, 22, of Queens, who charged she has suffered recurring facial swelling since receiving the injections four months ago.

'I don't know what the future consequences of this will be,' the St. John's University student said. 'I am already suffering.'

Izadeli Montalvo, a student at St. John's University in Queens, was worried to be told she looked 35.

She is only 22.

Izadeli put such faith in the woman who gave her the bad news, beauty specialist Olga Ramirez, 34, that last December she paid $600 for three injections she was assured would make her look more youthful and prevent wrinkles.

It was a disaster. Izadeli's face swelled up painfully time and again over four months. She had suffered a severed facial nerve that may require surgery to repair, according to her lawyer Mason Pimsler.

The trouble was that Ramirez – professionally known as Madame Olga – was licensed by the state only as an esthetician to do makeup work and suggest

For at least four years, Ramirez worked out of her College Point home, where investigators seized hundreds of needles, containers of medicines and a small amount of hormones, authorities said.

Ramirez, who had business cards claiming the title doctor, 'operated for some time with reckless disregard for the people who turned to her for help,' Brown said.

Ramirez was charged with assault for giving injections to Montalvo, who told the *Daily News* she went for a consultation with Madame Olga in December and was informed she looked 35.

She said she paid $600 for three injections, which Ramirez promised would make her skin look more youthful and prevent wrinkles.

Instead, Montalvo said, she was left with swelling and numbness in her face. 'It was very painful. It was a very bad experience,' she said.

Brown said Montalvo was temporarily disfigured by the treatment. Her lawyer, Mason Pimsler, said she suffered a severed facial nerve that may require surgery to repair.

Investigators are not yet sure what the injections contained, but suspect it may have been a collagenlike substance. They seized bottles bearing the names over-the-counter medicines. She was not qualified to prescribe or administer drugs – or use the title 'Dr.' as she did on her business card.

So yesterday the Queens District Attorney, Richard Brown, shut down Madame Olga's illicit medical practice and accused her of practising medicine without a license. 'She operated with reckless disregard for the people who turned to her for help,' said Brown. He alleged Montalvo was 'temporarily disfigured'.

Investigators at Madame Olga's home in College Point, her workplace for four years, seized hundreds of hypodermic needles, containers of medicines bearing the names 'biopolymer' and 'biopolymere', and a small amount of hormones. They are not sure what was in the injections given to Izadeli, but suspect it may have been a collagenlike substance.

'All I know,' said Izadeli, 'is that I am very upset. It was a bad experience.'

259 words

'biopolymer' and 'biopolymere', authorities said.

Ramirez is licensed by the state as an esthetician, enabling her to do makeup work and apply over-the-counter medicines, but not to prescribe or administer drugs, authorities said.

322 words

Here is another story where readers already knew that the woman had died on the operating table in the presence of a medical salesman. On the left is the news report of the campaign by the relatives. It is a valid piece of writing, but might be compared to the same story told in narrative style. There is a saving of 19 lines.

Relatives of a woman who died after a botched operation hope her death helps others live.

Lisa Smart, a 30-year-old financial analyst, died in 1997 at Manhattan's Beth Israel Medical Center after routine outpatient surgery to remove a benign cyst.

A year later, the state Health Department blamed Smart's death on negligence by two doctors, who used unfamiliar equipment and allowed a Johnson & Johnson salesman to assist with the operation.

One of the operating surgeons – her doctor's partner – was on probation for a long list of violations.

Had this information been available, Smart might be alive

When Lisa Smart, a 30-year-old financial analyst, was wheeled into the surgery at Manhattan's Beth Israel Medical Center for the removal of a benign cyst she did not know that one of the operating surgeons, her own doctor's partner, was on probation for a long list of violations.

And she did not know that a Johnson & Johnson salesman would be there during the operation showing the doctors how to use new equipment.

Lisa died. The state Health Department blamed the two doctors for negligence.

Her husband travelled to Albany yesterday to press for 'Lisa's Law', a bill to give patients the right to know about

today, her husband, Anderson Smart, said yesterday.

'We don't want this to happen to anyone else,' said Smart, who travelled to Albany to press for a measure to give patients access to more information about their doctors.

Dubbed Lisa's Law, the bill would require the state to provide a profile of each of the state's licensed doctors, including information about lawsuits, their training and work history. The state collects the information, but does not make it available.

The bill has been introduced in the Assembly twice, but has gone nowhere.

The head of the Senate Health Committee, Sen. Kemp Hannon (R.Nassau), said he agrees there's a need to provide patients with more information about doctors.

'The trick is trying to balance what's appropriate and what's not going to deter physicians from practising in New York or turning down risky patients,' said Hannon.

The powerful Medical Society of the State of New York remains fiercely opposed to providing information about malpractice lawsuits, insisting it's an unfair gauge of competence.

'Many of the best doctors have the worst malpractice experience, because they take the the lawsuits, training and work history of state licensed doctors – information the state collects but does not make available. 'We don't want this to happen to anyone else,' said Anderson Smart.

Lisa's Law has been introduced twice in the assembly but has gone nowhere. The powerful Medical Society of the State of New York is fiercely opposed. 'Many of the best doctors have the worst malpractice experience, because they take the patients with the most difficult problems,' said Liz Dears for the Society. The head of the Senate Health Committee, Kemp Hannon (R.-Nassau) commented: 'The trick is trying to balance what's appropriate and what's not going to deter physicians from practising in New York or turning down risky patients.'

225 words

patients with the most difficult problems,' said Liz Dears, a Medical Society lawyer.

292 words

Here is a story which offers us a chance to experiment with different styles of newswriting. The original intro read:

> A Brooklyn rabbi stole $6 million from the Board of Education by putting 81 no-show employees on the board payroll in a 20-year scam that benefited his religious school, Special Schools Investigator Ed Stancik charged yesterday.

This is a classic example of an overloaded intro, and one obsessed by source. You have to read it twice. And even then, it is not immediately apparent what the rabbi has been up to.

The story might have been treated in any one of three ways. On the left is a straight narrative style. On the right is a modified narrative which focuses on the three principals in the conspiracy. Both these treatments, as it happens, are shorter than the original report by some 37 lines. The narrative style, far from being longer, has saved space by the avoidance of repetition and incidental explanation.

Hertz Frankel, an Hasidic Rabbi, was very busy as the devoted principal of Beth Rachel, his girls' school in Williamsburg.

He was responsible for 4,000 students and their teachers, and also for hiring and overseeing 30 security guards for the school vacation camp and another 51 paraprofessionals. He was so conscientious about these extra staff that he delivered their signed time sheets to the district office himself, picked up the

Hertz Frankel, a prominent Hasidic Rabbi, cared deeply about religious teaching at the Beth Rachel Jewish Girls' School in Williamsburg where he was principal. William Rogers and Mario DeStefano cared deeply about keeping their jobs as District 14 Superintendents, which they thought depended on the support of three Satmar Hasidics on a nine-member board.

The interests of the three men led them into a conspiracy that has only now been exposed after

checks, and distributed them himself – for twenty years.

But in all those years there never was a vacation camp.

And there never were jobs for paraprofessionals or security guards. The fake workers – Hasidic housewives and Beth Rachel teachers – were paid salaries from $5,000 to $144,000 a year, but gave the money straight back to Rabbi Frankel. And he, in turn, spent it on Beth Rachel.

Rabbi Frankel, 68, and his 'no-shows' were all part of a conspiracy that siphoned off $6 million of public money – $4.3 million in salaries and $1.9 million in medical benefits. But they could not have managed the scam without the help of two District 14 Superintendents, William Rogers and Mario DeStefano, both now deceased. They believed that helping Rabbi Frankel would keep them sweet with three Satmar Hasidic members on the nine-member district board. So they certified the fake employees, even taking them to the central board office for fingerprinting formalities.

The two-decade scam was exposed after a two-year joint investigation by Special Schools Investigator Ed Stancik and the U.S. attorney's office. On Friday, Frankel, pleading guilty to a felony charge to commit mail fraud, was given three years' probation and ordered to repay 20 years.

In the late seventies, Rogers and DeStefano invented fake jobs for 51 paraprofessionals and also for 30 security guards at a non-existent vacation camp, Frankel provided the names of people who would pretend to be workers – Hasidic housewives and Beth Rachel teachers. Then the superintendents took the fictitious employees to the central board office for fingerprinting formalities.

Once they were enrolled – at salaries ranging from $5,000 to $144,000 a year – they never did any work, but Frankel would deliver signed time sheets to the district office, collect the checks, and give them to his fake workers.

And the no-shows would give Frankel the salary money, which he put into Beth Rachel school.

The no-shows used the medical benefits to the tune of $1.9 million. Some $4.3 million in salaries went into school funds. 'At no time did I personally make a single penny from this arrangement,' said Frankel yesterday. 'All funds received were used for secular programs at the school.'

He had pleaded guilty to a felony charge to commit mail fraud – Rogers and DeStefano are dead. Judge Eugene H. Nickerson put Frankel, 68, on proba-

$1 million.

Stancik, calling it 'a conspiracy of staggering proportions,' said none of the people involved ever set foot in a public school. About half the cash was still missing. Frankel said the money went to legitimate, secular remedial programs at Beth Rachel and he was unaware of 'anything illegal'. 'At no time did I personally make a single penny from this arrangement.'

Beth Rachel has returned $1 million and Schools Chancellor Rudy Crew said he would press for more. He would discipline any staff involved.

Yesterday Stancik demanded that Crew dismiss Acting Superintendent John Musico, whom he accused of destroying evidence. Musico did not return calls.

tion for three years and ordered him to repay $1 million.

The two-decade scam was exposed after a two-year joint investigation by Special Schools Investigator Ed Stancik and the U.S. attorney's office.

Stancik, calling it 'a conspiracy of staggering proportions', said none of the people involved ever set foot in a public school. About half the cash was still missing.

Beth Rachel has returned $1 million and Schools Chancellor Rudy Crew has said he would try to recover more. Staff involved would be disciplined.

Yesterday Stancik demanded that Crew dismiss Acting Superintendent John Musico, whom he accused of destroying evidence. Musico did not return calls.

Both of these examples are subject to the criticism that the news point has been unduly delayed. What now follows is a modified narrative where the news point has been pithily encapsulated in the first sentence, and the narrative develops with explanation. This hybrid narrative-news style has much to commend it. But of course it's essential to have a first sentence in the intro that really epitomises the news without getting bogged down in sources and detail.

Rabbi Hertz Frankel was a thief – for a good cause. He siphoned off $6m of public school money but did not keep a cent for himself. He put it all into his private Jewish girls' school, Beth Rachel in Williamsburg.

The 20-year conspiracy, which involved two district officials, was exposed yesterday when Frankel, 68, was put on probation for three years and ordered to pay $1m back.

Topical hard news point.

It began in the seventies. Frankel, a prominent Hasidic rabbi, cared deeply about religious teaching at his school. William Rogers and Mario DeStefano cared deeply about keeping their jobs as District 14 Superintendents, which they thought depended on the support of three Satmar Hasidics on a nine-member board.

Narrative recapitulation.

Rogers and DeStefano invented fake jobs for 51 paraprofessionals and also for 30 security guards at a non-existent vacation camp. Frankel provided the people who would pretend to be workers – Hasidic housewives and Beth Rachel teachers. Then the superintendents took the fictitious employees to the central board office for fingerprinting formalities.

Once they were enrolled – at salaries ranging from $5,000 to $144,000 a year – they never did any work, but Frankel would deliver signed time sheets to the district office, collect the checks, and give them to the no-shows.

And the no-shows would give Frankel the salary money, which he put into Beth Rachel school.

The no-shows used the medical benefits to the tune of $1.9 million. Some $4.3 million in salaries went into school funds. 'At no time did I personally make a single penny from this arrangement,' said Frankel yesterday. 'All funds received were used for secular programs at the school.'

The scam was exposed after a two-year joint investigation by Special Schools Investigator Ed Stancik and the U.S. attorney's office.

Stancik, calling it 'a conspiracy of staggering proportions', said none of the people involved ever set foot in a public school. About half the cash was still missing. Schools Chancellor Rudy Crew said the staff involved would be disciplined and the board would try to recover more money.

Yesterday Stancik demanded that Crew dismiss Acting Superintendent John Musico, whom he accused of destroying evidence. Musico did not return calls.

Follow-up news points.

News-features Editing

These last snippets are really in the no man's land between news and features, the writer making the most of flimsy material. But the story-telling technique is not simply a gimmick the text editor should learn from popular papers. Here is an example from a serious feature where the delayed intro is well used to contrast the start and the pinnacle of a man's career.

When he was growing up in Stoughton, Wis., during the early 1920s, H.I. Romnes used to think of himself as a 'lucky fellow'. As the oldest of five children, Mr. Romnes was what he calls the 'front man' and did the selling in his father's bakery shop while the others stoked the fires and kneaded the dough.

Last week, after two years as president, Mr. Romnes once again became the man up front when he was named chairman and chief executive of the American Telephone and Telegraph Company.

News magazines and serious weekly newspapers have to use delayed intros and story-telling techniques to do justice to assessments and complicated investigative reports. If the subject has not been running in the news but comes from the paper's own inquiries, it may be essential for the writer to put the conclusions into context. In this article the delayed intro does just that – and it effectively contrasts promise and performance two years on:

In July, 1964, Peter Thorneycroft, then Minister of Defence, rose to answer an awkward Parliamentary question about the size of the Ministry's senior staff. 'I have been able to take certain actions,' he told Labour MP James Boyden, 'which ensure that Professor Parkinson is removed from the establishment.'

Three months earlier Thorneycroft had proudly introduced his 'revolutionary' streamlined Ministry, designed to impose greater central control on defence policy. Two and a half years after the revolution, an Insight inquiry has found that the Ministry, under Thorneycroft's successor, Denis Healey, is not the streamlined instrument it should be. Parkinsonism, far from being uprooted, is spreading.

Instead of fewer senior officials there are more. Instead of a controlled system of decision-making on a tri-service basis, decisions are made tortuously by an elaborate and inefficient committee system. Instead of the service cutting their inflated strengths, they cling stubbornly to an archaic career structure.

This article is neither straight news nor feature; it is a mixture of news and opinion. A straight news intro would have said 'There are more officials in the Ministry of Defence instead of fewer promised by Mr Peter Thorneycroft in July 1964.' That would have been all right as far as it went, but it would have been thin and flat by comparison with the story-telling style. The writer properly preferred to use the jaunty scene in Parliament two years earlier as an overture for the repetitive discordant notes in the third paragraph. The three separate sentences there, as well as adding emphasis by the use of 'instead of . . .' also come to grips with a rather more complicated set of conclusions than could comfortably be housed in a straight news sentence.

This third paragraph is what is often called a 'taster' – a taste for the reader of things to come. It is a kind of trailer, a come-on to the reader confronted with a lot of words. Where you are editing a very long feature report, say 2,000 words or more, you should see that the structure accommodates early appetisers of some of the good things developed later in the narrative:

At 9.30 a.m. on his last day in England, May 25, 1951, Donald Maclean was walking decorously from Charing Cross station to his room in the Foreign Office. Guy Burgess, never a devotee of early rising, had only just got out of bed in his New Bond Street flat by Aspreys. He was reading *The Times* and drinking tea made by his friend Jack Hewit. Everything was relaxed and unhurried.

By 10.30 everything had changed irrevocably. Burgess, warned through Kim Philby in Washington that Donald Maclean was about to be interrogated, made a vital decision. By that evening Maclean had gone,

Opening with a dramatic human highlight. It is out of sequence in the article but essential to capture interest.

in a cloud of mystery – and Burgess had gone with him.

But for Burgess's excited and unnecessary flight, things might have been very different for Kim Philby. Conceivably, the most remarkable Soviet spy ever to penetrate the Western intelligence community might have remained undetected for another ten years. Certainly it is now clear that it was only his fortuitous double link – with both Burgess and Maclean – which turned suspicion on him.

Had the cool, untrusting Philby been finally betrayed in 1951 by the bonds of Burgess's impulsive friendship, it would have been an ironic finale. But the damage Burgess did to him was more than compensated by the inflexible loyalty of his friends in the Secret Intelligence Service. Insight's inquiries have now established in detail that Philby, publicly sacked from the Foreign Service in 1951, was in fact secretly employed by the SIS – even during the shadowy period before he became an *Observer* foreign correspondent at the request of the Foreign Office.

Feelings about Kim Philby vary sharply among his old colleagues in the British Secret Intelligence Service. Some preserve a degree of affection and ruminate upon the 'misplaced idealism' which led him to work

Recapitulation. Early presentation of an important conclusion.

for the Russians. Some see his career largely as a technical feat. 'He was an agent who really lived his cover', they say.

Others take a more impassioned view, like the man who said to us: 'Philby was a copper-bottomed bastard, and he killed a lot of people.'

Espionage and counter-espionage can seem so much like civilised office games that the blood can get forgotten. But in this account of Philby's career from 1945 to 1951 there are two crucial episodes which luridly illuminate the realities of the game.

The first case is a man alone: a Soviet intelligence officer caught in the act of trying to defect to the West. That story ends with a bandaged figure being hustled aboard a Russian plane in Istanbul.

Taster No. 1. Will be told in detail later.

In the second case, there are some 300 men in armed parties, slipping across the Iron Curtain border from Greece into Albania. This was a scheme designed to test the feasibility of breaking Communist control of Eastern Europe by subversion: the story ends in a crackle of small-arms fire on bleak hillsides, and the total discrediting of a policy which might have caused the Soviet Government a lot of trouble.

Taster No. 2. Will be told later.

Behind each case is the shadow of Kim Philby – the Soviet penetration-agent at the

Recapitulation, to remind readers of the essence of the story. New development indicated.

heart of the Secret Intelligence
Service whose loyalty went
unquestioned for so long.
Indeed, it might never have
been questioned, but for the fact
that Philby was caught up in the
complex aftermath of Donald
Maclean's espionage for the Russians.

Most good news and feature leads have one thing in common:
they are specific and human. Indeed, the way the news
magazine or weekly copes with beginning a story that has
been running in the daily papers is to be more specific and
detailed about some element in it. The news stories had
already said, for instance, that King Constantine of Greece
had tried to overthrow the military government and had
flown to Rome after his failure. A later news-feature report
begins on the most vivid sequence in the whole chronology of
the story. The magazine began its report of the king's revolt
like this:

To the astonishment of a handful of passengers waiting at
Rome's Ciampino Airport at 4 a.m. squads of Italian police
suddenly materialized and took up positions around the field.
Moments later, a white turbo-prop jet taxied to a stop on the
apron. In the plane's doorway appeared a young man in the
red-trimmed uniform of a field marshal. Limping slightly from
fatigue, his face ashen and heavily bearded, King Constantine
of Greece, 27, walked down a ramp on to Italian soil. Behind
him, glum and red-eyed, came his Danish wife, Queen Anne-
Marie, 25, her mink coat still smelling of the mothballs from
which she had hastily removed it.

With them were their two infant children, Queen Mother
Frederika, the King's 25-year-old sister Irene, and several loyal
followers.

Thus last week, after an abortive royal countercoup that
may go down as one of the most inept conspiracies in history,
the King of the Hellenes fled his country, leaving in control

more firmly than ever the military junta that had seized power last April in a lightning coup.

Where the news result is familiar to readers, detail is the only answer. A Sunday paper reconstruction of the Rhodesian talks between Harold Wilson and Ian Smith on board HMS *Tiger* began like this, with new detail of a dramatic moment in the talks:

> The first intimation that the *Tiger* talks might be a flop came just three hours before the end of the seaborne confrontation. Mr Ian Smith, the Rhodesian Premier, was showing extreme reluctance to put his signature to the working document that he had personally elaborated with the British negotiators in the previous day. 'If you won't sign,' said Mr Wilson, settling for half a loaf, 'you will of course commend it to your Government colleagues in Salisbury.' 'I'll have to commend it to myself first, won't I?', said Smith.

Detail, not chronology, must be the master in feature leads. The detail can even be a development since the hard news was first told. This was the beginning of a feature telling how commercial television companies had competed for new franchises in Britain:

> Every morning on a private line between the commercial television companies there is a grandly-styled Red Telephone Conversation: the network planning officers of the 14 companies use it to synchronise their complicated programme swaps. Last Thursday the exchanges were somewhat chilled.
> Rediffusion, in the chair, was attempting to explain how the night before it had managed to help perpetrate one of the network's biggest programme muddles. Bewildered viewers outside London had been treated to a discussion of the documentary 'Famine', which they were told they had just seen – but, which, in fact, had gone out only to London viewers.
> The 'Famine' mix-up seems to have been the first unlooked-for product of last Sunday's announcement by the Independent Television Authority of the new franchise deal for 1968 –

bringing three new companies into the business; deposing Television West and Wales and cutting Rediffusion's programme days effectively from five days to two. Rediffusion just has not been the same since.

The features editor should study the structure of the best feature stories in the newspapers and news magazines. Features text editors are not there to write features: that is the job of the writers. But the features text editor should be able to tell a writer what is wrong with the structure of a story; and should be able to make suggestions for improvement. I say 'suggestions' because there should be time in features editing to discuss improvements with the writer. Features text editors can make real improvements in both the language and the structure of pieces presented even by brilliant writers; occasionally the specialist overlooks the ignorance of the average reader; new features writers are often on an adjectival spree or simply out to show their skill.

Features editors should always put their observations to even the best writers – but where there is a margin of doubt they should give the writer the preference and they should not hack good writing to preconceived notions. If you have gone to features editing from straight news editing, beware the reflex actions you have rightly cultivated as a straight news journalist. In features, the mood, the style may be everything. This is also true of the news-features which can appear on a news page, the occasions when a descriptive commentator is covering a news scene and there is no hard news at that precise moment. For instance, here is a news-feature intro from Aden by David Holden:

> 'Gone away' says the sign painted on the wall of Aden's biggest prison by some waggish British soldier a couple of months ago when the last of South Arabia's political detainees were released. 'Gone away – no milk, no papers.'
>
> The sign is still there; and in two or three weeks from now when the last British troops leave Aden for good, it may well serve as a mocking epitaph for 128 years of empire in South Arabia.

In Aden, the empire was never very imperial and, apart from 'Ali Baba's' mobile chip shop, it is not leaving much behind. Already this is a half-abandoned city.

A sub with itching fingers might have been tempted to rewrite a hard news intro: 'Already Aden is a half-abandoned city'. That would, of course, have ruined an evocative intro which had woven into it some of the background and a news point which was much more tellingly made in the context. Gone away, gone away . . . the desolation is vivid.

As a final caution, read this intro. The hard news was simply that Irish people were being asked to stay in England for Christmas because of the risk of spreading foot-and-mouth disease. Peter Dunn had visited some of the Irish stranded for Christmas, and he might easily have begun: 'Christmas dinner has been specially laid on for some 250 Irish stranded in London by the foot-and-mouth restrictions.' Instead he chose a detail – a specific human Irish detail which makes us want to delve deeper:

Mr. Allen C. Breeze, Irish poet, author of Tshombe's Lament and owner of T.S. Eliot's false teeth, will not be going home to Ireland this Christmas, though he had planned to. He has given his air ticket to his friend, Charlie, a tall serious man who is in commerce.

Intros like this still the itchiest subbing fingers.

CHAPTER EIGHT

Headlines

What the News Headline Says

If I choose to head an article 'An Inquiry into the Conditions of
Mycenaean Civilisation in the Heroic Epoch, with Special
Reference to the Economic and Domestic Functions of Women
Before and After the Conjectural Date of the Argive Expedition
against Troy', – if, I say, I choose for my article some snappy
little title like that, I really have no right to complain if (when I
send it to the *Chicago Daily Scoop*), they alter it to 'How Helen
Did the Housekeeping'.

G. K. CHESTERTON

They might nowadays have changed Chesterton's manuscript
to the even pithier 'How Helen Kept House'. But Chesterton
would clearly have made a brilliant features sub-editor. The
difficulty in writing headlines is precisely in conveying in a
few attractive words the essence of a complicated set of facts.
I would say that writing good headlines is 50 per cent of text
editors' skills. They have to catch readers on the wing. In half
a dozen words they have to inform them tersely and
accurately of a shattering or confused event, or arouse their
curiosity in a subtle manifestation of human behaviour. This
skill can be developed because there are certain principles for
good headline writing; a text editor of genuine flair may
occasionally break all the rules, but no more than the
composer who deliberately introduces discord into harmo-
nies. Every bit of available time spent chiselling out the right
words in the right sequence is time well spent.

The headline gives emphasis to a few words in bold type

and every word must be weighed. There is a double responsibility on headline writers. They have to attract as many readers as they can into the text of the story, or condemn it to unread obscurity; but even where they fail they have an effect, for many who do not read the story none the less retain an impression from scanning the headline.

Accuracy, intelligibility and vigour are the requirements, and any newspaper which is careless with its headline writing is careless with its own purpose and vitality. Where headlines are wordy, vague or confused, the newspaper seems to be in its dotage. Where every headline goes unerringly to the point with precision or wit, the whole newspaper comes alive. The art of the headline lies in imagination and vocabulary; the craft lies in accuracy of content, attractiveness of appearance, and practicality.

The Headline's Purpose

A prize young bullock escaped one day from the cattle market in Darlington. The bullock was chased by nine men along several shopping streets in town until it was recaptured. The bullock did no damage but provided a lot of temporary excitement. The reporter duly described all this with quotes included, and the copy came to the text editor for a headline. On it, after deliberation, the text editor inscribed the following headline, which passed into print:

NO DAMAGE AND
NO ONE HURT

The reporter the next day complained that his story had not been used. Clearly if he had been extraordinarily assiduous he would have found it, but only the more dedicated readers of the text that day would have been drawn to the story of the bullock.

The headline was not merely negative. It could have been written about the bulk of the proceedings in Darlington that day. It was undistinctive to the point of extinction: but it will survive in the pages as one of the finest examples of a headline that wasn't. The headline must tell the news; the text editor who writes it must have a sense of what news is, just as much as the reporter. What is it that has happened to arrest attention? What is new and interesting? What is different? The *result* of the activity is none of these things. 'No damage and no one hurt' could be news if it happened after an explosion or if it recorded, say, a day without traffic accidents. But here the result of the activity is not surprising; it is the *cause* of the activity which is different.

A bullock in its normal way will be expected to do no damage and hurt nobody. But a bullock does not run through the shopping streets every day. The headline writer, then, must at least begin by using the word bullock. Should the headline then be 'Bullock does no damage'? That headline is certainly accurate. But has it told the reader what the news really is? Is it the bullock's failure to decimate the population which is surprising – or is it simply the diversion of the bullock's chase through the streets?

The trouble with 'Bullock does no damage' is not that there is anything in it which is wrong but that there is not enough in it which is right. It is not related enough to the events of the day. It does not tell the news. The headline will have to be built on the simple news fact of a bullock running loose through shopping streets. We could write 'Men chase loose bullock'. But again that is too unspecific, too unrelated to the story. It would be much better to write 'Nine men chase bullock'; or, if there is room 'Nine chase bullock in town'. Better still, we could change the tone of the headline to emphasise that the news lies in the antics of the bullock rather than in any heavy drama: 'Prize bullock goes shopping'.

I have explored the case of the galloping bullock because I want to stress that the headline must sum up the news in the story it serves – and no other. It must distil the news. It must be specific. The first task, then, in writing a good headline is to read the copy carefully and decide on the basic news point. This may not be in the first paragraph. With most news stories it should be there, and if it is not, you may have to reorganise the story to bring the news to the top. But sometimes the news point is legitimately delayed and often the news is a complex of various facts in the story, so that enjoining the text editor to write a headline based on the first paragraph is not enough.

The headline writer must think hard on what single element in the story it is which makes it new, different, and worth its space in the paper. To make this judgment text editors need to know the background to the news item they are editing: if it is a developing story they must be fully aware of the previous developments and how other newspapers assessed the news point at their publication time. Unimportant details and subsidiary information are put aside, to focus on the real significance of the story. As they read the copy, text editors sum up the news in their mind, and note the sentence, words, phrases or ideas at the heart of the story. These notes will serve as the basis for constructing the headline.

We will try this technique with a simple hard news story.

> Groups of Royal Marine Commandos came under heavy mortar and small arms fire in Steamer Point, Aden, today. One Marine was wounded as NLF guerrillas fired on six posts simultaneously.

We have now to write a headline for this. Strip away the secondary details and the articles and we can write down a sentence which sums up the news: 'Royal Marine Commandos under heavy mortar and small arms fire in Aden today'. This is our sentence capturing the news. It is, of course, much too long for a headline. What can we cut out? Royal Marine Commandos can become 'Marines'. The location in Aden can be dropped since stories on troops in Aden have been running through the news for weeks. We can omit 'today' because in a news context the reader takes it for granted the item is about current events.

So now we have 'Marines under heavy mortar and small arms fire'. This may still be too long to fit in the space allocated. If we eliminate the description of the attack as 'mortar and small arms' we have a headline:

MARINES UNDER HEAVY FIRE

There may be room for further refinement. We can take out the word 'heavy' and put back the more specific word 'mortar'. Mortar fire is, in any event, more significant than small arms fire:

MARINES UNDER MORTAR FIRE

This headline meets all the requirements: it fits; it makes immediate sense; it attracts readers; it tells the news.

How Many Ideas?

What we have just done is to write a headline by editing a sentence. That was a simple story and a simple one-line headline, but the same technique of sentence-editing serves for more elaborate stories and more elaborate headline structures. Let us write a headline now of three lines on the following story:

> Teams of rescuers brought an injured woman of 25 to the surface at the Giant's Pothole near Castleton in the Peak District of Derbyshire yesterday, after a perilous 14-hour struggle through icy water and narrow rocky passageways 450ft underground.
>
> Caked in mud and swathed in a special insulation suit, Miss Donna Carr was carried from the hole at 5 a.m. by grimy-faced rescuers. She is believed to have a fractured skull and leg injuries after falling 30ft soon after entering the 1,317ft hole at 4 p.m. on Saturday. Last night, as she was reported fully conscious and fairly comfortable at Sheffield Royal Infirmary, some of the 50 rescue workers told of what they had done and of two heroes, Dr G. Kidd, and a nurse, Mrs Margaret Aldred.

We cannot cope with all these details in the headline. The woman's age and the pothole's location are secondary. Shorn of such secondary information, what is the core of the news? In a sentence it is: 'A woman down a pothole has been rescued after 14 hours'. Leave out '14 hours', 'has been' and the indefinite articles and we have a truncated sentence which becomes the headline, 'Woman down pothole rescued'. This splits into three lines as:

WOMAN DOWN
POTHOLE
RESCUED

This fits easily, but is rather drab. It is also slow. We want to relay the news as quickly as possible. This structure delays until the third line the news that the woman has been saved. We should hasten to an earlier line the introduction of this news point. So for the first line let us write:

WOMAN SAVED

That truncated sentence leaves a lot of questions. In what circumstances? Where? This time when we answer these questions let us try to flesh the skeleton with something specific: 'She has been saved after 14 hours down a pothole'. Delete the repetition and the indefinite articles and we have 'after 14 hours down pothole'. This could be split as:

AFTER 14 HOURS
DOWN POTHOLE

The trouble now is that the second line won't fit. Clearly rearranging the same wording on different lines does not help:

AFTER 14
HOURS IN POTHOLE

We have, therefore, to change the wording. Is there any other way we can express the same idea of 14 hours? Yes, there is. The woman spent *the night* in the pothole, so we can write:

```
WOMAN SAVED
AFTER NIGHT
IN POTHOLE
```

This is an adequate headline, but it would be improved if we could inject one detail of drama, something, say, about the icy water down there. We cannot do this with the existing line structure since the phrase 'after icy night' would be too long as a second line. If we are prepared to delay the core news point to the second line we can try:

```
WOMAN IN POTHOLE
SAVED AFTER
ICY NIGHT
```

Fine, but now the first line 'Woman in pothole' is too long. There is a device which will make it fit – a device which should be used sparingly, but which is legitimate and is accepted by the reader when it makes sense within the headline sentence. This is the device of the compound noun. 'Woman in pothole' becomes 'pothole woman':

```
POTHOLE WOMAN
SAVED AFTER
ICY NIGHT
```

Grammatical Traps

In each of these instances we have taken the core news point, expressed it in a sentence, shortened the sentence, and then simply transcribed the sentence, in the same order, into lines of headline. Where the words fell on the lines was determined simply by whether in that sequence they fitted the space available. If a newsy sentence has been edited comprehensibly there is no need to worry very much where the words fall. There is one caution, which I will give in a moment, but there is certainly no need for the fuss made by some newspapers in the United States. They insist on each line having its own grammatical integrity, and therefore ban headlines where, say, a preposition is on one line and the object is on another. Rules like this are a pedantry which has developed from one soundly based restriction on the word pattern in the multi-line headline. This simple real difficulty is one of meaning. There are a few occasions when you must watch the way the words fall between lines because this can change the meaning of a clear basic headline and the two-line headline of the same wording:

JUDGE GETS DRUNK DRIVING CASE

JUDGE GETS DRUNK
DRIVING CASE

That sort of split stands out as objectionable. Equally so if not as potentially costly are headlines where the writer splits hyphenated words:

'MORE TIME' CALL
FOR HELP-
JOBLESS SCHEME

Never split a hyphenated word; look for another way of saying the same thing without using a hyphen at all. There usually is one:

'MORE TIME' CALL
FOR SCHEME TO
HELP JOBLESS

Splitting a compound verb produces the effect of marching the reader in two different directions:

GUNMEN HOLD   HEAVY TAXES WILL GO
UP BANK   ON BEER, WINE

WILSON: SMITH RIGHT
OFF COURSE

As a general caution, then, never split compound verbs or compound nouns between lines. But the simplest test is to read each headline to oneself, pausing slightly at the end of each line. If there is awkwardness or doubt, rewrite. For instance, the text editor who wrote this one would have detected the trap by *saying* it:

VIETNAM VOTE: US
MIGHT WILL WIN

Impartiality

Accuracy and impartiality are the most important basic constituents of headlines. First, look at impartiality and ways of maintaining it. A news headline expresses the news, not the text editor's views. Curiously, in five years of provincial editorship when I trained scores of sub-editors, this simple point was the one I never seemed able to put across. There were moments, it was true, when there was a certain arresting quality about the result:

TEACH SEX TO
NORTH-EAST
BOYS' BRIGADES

Headlines which seem to put the newspaper solidly behind some outsider's expressed opinion, however enticing, have no place in the news columns. The worst tendentious headlines seem to commit the newspaper to a particular political policy when in fact it may be merely reporting someone else's views:

STEEL BILL   ELECTIONS NOW
APPALS WORLD   A CLEAR DUTY

This kind of editorialising must be avoided by using quotes or naming an authority in the main deck of the headline. It is a simple mistake. More reprehensible still are the headlines where the writer lets either cleverness or prejudice prevail:

'I'M NOT THREATENING',
BROWN THREATENS

It is a step from this twisted headline writing to the odious
practice of using loaded words in heads:

SMITH GLOATS   STRIKERS WHINE
OVER RACIAL   FOR MORE TIME
POLICY

Headline writers must put their personal opinions aside.
They are there to reflect as accurately as possible the content
of the story. Headline writers are neither for nor against.
They are neutral – and when they are headlining a controversial debate in Parliament or Senate in a dispute of any kind,
they should be balanced in their choice of points for the
headlines. Some of the trouble arises because headline
writers are hypnotised by a good headline phrase. The
Conservatives at one local council attacked a Labour airfield
project as a 'white elephant' so when the decision was
reached the sub-editor wrote:

THORNABY LABOUR MEN
BACK WHITE ELEPHANT

This headline seemed to accept the 'white elephant' tag
without question. Even with quotes around 'white elephant' it
would hardly have been a fair headline because the words are
so strongly biased (despite their merit of suggesting controversy).

Accuracy

The headline must be accurate in its detail and true to the
meaning of the whole report. It is easy to escalate the
meaning of the story by choosing the wrong heading: 'Worst
unemployment rate in country', said the headline. The story
said: 'One of the highest unemployment rates . . .' which is
not the same thing. 'Boots take over Timothy Whites' said the

headline when the bid had been made, but before the deal had gone through. On a story about a court delaying a pay rise by three months it was inaccurate to write 'Court cancels pay rise'.

How the News Headline Says It

The legendary *Daily Express* editor Arthur Christiansen defined effective headlines thus: 'Good headlines are written in vigorous, conversational, idiomatic language. Good headlines should be capable of being read aloud – which the mind does subconsciously.'

Having discussed the general principles of news and accuracy which are the foundations of the headline, we now examine some of the detailed techniques for making the headline effective. Let us first, however, dispense with Helen of Troy, whom we left at the beginning of the chapter. 'How Helen did the Housekeeping' is an acceptable headline on the feature text in mind there, but it is not the kind of headline we shall spend most of the time discussing. It does not tell us how Helen did the housekeeping. It only holds out the promise that the text will. It does not inform. It tempts. The distinction of the hard news headline is that it always gives information. How to give the crucial information quickly and intelligibly within the confines of a column is the major skill of news-headline writing.

The Helen type of headline is more appropriate for the longer feature or news-in-depth piece, where the aim is not to give immediate information but to explore, discuss or relate a rich narrative whose ideas are too complex and diffuse to be done justice by a hard news headline focused on a single key point. There are a few other occasions when you will want to write a Helen-type headline in the news columns, to use temptation rather than information. It will never happen with a real news story where the emphasis is on quick communication of information – where information is a real attraction to readers.

But on lighter stories in the news columns it may be better

for a change of pace to write 'Why the General saw red' rather than 'Painted flagpole angers General'. That might be enough for many readers without their reading further; and the hard news heading might also seem to give such newspaper trivia an undue sense of importance.

A better guide for news headlines than Helen of Troy is the newspaper adage 'Man bites dog'. It is not merely a good story. It is also a good headline, in its own right, for reasons I will adduce. It may seem odd to be writing about 'the headline' when you consider the rich and often comic differences in the headlines of different papers. The headline writer stands in the middle between the newspaper's sense of its identity with its attitudes to life and news, and the newspaper's audience with its levels of education and knowledge.

It is not surprising that newspapers sometimes disagree about what is the most important feature of a news report, still less that they find themselves expressing this in different tones. 'Mr Charles Chaplin returns', says one in the manner of a butler at a banquet. Another shouts 'Charlie's back!' But the differences in news selection and even in tone do not mean there are two sets of opposing principles for headline writing. All good news headlines follow certain rules, in what they say and how they say it. What they say is the single most urgent news point (as the newspaper sees it), accurately, intelligibly and impartially. How they say it varies much less than appears.

Verbs

Here are some headlines which say the same news point in different ways – but there is something common in the construction of all these headlines and you should see if you can spot what it is. There are three pairs of headlines for three separate stories, and in each case the 'serious' headline is on the left and the 'popular' headline on the right.

RADIO RELAY	UP GOES 'FLYING POST
SATELLITE	OFFICE'
PUT IN ORBIT BY US	

STUDENTS CHALLENGE	DANNY THE RED
DE GAULLE'S RULE	HUMBLES DE GAULLE

BENN ACCUSES	US ATOM BRAIN
US FIRM	POACHERS WARNED

The popular papers were trying to emphasise the personal, dramatic or romantic elements. But every headline had a single common characteristic – a verb. News is activity and a verb represents action. It could be an excellent rule always to have a verb in the headline: but there are occasions when it is better to include the verb by implication, rather than by statement, and others when a rich phrase without a verb may be preferred. But these are the exceptions. Headlines must live. Most headlines without a verb are only half alive. They tell readers nothing and produce an effect of dullness and monotony: no news today. The deadest kind of news headline is the simple generalised label:

FRANCE AND	AMERICAN VIEWS
THE CONCORDE	ON CHINA

Well, thinks the reader, get on with it. What about France and the Concorde? What are America's views on China? There always have been American views on China; what the headline should be telling is what is new or significant about them.

It is odd the way the label has persisted. It does not follow naturally from regarding a headline as a truncated sentence. It is an artificial form, a legacy from a more pompous age. Who would ever dream of transmitting news verbally in the way these headlines do in print:

CLIMBER'S	GREEK PURGE
400 ft	OF CIVIL
DEATH FALL	SERVICE

It is much more natural and fresh to write as you would say:

CLIMBER	GREEKS PURGE
DIES IN	CIVIL
400 ft FALL	SERVICE

Active verbs

It follows that if the verb is the secret of the active headline, it should be the most active verb which fits the facts. If the verb is weak, the headline is weak. The normal headline has no room for adjectives. Its colour and spice must come from a rich verb. If a wife goes to court to make an emotional appeal for her husband, who has not stopped after a road crash, it is too pallid when you say in the headline 'Wife asks judge for leniency'. A livelier and more informative headline might be: 'Wife pleads for hit-and-run driver'. The verb 'pleads' gives an immediate and arresting impression of what happened; and the construction of the headline then allows room for the added information that he is a hit-and-run driver.

A verb is better than no verb, but vague portmanteau verbs will not do. Avoid, for instance, saying: 'Archbishop gives views on racial policy' when what the Archbishop has done is *condemn* the policy in vigorous terms. Do not say 'Lorry damages shop' when in fact the lorry has *wrecked* the shop completely (and vice versa). Avoid, when you can, using parts of the weak verb 'to be' and 'to have' as the main verbs in headlines. A headline gains in strength when a stronger verb is used:

ISTANBUL HAS	EARTHQUAKE ROCKS
EARTHQUAKE	ISTANBUL
TORY IS OUT	TORY BEATEN

Nor are parts of the verb 'to be' and 'to have' needed as auxiliaries. An intelligible headline is often much more emphatic without them. For instance, 'Jones arrested' is more urgent than 'Jones is arrested', and 'Miners told to quit' is better than 'Miners are told to quit'. There will be occasions, too, when the verb 'to be' should be omitted even though this seems to leave the headline without a verb. In headlines like this the verb 'to be' is clearly implied:

TOWN HALL (*IS*) POLICE (*ARE*) IN
IN DANGER GUN DRAMA

(*THERE ARE*) SHADOWS OVER
PEACE TALKS

Present and future tense

A further point about the verb in the headline may already be apparent. The headlines have used the present tense to describe events that have already happened. There are good reasons for this. First, the present tense is active. It puts readers into the middle of the action. It gives them a feeling of participation. Secondly, the event may be past, but it is recent past, and readers are learning of it for the first time. They perfectly well understand the convention and will infer from a present-tense headline that the event occurred within the publishing time of the newspaper: that a headline in the present tense in the morning newspaper is presenting the news of yesterday. Similarly, a weekly newspaper is understood to be presenting the news of the week and may use present tense for the events of the week. There is a point at which it will no longer do. It cannot be used in a report of a court case based on earlier events where it would suggest that the offence was being committed again: 'Baker sold loaves underweight', not 'Baker sells loaves underweight'. And any heading with a past time element built into it must carry past tense in agreement: 'Attlee backed Truman in 1946 dispute'. (Further, there is one headline construction, of which more later, which reports even contemporaneous events in the past tense: 'The girl who hid under the bed'.)

The way the tenses are used may be illustrated by an imaginary example. A speaker who on Thursday denounces a current dock dispute may properly on Friday be headlined:

'Dockers strike for selfish reasons, says union leader'. The remarks were made the day before, but they earn the present tense.

Imagine now that the dockers' dispute had ended a few days before. The union leader's remarks would then be headlined: 'Dockers struck for selfish reasons, says union leader'. To have retained the form 'dockers strike' would have suggested the strike was continuing, or that the union leader was referring to a more general attitude of dockers. Past time is rarely specified. 'Yesterday', for instance, is a word almost never justified in a morning paper headline because almost every item could be headed 'yesterday' and readers, anyway, take it for granted it was yesterday. But since a newspaper's future is infinite, it is generally best to specify future time: 'Dockers will strike tomorrow/next week/next month'. Note here how the omission of 'will' could still imply future tense, thanks to the specific future date.

Most headlines are in the present or future tense. Deaths happen in the present: 'Mayor dies' is better than 'Mayor has died', or, of course, 'Death of Mayor'. But there is one caution: it would be macabre to add a time reference to such a headline: 'Mayor dies today'. After a death, headline references to the person naturally carry past tense – except that a headline on a will may be present tense, since the legacy when declared is a contemporary act: 'Johnson bequeaths park to town'.

The active voice

Above all, prefer the active voice to the passive. In other words, write headlines with somebody saying something or doing something, rather than having it told to them or done to them. 'Boy falls into well' is what people say and what text editors should write as a headline, rather than this published but unnatural back-to-front headline:

FALL INTO WELL
INJURES BOY

Compare the active voice of the first version with the wordier passive of the second:

US DEMANDS RELEASE OF SEIZED SHIP

RELEASE OF SEIZED SHIP DEMANDED BY US

Notice how the passive voice breeds extra words, excess weight which exhausts the headline. Given the same headline constituents, the active voice can say more. Rejecting a passive construction can lead to a more vivid construction altogether, because it may offer a chance to exploit better the amount of headline space available. For instance:

WOMAN FOUND DEAD BY HUSBAND

'Husband finds woman dead' is the active voice. This more direct approach immediately opens up other possibilities. 'Wife' is a shorter word than 'woman' and also shows that she is married. There may be room for a better headline altogether:

CITY BANKER FINDS WIFE DEAD

or

MAN FINDS WIFE DEAD IN CAR

Subject Omitted

So far I have argued that we want a verb; a verb in the present tense; and, as a rule, a verb in the active voice. Considering the headline as an edited sentence leads us now to another important element: the subject of the sentence, the 'who' of the headline. Failure to appreciate that the headline is really a truncated, but still meaningful, sentence, and that the reader understands it as such, is the reason for the appalling habit, spread from North America, of writing headlines where the subject is casually omitted and the headline begins on a verb. This has grown not from any urgent theory about bringing in the verb first, but because it is easier to make a heading fit if you can drop the subject. It is indeed easier – easier on the text editor but harder on the reader. A headline is not a choice number of words arbitrarily bolted together. It has its own integrity. It is a crisper version of the way we communicate by speech and prose. In prose we omit the subject (though it is understood) only for injunctions or commands. To do the same thing for a narrative headline in the present tense is to do violence to the language:

HUNT BOMBS IN GREENLAND

What does that convey? The reader is to go off and hunt bombs in Greenland. But what the headline was trying to say was that American air force search parties were already looking for bombs in Greenland. 'Airmen seek lost bombs' would have made sense and it would have fitted. Headlines exist to serve the news and not the other way round. If a story is so difficult with a word like 'radiographer', say – then a good layout editor will change the page so that a meaningful headline can be written. If one is going to write a headline without a subject it should not be done merely by writing the full headline ('Radiographer steals pistol to end life' and then deleting the excess word 'Radiographer' – 'Steals pistol to end life'). Indeed, 'end life' in the subjectless headline does not make it clear whose life it is. It is possible in this instance to write an acceptable headline, admittedly with a compound noun, but none the less a headline which is intelligible and tells more of the story than the subjectless heading:

WOMAN STOLE GUN FOR SUICIDE

Who's Who

The subject should be there. How you describe the 'who' of the story is a matter for further discussion. There are all sorts of ways. John Jones, say, is at once a Welshman, a baker, a Unitarian, a driver, a father, a golfer, a man, an objector to a road proposal, a rescuer in a river accident, or simply 'he'. Which of the words you use to describe him in the headline must in part depend on the nature of the news. A name will rarely be used in a headline: it has to mean something to readers. Thus 'Mr Jones protests at shop closing-hours' says less than 'Baker protests at shop closing-hours'. If Mr Jones the baker is chased by a bull while playing golf he would become 'Golfer chased', rather than 'Baker chased' since the latter headline would give the impression the bull was in his bakery. A name should, of course, be used in a headline when it gives authority to the news. If the name is known, use the name and not other titles. If there is doubt about whether somebody is well enough known the good text editor will use a title, since this doubt will become a certainty for the average reader. But there is one exception to this: to err generously on the side of headlining the name in an obituary. The most important piece of information is who has died, and it is a contortion that produces a headline such as:

HE LED JUNGLE
GUERRILLAS

when the news is

CHE GUEVERA
SHOT DEAD

The 'he did this or the other' headline is justified only when it concerns the death of a person who has become obscure but who once did something outstanding or bizarre: 'He rode Niagara Falls in a barrel'. Otherwise stick to names in obituaries. Almost as fatuous as the 'he did' variety are the formulae:

FAMOUS MANCHESTER-
BORN COMEDIAN DIES

DEATH OF WELL-KNOWN
CHESHIRE PEER

These confuse the purpose of a headline with the purpose of a contents bill. The concealment on the bill may induce people to buy the paper. But in the page it does not invite them to read it.

The weakest form of subject in a headline is 'he' or 'she'. It is not an identification.

HE FORECASTS A
30 HOUR
WEEK SOON

That story turned out to be about a Labour MP and former cabinet minister. 'MP' would have been more specific and would have given the headline more authority. There is a rule for identification. 'Man' or 'woman', for instance, is weak, though sometimes inevitable. 'Wife, father, mother, husband', are better because they narrow the field – always provided the story is something to do with the individuals as wives, fathers, and so on. It is not good practice to use the word 'husband' as another word for 'man' or 'driver' when the fact that he is married has nothing to do with the story.

HUSBAND
BANNED
AT RACES

This suggests his wife can go in and he has been barred – it could even be for some matrimonial reason. But, given that the specific description does not introduce a distortion into our understanding of the story, always prefer the specific. Do not say 'child' in a headline if the child is not yet two. Say 'baby'. For instance:

TERRORISTS KILL YOUNG ISRAELI

'Young' is too vague. The story is that terrorists killed a three-year-old boy. 'Israeli boy' would have been better here, and altogether better:

RAIDERS KILL ISRAELI BOY OF 3

There is one final device affecting the subject in the headline. This is the construction of headlines beginning 'The man . . . who'. This formula is acceptable when identification is important:

THE MAN WITH BRIGHT IDEAS
DOES IT AGAIN FOR £1,000

It is more appealing to say 'The man with bright ideas' than 'Factory worker', or the man's name which is not widely known. 'The man who' formula can also be used on headlines over pictures of the subject or on lighter stories where the headline relaxes:

THE BOY WHO PULLED OUT A TOOTH
WITH AN E-TYPE JAGUAR

The odd circumstances can themselves be enough to justify this, but not always. The implication of this style of headline is that the reader is going to be given extra details about the subject, and so it will not do on a news report which merely states a fact without elaborating any personal details.

Be Specific

The vaguer the description the duller the head. What is there in this to make the skimmer of the headlines stop and read the story?

DEVELOPMENT PLAN HELD UP

Every rebuilding story could be headed 'Development' just as the architect's model of a redevelopment scheme could be headed, as I once saw it, 'Development in miniature'. Nobody is interested in 'development', but they are interested in new schools, roads, shops, banks, parking, swimming pools. They are interested in specifics, in short, and not the abstract and the general. The head 'Development plan held up' was on a story which really said:

NEW SCHOOL DELAYED

'Plan' itself, of course, is another headline killer. It is so general, so vague, so meaningless: '£500,000 plan inquiry'. Figures rarely sing in heads. This headline seems quite remote from the real world of the reader. In fact the story announced that there was to be a public inquiry into a proposal to build a hotel near York Minster – a hotel with a shopping precinct and a bank. Any one of these specifics – hotel, shops, Minster – would have sent a signal to the reader. Always look for the specific which will illuminate a head, which will give an instant picture of the activity: not that someone has a 'big new appointment' but what it involves; not 'river accident' or 'road tragedy' or 'daring raid', but what happened. For instance:

CITY
GANG
MAKE
BIG HAUL

might be anything from stealing the Crown Jewels to robbing the Bank of England. Contrast the interest of the headline based on the real specific activity in that story:

GANG ROBS
400
PARKING
METERS

These injunctions apply especially strongly to headlining speeches. It is never enough to say 'Opposition attacks

Government'. That is what we expect. Only by pinpointing the detail can the headline hope to prove interest.

Saying Where

The injunction to be specific means specific about genuine news and not about irrelevancies. Of these the most intrusive in the headline is the location of the news; the 'where' of the story. It should only be included when the location is an integral, rather than an incidental, part of the news, and this should be the rule for local as well as national newspapers. Where something happened is usually less newsy than what happened.

It is normally said that foreign stories should carry locations and home stories should not. This is of some help, but it needs refining: How specific a foreign location? And when does a domestic place name warrant inclusion in the head? The real test must be whether including the place name adds significance. There is clearly no need to say 'De Gaulle condemns rioters in Paris speech'. It will do just to say 'De Gaulle condemns rioters'. But the rule of significance does from time to time necessitate inclusion of a precise foreign place name. When de Gaulle made his speech in Quebec advocating French nationalism it was essential to the headlines to say that he made it in Quebec. The fact that he addressed French Canadians in this way in a French-speaking city while a guest of the Canadian Government was not incidental to the news: it was an integral part of it.

The test of significance should be carried over into home and local news. It is right for a national paper to headline a story 'Epidemic moves into Cheshire' because *where* foot-and-mouth disease spreads is the news. A local paper would be right to refine that further, since doing so would add significance for local readers: 'Foot-and-mouth spreads to Tarporley farm'. But I would suggest that local papers should pause before automatically thrusting locations into headlines irrespective of significance. The theory is that local readers will be drawn to the story because it has a local place name.

For sports stories there are special considerations but the practice of including place names in every news head needs rather more than custom to justify it.

Broadly, there are two types of local paper: those circulating in a limited local area, usually evening and weekly newspapers in Britain; and those circulating in a wide area, over two or three counties for an English provincial morning or part of a state, say, in the United States. If the paper with a concentrated circulation area is doing its job properly and cramming the inside pages with local news, its readers should safely be able to assume that headlines there automatically refer to local news. There is no need to labour the fact by putting in the town every time. Moreover by encouraging the reader in this assumption, by proper grouping of the news, the headlines can be made to work harder. Without monotonous repetition of place names, heads are at once livelier and there is more space to say something meaningful.

Now consider the paper circulating over a wider area. A local name is only local to a limited number of people in each wide edition area: in other words by including the local name you are as likely to repel as many readers as you attract, or even more. And local names in heads give an inhibiting and parochial air when the stories themselves are good enough to survive on their genuine news merits.

ELWICK MAN ON MURDER CHARGE:
REMANDED AGAIN AT HARTLEPOOL

This was a story which might have been headlined:

FARM WORKER OF 21 DENIES
MURDERING TEACHER

Again, 'Two-car crash at Middlesbrough' might have been headed 'Baby escapes unhurt in two-car crash'. And when a good headline also has a place name, does the place name really ignite more interest? 'PC bitten by howling Alsatian' is enough for most people wherever they live; the addition of 'at Gateshead' can be something of an anticlimax.

Be Positive

Be specific, then: but also be positive. Some stories must carry a negative statement in the headline ('Dockers refuse pay offer'), but there is nothing more deadening than a series of abominable 'No' headlines, which merely say 'No news today'.

NO CLUES REPORTED
ON MISSING BANKER

New York City Police yesterday reported 'no luck' in their hunt for a missing Lockport banker and attorney who disappeared from his home on August 26. 'We've got no clues', said a Missing Persons Bureau spokesman in the search for 44-year-old Joseph Thomas Symes, married and the father of three. 'The mystery just gets deeper', etc.

NO RECORD IN
DUBLIN

Alan Simpson, the United Kingdom mile record holder, produced another blistering finish to win the international mile event in three minutes 56.9 seconds at the John F. Kennedy Stadium last night. But any hopes of the Yorkshireman breaking Michel Jazy's recently set world record of three minutes 53.6 seconds faded on a slow second lap.

These are different types of 'No' stories. The first would clearly be news if there was a clue. The other depends for its justification on the degree of expectation of Simpson breaking the record. But both could convey their information more positively, the Simpson headline by highlighting the 3 seconds from a record:

MYSTERY OF MISSING
BANKER GROWS

SIMPSON 3.3 OFF
RECORD

If the line about the mystery had not been in the banker story the head could still have been expressed without the direct negative: 'Police draw blank on missing banker'. In the sports story, the 3.3 will be understood in context – but it would be necessary in editing the text to write in that Simpson missed the record by 3.3 seconds. The text should immediately support the head without the reader having to do a calculation. The most frequent source of a 'no' head is the denial story:

EPIDEMIC 'IS NOT
THREAT TO MEAT'

A report that the foot-and-mouth epidemic was threatening the domestic meat supply was described by the Minister of Agriculture yesterday as premature.

This story could carry the news more actively and positively:

MEAT SUPPLY IS
STILL SAFE

It is harder to avoid hesitant headlines, but do ration the insipid 'may'. Obviously neither text editor nor reporter must press the facts for a headline, but some stories which invite a 'may' headline could often carry a more positive emphasis.

'Bloggs likely to earn place in first Test' is better and may even be more accurate, too, than 'Bloggs may . . .' 'Forecast', 'expects', 'fears', 'considers' are equally useful variants.

A succession of polysyllabic words slows the reading and comprehension of a headline. Consider the opposite:

GIRL LOST TEN DAYS
FOUND DEAD
IN LOVERS' LANE

That is nine words and ten syllables. It gives all the information quickly and coherently. It does no violence to the language. Without twisting the facts it is possible to insist on short, simple words. English is rich in them. *Banned* is acceptable for *prohibited*; *neutral* for *uncommitted*; *talks* does express the meaning of *negotiations*; *goods* are *commodities* (except perhaps in the business pages). Consider the way long (and often abstract) words obscure the facts; and the way short simple words charge the heads with meaning:

IMPLEMENTATION OF
SCIENCE EDUCATION
PROGRAMME

MORE SCIENCE TEACHING
IN SCHOOLS SOON

A good test is to say the headline aloud. Does the wording trip off the tongue? If instead it trips up, try writing another.

Single Thoughts

Simplicity in headlines does not merely mean simple words: it equally means the simple expression of a single thought. Effectively to convey one single idea in the limited space of a headline requires skill; to convey two ideas in the same space, with the same intelligibility, requires a rare genius. Just as a sentence becomes difficult to follow when it is overloaded with separate ideas, so does a headline. Two breaths are needed for 'Gambling ice-cream man's brain operation called off as he seeks group help'. The 'as he' construction generally means that the writer is wandering too far from a vivid single news point. The next head suffers from trying to say too much in one breath and the separated form of attribution increases the confusion.

CRITICAL SIX MONTHS, BUT, DESPITE
PRESSURE, NO REFLATION – CHANCELLOR

It is best to omit one of the thoughts in the headline and simply say:

CHANCELLOR RESISTS PRESSURE
FOR QUICK REFLATION

Text editors handling a complicated story which creates difficulties for headline writing should mentally stand back from its intricacies and ask themselves: what is the simple effect of all these words? Without retreating into meaningless generality it may then be possible to write the head on the broad intent of the story.

We have now analysed all the basic constituents of a good headline sentence, which can be edited into the actual headline. To recapitulate, they are:

An uncluttered single thought
which is positive
and specific
expressed with a strong verb
in the active voice
in short simple words.

These ground rules are summed up in the adage mentioned earlier:

MAN BITES DOG

That is a good news story – but also a first-class headline. It expresses a specific and single item of news positively, with an active verb and in simple words. Some of the headline deficiencies I have discussed would produce this version:

INFLICTS WOUND
ON CANINE,
AVER POLICE

The Key Word

We know what the constituents of the news headline should
be, and the general rules. These are a guide for livelier,
clearer headlines, not a prescription for monotony. The rules
are not meant to restrict your native genius or torture the
news. A rule can be broken – if you know why you are
breaking it. Before moving on to specialised headlines and
variations I would like briefly to discuss the label headline
and suggest another technique which may help towards the
right headline.

I advised earlier that the first thing to do as you read the
text is to note separately the sentence summing up the news
and then edit it for a headline; a headline sculpted from a
sentence should have a better chance of retaining some
grammatical integrity and intelligibility. There is another
technique for headline construction, which is to note down
the individual words that make the story unique, that make it
news. Sometimes a single word is the key to the headline and
however the headline sentence is constructed, the head will
be weaker without the key word, whether it be noun, verb or
adjective. Flaubert put the matter more elegantly to Maupas-
sant:

> Whatever one wishes to say, there is only one noun to express
> it, only one verb to give it life, only one adjective to qualify it.
> Search, then, till that noun, that verb, that adjective are
> discovered; never be content with 'very nearly'; never have
> recourse to tricks, however happy; or to buffooneries of
> language to avoid a difficulty.

This is too idealistic a doctrine for headline writers, and too
extreme as well: headline writers denied all synonyms might
occasionally create prose but they would risk their sanity in
the process. What we should do, in approximation, is to seek

out the single word or words which at least make this headline different from any other.

Two cinemas in New York were told to take off 'strip' or 'nude' films; yet the key words were crowded out with a head about unspecified films being 'rescheduled'. A policewoman chased a boy who was brandishing a bayonet and was rewarded with 'Policewoman stuck to duty'; a label heading without the inappropriate verb would have been better – 'Policewoman and bayonet boy'.

Labels That Work

There are times when we have to take this middle course, retaining the key words and relinquishing the verb. This produces a label headline, but there are labels and labels. There are times – perhaps one news story in a hundred – when one may with a clear conscience use a label. There may be a mixture of reasons: to avoid a weak verb while retaining key words; to fit into a tight space; to suit the text when there is no active news point; or to create a change of pace. But the words of the verbless label must be potent. If they do not actually tell the news they should indicate it. A few varying examples will illustrate the essential points.

When the first British heart transplant patient was recovering on the day after the operation, the doctors reported that he was well and added that he had given them a thumbs-up signal. Now a headline merely saying that the heart transplant patient was well would have been accurate but it would also have fitted several other operations. The key phrase for every headline was 'thumbs up'.

HEART MAN GIVES THUMBS UP
(active but too long for the space available)

HEART MAN DOING WELL
(active and fits but too weak with omission of key words)

HEART MAN'S THUMBS UP
(a label, but it fits and with the key words it is quite strong)

HEART MAN: THUMBS UP
(an awkward split but newsy)

The label using the possessive to carry the key words is a useful economy device. Another story, in the middle of a period of Labour Party disaffection, says that MPs face a crucial test of their loyalty in a vote on the Government's incomes policy. The active verb would be:

LABOUR MPs FACE LOYALTY TEST

But if the active head is too long you can get by with the label bearing the key words:

LABOUR'S LOYALTY TEST

A light story on what a champion jockey was dreaming of doing on retirement might have carried the active head 'Champion jockey dreams of . . .' but that was already occupying all the available space. The possessive label 'The champion jockey's dream' did not tell the news but it indicated its area in a fairly tempting way by retaining the key words. These are all instances where the label has been acceptable but second best. Very occasionally it is better, for instance on a story which relies on suspense:

> It looked like a big raid. Suddenly ten detectives including two chief inspectors moved into the garden of a semi-detached house yesterday. Methodically, they set about their business . . . with two motor mowers, garden forks, spades, rakes and clippers. But it was not a murder hunt. They were not looking for clues. The detectives were giving up a day off to tidy the overgrown garden of one of their colleagues who has been in hospital for six months . . .

An active news head on this story spoils the suspense and reads flatly:

DETECTIVES TIDY GARDEN

But a verbless label can make something of the suspense idea using the familiar CID for Criminal Investigation Department:

SECRET OF A CID DIG-IN

Words like 'secret' and 'riddle', if used sparingly, can rescue a difficult label head: 'Riddle of Russian diplomat'. A combination of evocative key words may also be superior for a complicated story where no single news point merits a central position: 'The monk and the mystery of the Mussolini diaries'.

The choice between a label and an active head requires judgment. Remember it is the label which is the exception and which needs justifying. This unjustified label, for instance, rouses no curiosity at all:

MEDICAL HAZARDS
ON THE ROAD

I find myself reading another newspaper's version headed:

HEALTH TESTS URGED
FOR OLDER DRIVERS

Similarly, the active news heading 'Girl strangled with dog lead' is at once more intelligible and forceful with all the key words, than the confused label: 'The missing dog murder hunt'.

Headlines in Practice

But let us now take the concept of the key word and apply it to a story, seeing what headline emerges. Note, incidentally, how frequently it is the verb which is the prime key word.

A soldier, aged 18, got a barrack room friend to chop off his trigger finger with an axe so that he could get his release from the Army, Major M. Clarke, for the prosecution, said at a Colchester court martial today.

Privates M. and B., both serving with The Prince of Wales's Own Regiment, pleaded guilty to malingering. M. was sentenced to 112 days' detention and B. to 126 days' detention, both sentences being subject to confirmation.

Major Clarke said that on December 29 six soldiers were in a room discussing ways and means of getting M. out of the Army. Someone suggested he should lose his trigger finger, and B. agreed to chop it off for him. M. then lay down on his bed, put his right index finger on an upturned locker, and smoked a cigarette while B. chopped the finger off with an axe.

Captain A. B. Bower, in a plea of mitigation for M., said he was anxious to get out of the Army because his mother had lost her job, and was not getting enough money on which to bring up a large family.

For B., Captain Bower said that he thought M. was bluffing. When he realised, however, that M. was serious, he could not back down, otherwise he would have lost face with his fellow-soldiers.

The strong key words that spring from that story are:

FINGER
CHOP OFF
SOLDIER.

It is a simple matter to put these into coherent form and into a headline: 'Soldier got friend to chop off finger'. One national daily handling the story managed this: and another, with less headline space, wrote: 'Soldier got pal to cut off finger'. Here 'cut off' is distinctly weaker than 'chop off' because it suggests the action of a knife rather than an axe. Another, subjectless, heading was less satisfactory, with the unattributed, unquoted head 'Please chop off my trigger finger' (though the word trigger would just suggest the context). Two other national papers, however, headlined the story in this way:

SOLIDER 'LOST TRIGGER FINGER FOR RELEASE'	WHY A SOLDIER LOST HIS TRIGGER FINGER

We see at once how a head fails without the key verb 'chop off'. 'Lost' is dreadfully weak for the sudden violent action of an axe on a man's finger. The first head, incidentally, also illustrates the troubles that arise from trying to say too much. 'For release' so close to 'trigger finger' gives a momentary but disconcerting impression that the finger was somehow trapped and needed releasing. It does not convey 'to get out of the Army'. (And why the quotes in this headline?) The second head fails by resorting to feature-style treatment, which is all right on a featurish story without much news, but out of place on a hard news story. Why the soldier lost his finger is, in any event, less compelling than *how* he lost it.

Free-style Headlines

We have been writing headlines to a strict discipline. The words we could use have been suggested by words in the text carrying the most important news point; the number of words has been limited by the amount of space available, as it must be for a newspaper handling a multiplicity of news stories, the staple of the newspaper. There are occasions when a news heading of a limited length is not suitable:

(a) When the ideas in the text are so rich and diffuse that a simple hard news head does not do them justice
(b) When the natural headline wording is so attractive (so funny, so apt) that it should be given whatever space it needs

These categories need a wide range of what I shall call free-style headlines. News-style heads always give information impartially. Free-style heads may not: they may ask a question or make a joke or be a general label. Most main features need free-style heads; but discussion under the traditional division of news and features is not really helpful to us. The text is primal. Free-style heads should appear wherever the text requires, on news or features.

Here is an example broadly in category (a):

> A schoolgirl is told she has failed her advanced GCE examination. Her father complains, in a complicated series of events, and at the end of it all she has her marks approximately doubled to give an excellent grade B with merit.

Now reducing that story to a hard news head with limited space produces this:

GIRL'S FAILURE
BECAME PASS
WITH MERIT

But the story is suffocated by this condensed form. The story only really came alive in a detailed free-style headline:

IT TOOK SIX LETTERS AND FOUR
EXAMINERS TO SWITCH JULIA'S
A-LEVEL FAILURE INTO A PASS WITH MERIT

There are a lot of words in that free-style head but it is easy to read because it is a complete clear sentence. But note: the free-style headline must read coherently like a sentence with punctuation marks – and no words omitted. This attempt at a free-style heading falls flat:

NOW, CAN YOU THINK OF NAME FOR
LONDON MOTORWAY BOX?

The omission of the word 'a' quite spoils the ring of that headline. Exceptionally vivid quotes are worth free-style treatment: when the Pope addressed the United Nations one paper soared over the commonplace headlines of its competitors (Pope pleads for peace at UN) by running his actual words across the top of the page:

'IF YOU WISH TO BE BROTHERS
LET THE ARMS FALL FROM YOUR
HANDS . . . SWEAR: NO MORE WAR'

And again with the next story about a trawler going down.
The crew is given up for dead. But one man comes ashore
alive in Iceland and his wife flies to see him. A straight news-
style head (Wife rejoins 'dead' husband) would have failed to
capture the richness of the reunion in the way this paper did
with a free-style head running beneath the reunion picture:

HONESTLY, DEEP INSIDE ME
I THOUGHT I WOULD
NEVER SEE YOU AGAIN

Letting the Words Take Over

Let us now venture into the disputatious area where it is the
inspiration of attractive wording which breaks the bonds of
the news-style head. There is no limit to innovation here:
puns proliferate and allusions abound. Of course, what I
think funny you may regard as the bore of the century; and
what both of us agree is hilarious may be a stroke of genius
from which no general guidance can be drawn. Accepting
that, it may be worth saying that pun, allusion, irony, wit,
metaphor, alliteration and anticlimax are all acceptable
fathers of free-style heads which are better than straight news
heads. Borrowing a current catch-phrase for a heading, be it
from a pop song, an advertising campaign, a film title, a novel
or a TV comedian, requires superb timing.

The moment perhaps lasts a week. 'Hard day's night', 'Back
to the future', 'No room at the inn' and numerous others too
painful to mention have seemed to survive as if pickled. But –
and it's only my opinion – a very ancient catch-phrase may
be revived successfully in a head. A small illustration will
suffice. When a new hotel was opened, small sections of the
plasterboard ceiling fell down at a celebration lunch. These
were the straight news heads:

CEILING COLLAPSES AT £2M HOTEL OPENING

CEILING FALLS AT HOTEL OPENING

CEILING COLLAPSE PROBED AT HOTEL OPENING

CRASH GOES CEILING AT £2M HOTEL

These are all right as far as they go, but they suffer by being cast in the straight news mould; they tend to overdo the seriousness of the incident. 'Ceiling collapse' conjures up a calamity and this is why the label 'The day the ceiling fell in' would be softer, the Thurber style being a hint that nothing really serious happened. But a free-style head with allusion to an old joke tells the news perfectly in harmony with a formal lunch:

WAITER!
There's part
of the
ceiling
in my
soup

A good light head has a core of news; and writers must not be caught giggling at their own joke by exclamation marks, quotes, underlining italic or any other red-nose devices of prose. If you are in doubt about an allusion, a good test is to ask yourself whether the head, in making its joke, also indicates the news. If it does not, you have almost certainly strayed too far in your enthusiasm.

Good and Bad Puns

Most injury is caused by clumsy puns or ill-kempt metaphors. On a story about tyre regulations: 'Motorists "tyre" of these regulations'. On a story of a road offence: 'Kerbing his exuberance'. On a story of cemetery vandalism: 'Two youths given grave sentences'. The metaphors are self-conscious and contrived – and puns which have to be trussed in quotes should not be allowed out.

Puns on people's names should be avoided. They and everyone else stopped laughing at that one at the christening. I am not against puns in heads. Let Fowler set the standard: 'The assumption that puns are *per se* contemptible, betrayed by the habit of describing every pun not as *a pun* but as *a bad pun* or *a feeble pun*, is a sign at once of sheepish docility and desire to seem superior. Puns are good, bad and indifferent, and only those who lack the wit to make them are unaware of the fact.' So some good puns:

A debate in the Indian Parliament on whether saris too revealing should be banned:

A SARI WITHOUT A FRINGE ON TOP

A film review:

JAMES STEWART FASTER ON THE DRAWL

Feature Headings

Most main feature heads should be free-style in the sense that the wording should dictate the layout. This does not necessarily mean long wording. Two or three words may be the most apposite and then the typography should be adjusted to display them. Many news text editors seem all at sea writing feature heads. What can they grasp for projection? There is no news to tell in the traditional way, so the simplicity, urgency and stridency of the news head will be wrong unless it happens to be an exposé feature. A few guides may be offered. If the feature has an especially colourful phrase, let that be the head. If the feature sets out to answer set questions, pose the questions. Just who are the speculators? Well what really goes into a meat pie? What is the cost of a night out? For general feature heads, there are certain formula constructions which come to the rescue provided they reflect the emphasis of the text. These formula headings are based on the how, what, wherefore syndrome. For instance:

WHEN IT PAYS TO LIVE IN SIN

WHEN LOVE TURNED SOUR

WHY YOUNG GERMANY EXPLODED

HOW THEY PLANNED THE HEART TRANSPLANT

THE TRUTH ABOUT BUST DEVELOPERS

WHERE MAJOR WENT WRONG

Making these formula headings live means choosing key words after the initial word sets the scope of the piece. It might be helpful to analyse a feature headline on text which told how Francis Crick and James Watson worked out the structure of deoxyribonucleic acid, universally called DNA. The paper they published won each of them a Nobel Prize; and the text says it has proved to be the key for unlocking some of the fundamental secrets of life. They were in competition at one stage with the celebrated chemist, Dr Linus Pauling. Here are some of the stages to an accepted popularised feature headline for two articles:

HOW THEY WON A NOBEL PRIZE

Too unspecific, could apply to all Nobel prizewinners.

HOW THEY DISCOVERED DNA

DNA will not signal a great deal to all readers. Can we say: secret of life? A good phrase but needs care.

HOW THEY HELPED TO DISCOVER THE SECRET OF LIFE

Too strong: the text says it was the key to unlocking some of the fundamental secrets of life. They have taken one stride, but others must follow, so the headline must not suggest we know all there is to know about life.

HOW THEY HELPED TO DISCOVER THE SECRET OF LIFE

More nearly accurate, but 'helped' is a weak word. So is 'aimed' which underplays their success. Can we make a feature of the competition with the other scientists? Yes, the text seems to support this even to the extent of the word 'race'.

HOW THEY RACED TO DISCOVER THE SECRET OF LIFE

Stronger wording but 'raced to discover' is wordy and may be open to the objection again that 'discover' suggests all was in fact discovered. We need a head which retains 'race', which is one element of what they were doing, and 'secret of life', which was their objective.

THE RACE . . . THE SECRET OF LIFE

becomes

THE RACE TO FIND THE SECRET OF LIFE

Feature heads, like news heads, are better when they have a specific element; where, when they are labels, they use key words. Just one piece of colour from the text will do. 'The deal in Chicago' is less vivid than 'The deal in Room 410'.

Specialised Pages

All the injunctions for active news headlines apply to sports and business headings. Business people prefer restrained treatment of business news and they should have it. But confidence in the financial pages is not a matter of avoiding verbs and simple words. It is a matter of tone, moderation and simple accuracy. Business shares with sport one special headline requirement: names. The names of the companies and the names of their leaders are the essential signal. Shun the more general headings such as 'Pieman and the baker in merger talks' and write simple active specific headlines:

ASDA KINGFISHER MERGER FEES TO HIT £72M

BOWKETT QUITS AS BERISFORD PROFITS LEAP

OPPOSITION TO COKE DEAL HITS CADBURY

Similarly with sports headings the names of teams, players, managers, horses and jockeys are essential headline material. Sport is vigorous and the headline should be vigorous. The point you select for the head will depend on whether you are headlining a rush evening sports special, or a morning or Sunday sports page. With the first, you can safely assume that the head should concentrate on the result of the game, since the readers will primarily be buying the paper for that. In the second instance, with the results having been broadcast several hours before, the sports readers should be given headlines which concentrate on a feature of the game, leaving the result to be implied:

PRIDE NOT ENOUGH TO LIFT SAD FOREST

HIGH-SPEED SCOTS RUN RIOT

The best way to avoid clichés in sports headings is always to select an outstanding incident or player, rather than a generality.

Headlinese

The words individually are harmless enough, but in certain combinations there is a mutation which twists the headline horribly, and produces headlinese. Readers who expose their gaze to it are not exactly turned to stone, but there is a distinct glazing of the eyes and a buzzing sensation between the ears. Try this example:

SKYSCRAPERS PROBE HUSTLE

or:

HOMES PLAN FACTORY HOPE

We will come back to these in a moment. Even for them there is a diagnosis and a cure. The road to recovery begins by recognising the fundamental reasons for headlinese: compression plus haste. Headline writers have no malevolence for the readers they are about to assault; they do it because, as Theodore Bernstein put it, they have a desperate need to fit size 7 ideas into size 2 spaces.[15] So absorbed are headline writers in this, so preoccupied are they with extracting its essence in half a dozen words, so deep does every detail impress itself as they search the copy again for the unique combination of headline words, so familiar with the facts do they become, in short, that the headline they write does not mean a thing. What they should do when they emerge clutching the six words of truth is lay them aside for a moment, pause, and try to read them as if they were a reader the next day who, with a train to catch and mind preoccupied by an overdraft, comes across them for the first time.

If headline writers did this, few of the choicer varieties of headlinese would survive with their ambiguities and gobbledegook. Even the slightest doubt in the headline writer's mind should suffice to consign that headline to oblivion. But doubt should be reinforced by diagnosis and, as a warning to others who pass this way, the main inspirations of headlinese will be set out here.

The Seven Deadly Sins

There are ways of dealing with them if you know what they are: careless use of nouns as adjectives; the creation of the plural adjective, hitherto unknown to the English language; excessive omission of words; abuse of headline catchwords; extravagant metaphor; confusion of tenses; and clumsy construction. To these seven sins can be added another vice – slang, which can be dealt with summarily. It passes in a light heading when the slang is indeed common parlance and is one splash of vulgar procession of subject, verb and predicate. It fails when slang is piled on slang as in the classic American newspaper announcement that Professor William Craigie was joining the University of Chicago to direct the compilation of the *Dictionary of American English*:

MIDWAY SIGNS LIMEY PROF TO DOPE YANK TALK

Nouns and verbs

The most serious begetter of headlinese is unquestionably the abuse of the noun as an adjective. I approve of calling the man who has had a heart transplant 'heart man' in the headline, letting the noun 'heart' do the work of an adjective and identify the man. This is clear enough. The trouble comes when the word which is used as an adjective *can also represent a verb*. There are any number of words which can be either noun or verb according to sentence structure, whose role is revealed only by other words in the sentence. When these other words are omitted to form the compact headline sentence, the key word may become ambiguous. The first defence against headlinese then must be to have an early warning system which cautions headline writers as they deploy the noun-verb words as adjectives. In the headline vocabulary these are conspicuous:

tax, ban, plan, drive, move, probe, protest, bar, share, watch, cut, axe, ring, bank, rises, state, pay, pledge, talks, riot, attack, appeal, back, face, sign, jump, drug

It is the confusion of noun and verb which makes us stumble at this one:

POLICE STATE TAUNT BY HOGG IN ROW ON SEIZED PASSPORT

'Police state' we read here as subject and verb. So they gave evidence did they, about a taunt made by Hogg? No. The story tells us that during the row about a seized passport Mr Hogg accused the Government of setting up a police state. It is Mr Hogg who is using the word state and using it as a noun in the position of an adjective. He is quite entitled to do that because in his sentence the position of the words 'a police state' and the retention of the word 'a' make it clear that 'state' is being used as a noun and 'police' is a noun being used adjectivally to qualify the noun 'state'.

The headline writer cannot use Mr Hogg's 'police state' unless there is a clear indication of what it means: and there are ways of doing this even within the limited space of a headline. First, the headline could hyphenate police-state to indicate that it is a compound and not noun and verb. Or secondly, and preferably, the words should be enclosed in quotes:

'POLICE STATE' TAUNT BY HOGG IN ROW ON SEIZED PASSPORT

Very many of the wildest headlines, created by the confusion of noun and verb, can be tamed if headline writers recognise the beast as double-headed. Armed only with a hyphen or quotes they can bring the troublesome words to useful service, though some examples are so ferocious they have to be put down altogether.

PUNJABI WHO RUNS STREET PROTESTS

And so do all of us. The headline is supposed to indicate an article about a Punjabi who organises protests in the streets. Street is being used as an adjective. Hyphenating street-protests might just rescue this one.

'SPEED PROBE NEED URGENT'

It is not a call to speed a probe. It is a call to hasten an inquiry into speeding in a town. The two initial nouns as adjectives with a third which could be a verb take some digesting; quick work might just about produce a survivor, coupling speed-probe and leaving the quotes for the one word which needs them:

SPEED-PROBE NEED 'URGENT'

NIGERIAN TALKS IN LONDON

Did they grill him hard? 'Talks on Nigeria in London' would fit. (If tight, you might just get away with 'Nigeria talks in London'.)

DISASTER PLANNING THE EUROPEAN WAY

One asks: 'is it a disaster planning the European way?' But the article does not tell us. It is about the way the European Civil Defence plans for disaster in nuclear war. Disaster, you will have guessed, is a noun used as an adjective. Rather than create a hyphenated monster heading it should be written simply: Planning for disaster in Europe.

Plural adjectives

The English language does not recognise a plural adjective. We never say 'Ten beautifuls women' or 'Plums tart'. Absurd headlines like 'Skyscrapers probe hustle' are produced when we use a noun as an adjective – and then put the adjective into the plural. Here is another:

WHITE LINES EXPERIMENT ON ROADS

Very irresponsible of them. 'White lines' is being used adjectivally to describe the kind of experiment (just as 'skyscrapers' is being used to describe the kind of 'probe'). All such must be singular. 'White-line experiment on roads' is intelligible and not ludicrously ambiguous. And, of course, we understand there is more than one white line, just as we understand there is more than one road in road safety. Putting the noun being used as an adjective into the correct singular prevents many a nonsense, but sometimes this is only one fault. The most grotesque headline occurs when in addition to a plural adjective we have to cope with not one but three nouns as adjectives.

NUCLEAR PLANT DAMAGES PROBE BY POLICE

can be swiftly treated for its painful pluralisation:

NUCLEAR PLANT DAMAGE PROBE BY POLICE

This inactive headline with three initial nouns to describe the probe is best recast positively

POLICE PROBE NUCLEAR PLANT DAMAGE

When we are using a word in an unusual way the onus is on us to make sure the reader is with us all the way.

BEXLEY SCHOOLS BAR ROW SPREADS

The bar rows most people know about are not very pleasant. Is this an instance of alcohol being smuggled into the teachers' room? No, it is a decision to refuse to admit children to two schools – to bar their entry. 'Entry row' would have made some sense. And again:

PRODUCTION OVER MINE SAFETY, CLAIMS INSPECTOR

does not mean that output is over the level needed to keep the mine open. 'Over' here means 'put first': Pit output put before mine safety, says inspector.

Excessive omission

You read the text, you chisel out an acceptable headline, then it fails to fit by a few characters. This is the moment of temptation. If you omit just that one word, it still makes sense, doesn't it? A good test for excessive omission is to see if there is a chink in the wording where you can reasonably insert alternative pronouns or prepositions and change the meaning:

SIGNALS AT RED, SAID NOTHING

The omission is between the 'red' and 'said', and what might we legitimately imagine in there? 'They' said nothing? 'He' said nothing? 'I' said nothing? 'We' said nothing? 'Police' said nothing? 'Archbishop' said nothing? I suspect that what was originally written was:

'SIGNALS AT RED, I SAID NOTHING'

The text is that a fireman of a train which collided with another told the inquiry that after the train had begun to move he saw a signal gantry with all the signals at red – but he did not say anything to the driver about it. This admission is worth the headline, but the subject of the sentence cannot be omitted. Instead of trying to cope with the exact quotes here, the headline could have been:

RAILMAN SAW DANGER, SAID NOTHING

Two more with the missing word supplied (in brackets):

ST PAUL'S TRIBUTE TO LUTHER KING (CATHEDRAL)

VIETCONG FLAGS OVER SAIGON (FLY)

Abuse of catchwords

The ugliest headlines give the impression that a handful of words thought to be powerful in headlines have been taken at random without any attempt to create an intelligible headline sentence. Words like shock, ordeal, pledge, probe, are potent symbols, but like soup concentrates they need water. They cannot be served altogether and raw:

TRAIN RUSH HOUR SMASH ORDEAL

CAR PLEDGE MOVE HIT

In this category we must analyse our opening shocker

HOMES PLAN FACTORY HOPE

We have a noun–adjective double. Homes plan, which means a plan to accept industrialised housing in a new town; and a factory hope, which means there may be an industrialised housing factory. All these words are acceptable if used in a less constipated context. In addition, we have excessive omission. If we could insert a verb to separate the two sections of the headline we might just make sense:

HOMES PLAN RAISES FACTORY HOPES

But the truth is that this headline is guilty of a further offence: two thoughts in four words. Headlinese is best avoided here by settling for the main news thought. So, too, with this monster created by coupling five nouns together:

CORNED BEEF ON 'SECRET' SALE STORM

This was also an instance of too much in the headline and of the headline overtaking itself. The news was:

'TYPHOID' CORNED BEEF IN SHOPS AFTER ALL

Extravagant metaphor
Escalation robs headlines of authority. People who are worried about through traffic find they are living in 'terror road'; a mild disagreement becomes a storm; and anyone who makes a criticism is in danger of being pictured in the most ferocious posture:

BISHOP FLAYS MODERN GIRL

DIRECTOR SLASHES SEATS

TEACHER LASHES MEALS ISSUE

Related to this source of headlinese is the escalation of metaphor until it loses touch with reality.

KLONDIKE RUSH FOR WHITE GOLD

'White gold' is a metaphor here for uranium. And the rush is not in the Klondike. It would be all right to say:

'KLONDIKE' RUSH FOR URANIUM

This use of the metaphor would give an image of frenzy similar to the gold rush in the Klondike, and losing the 'white gold' metaphor hardens the headline without emasculating it. What happened was that the headline writer built on a good idea but left the reader behind.

Confusion of tenses

We use the present tense in heads for contemporaneous events; but we cannot retain the present tense throughout when there is a clear time-change built into the headline:

CID SUSPECT ARSON AFTER BABIES SAFE

I do not agree with the view that when a past time element appears in the head the only thing to do is use a verb in the past tense. That would produce 'CID suspected arson after babies saved', as though they no longer suspect arson. What we should do is recognise that in this clumsily constructed head, the word 'after' enforces past tense on what follows: 'CID suspect arson after babies saved'. We could avoid the past tense: 'CID suspect arson after baby rescue'. But it is also better to avoid the 'after' construction. This would fit:

BABIES SAVED IN FIRE: CID SUSPECT ARSON

Clumsy construction

To make heads fit their space there is some juggling you can do with word order without sacrificing meaning. But a halt must be called when the word shuffling produces heads such as

LONDON MODEL IS STRANGLING VICTIM WITH CITY MAN

The news can and should be expressed in normal sequence:

LONDON MODEL AND CITY MAN FOUND STRANGLED

or

LONDON MODEL FOUND STRANGLED WITH CITY MAN

And again:

TENANT HIT RAIDER WITH BOTTLE ON HEAD

Who bottle on head had?

Chapter Nine

Headline Vocabulary

Everyone must, for the most part, be his own analyst; and no one who does not expend, whether expressly and systematically or as a half-conscious accompaniment of his reading and writing, a good deal of care upon points of synonym is likely to write well.

H. W. FOWLER

Headline writers must have an armoury of synonyms. 'Can you think of another word for "requisition"?' Pleas like that are common as text editors try to avoid the long words and the abstractions which kill headlines. Practice in headline writing enforces acquaintance with a wide order of synonyms. Text editors will be their own analysts: in half a dozen synonyms only one may be quite right for the idea to be expressed.

For writing and editing there are a few useful dictionaries of synonyms; Roget's rich *Thesaurus* is especially valuable once its method of presentation is mastered. For headline writing, however, a different kind of vocabulary is useful – a list of words which commonly give difficulty in headline writing with headline alternatives. These must be shorter and, preferably, more specific. It is these that headline writers need to store in their minds, and which the following vocabulary attempts to supply.

The main headings throughout are the nouns, verbs and adjectives which give most trouble, followed by shorter alternatives. With the troublesome abstract nouns listed it is often better to change the headline thought so it can be expressed with a verb. The list is not a list of synonyms. It is a list of headline ideas. Some of the alternative words suggested will not fit the shade of meaning in every case, and the text editor must judge.

It is a good idea to make your own additions when a moment of headline inspiration finds a new way round a familiar tortuous abstraction. Words in italic should only be used in difficulties and then only if the style of the newspaper permits.

A

abandon (vb)
drop
give up
quit
skip
yield

abatement (n)
cut
decline
drop
easement
ebb
fall
slump

abbreviate (vb)
chop
cut
lop
shorten
slash
squash

abduction (n)
capture
kidnap
seizure

abolish (vb)
ban
bar
block
close
cut
drop
end
foil
kill
squash

abolition (n)
ban
bar
end

abscond (vb)
flee
leave
run

accelerate (vb)
bustle
dash
drive
hasten
hustle
press

push
race
rush
scramble
speed

acceleration (n)
drive
flurry
hurry
push
race
scramble

accident
(nouns)
blast
collision
crash
horror
pile-up
terror
(verbs)
blast
collide
crash
gut (fire)
ram
raze
smash
strike

accommodate (vb)
fit in
hold
house
put up
take in

accumulate (vb)
acquire
add (up)
amass
build up
gather
grow

accurate (adj)
exact
right
true

accusation (n)
allegation (n)
blame
charge
citation

accuse (vb)
allege
blame
charge
cite
indict

achieve (vb)
gain
get
grab

achievement (n)
gain
triumph
victory
win

acknowledge (vb)
admit

agree
OK/okay
recognise

acquire (vb)
buy
choose
gain
get
grab
inherit
pick
reap
take

acquisition (n)
benefit
bequest
find
gain
legacy
win

acquittal (n)
clearance
freedom
release
reprieve

adamant (adj)
enemy
firm
hard
rigid
tough

adjustment (n)
change

revision
shift
switch

administer (vb)
control
direct
manage
run

advantage (n)
benefit
gain
help
plus

aggravate (vb)
annoy
excite
inflame
kindle
provoke
spark
vex
worsen

agreement (n)
accord
bargain
bond
deal
pact
treaty

**agriculture
(nouns)**
crops (or be specific)
farm

farmers
food
land
(verbs)
farm
harvest
plant
reap
sow
till

allegation see **accusation**

alleviate (vb)
ease
lessen
let up
reduce

alleviation (n)
aid
help
let-up
lighten
relief
remission
rescue
succour

allocation (n)
cut
dole
quota
ration
share

amalgamate (vb)
bond

combine
fuse
join
link
merge
mix
team up
tie
unify
unite
weld

amalgamation (n)
link
merger
team
tie-up

ambassador (n)
envoy
minister

amendment (n)
change
revision
rewording
shift
switch

announce (vb)
notify
proclaim
report
reveal
tell

announcement (n)
disclosure

news
record
report

apartment (n)
flat
home

apathetic (adj)
aloof
cool
calm

appeal (vb)
ask
call
plea

appoint (vb)
choose
invest
name
pick

apologise (vb)
climb down
regret
repent
rue
say sorry

apology (n)
regret
remorse

appointment (n)
duty
job

mission
place
post

apportion (vb)
allot
divide
give out
share

apportionment (n)
deal
lot
part
quota
ration
share

appreciate (vb)
grow
increase
rise
value

appropriate (vb)
grab
loot
seize
snatch
take over

arbitrator (n)
judge
referee
umpire

argument (n)
dispute

fight
quarrel
row

arraignment (n)
case
charge
indictment
suit
trial

ascertain (vb)
find out
learn
seek

assistance (n)
aid
back-up
help
relief
rescue

attain (vb)
get
reach
secure

authorise (vb)
adopt
agree
allow
approve
back
favour
let
pass

permit
ratify
sanction
say yes to
sign
vote

B

bankruptcy (n)
collapse
crash
failure
fall

barrister (n)
counsel
lawyer
QC (not always)

beginning (n)
birth
dawn
début
onset
opening
start

bequeath (vb)
give
leave
will

bewilderment (n)
awe
puzzle
shock
surprise

business (n)
company
firm
trader

business premises (n)
company/plant
firm
shop/store/office

C

calculate (vb)
assess
estimate
rate
value

catalogue (n)
details
list
name
record

ceremony (n)
display
fête
pageant
parade
party
review
spectacle

cessation (n)
end
gap
lull
pause

rest
stop

challenge (vb)
contest
dare
defy
dispute
doubt
flout

championship (n)
award
crown
title

circumvent (vb)
balk
beat
cheat
defeat
dish
foil
outwit
stop

clemency (n)
mercy

clergyman (n)
minister
priest
rector
vicar

close (vb)
call off
conclude

end
finish
shut

coalition (n)
alliance
band
group
league
syndicate

comfortable (adj)
cosy
fine
good
snug

commendation (n)
acclaim
applause
backing
eulogy
good record
homage
praise

committee (n)
body
group
party

commodious (adj)
fit
roomy
spacious

communicate (vb)
pass on

reveal
tell

competition (n)
fight
race
rivalry

complain (vb)
accuse
growl
grumble
object
protest
resent

completion (n)
end
finish

conciliation (n)
good offices
peace move
talks
truce

confront (vb)
face

congratulate (vb)
commend
praise

conjecture (n)
guess

consider (vb)
discuss

look at
report on
study

consolidate (vb)
cement
combine
fuse
mix
unify
unite
weld

construct (vb)
build
form
make
put up

continue (vb)
go on
persist
remain
run
stay

contradict (vb)
deny
disown
dispute
dissent
reject
refute

contradiction (n)
denial
rebuff
rejection

contribution (n)
award
donation
gift
grant
present

co-operate (vb)
combine
help
join with
side with

criticise (vb)
abuse
censure
challenge
chide
condemn
decry
deplore
flay
rail at
rap
slap
slam

criticism (n)
blow
censure
rebuke
rebuff

D

damage (vb)
harm
hit

hurt
ruin
spoil
wreck

defector (n)
rebel
refugee
runaway

deflate (vb)
contract
crush
cut
pinch
squeeze

deflation (n)
cut
squeeze

demonstrate (vb)
march
parade
protest
riot
sit-in

demonstration (n)
demo
march
parade
protest
riot
row
scene
showdown

sitdown
sit-in

denomination (n)
name
religion
school

department (n)
civil service
ministry
office

deprecate (n)
attack
belittle
discount
discredit
knock
run down

description (n)
account
story
tale

designate (vb)
appoint
name
select

destruction (n)
damage
havoc
ruin
waste
wreck

determine (vb)
agree
find out
fix

disagree (vb)
argue
differ
fall out

disagreement (n)
battle
clash
conflict
dispute
fight
fracas
quarrel
rift
row
rumpus
wrangle

disapprove (vb)
ban
bar
block
deny
disallow
reject
say no to
throw out
turn down

discriminate (vb)
bar
block
favour

penalise
screen
segregate

discrimination (n)
bias
favouritism
injustice
leaning
prejudice

discriminatory (adj)
biased
partial
undue
unequal
unfair
unjust

dissolve (vb)
end

distribute (vb)
deal
dispense
give
issue
scatter

distribution (n)
dispense
issue
supply

domestic appliances (n)
devices
gadgets

E

earthquake (n)
'quake
shake
tremor

emergency (n)
aid call
crash
crisis team
disaster
SOS

employment (n)
job
work

endorsement (n)
acclaim
approval
backing
sanction
support

endowment (n)
donation
gift
legacy
offer

enfranchise (vb)
give vote to
liberate
set free

enjoyment (n)
delight
glee
joy
pleasure

entertainment (n)
fair
feast
fun
show

equivocate (vb)
delay
dodge
evade
shuffle

essential (adj)
key
main
must
necessary
needed

establish (vb)
fix
prove
secure
settle

estimate (vb)
conjecture
fix price
guess
judge
value

every (adj)
all
each

exacerbate (vb)
irritate
vex

exaggerate (vb)
amplify
blow up
enlarge
increase
magnify
overstate
swell

examine (vb)
inspect
look at
question
quiz
search
study
view
watch

examination (n)
inquiry
probe
quest
scrutiny
study
trial

exemption (n)
exception
immunity

exhibit (vb)
display
show

exonerate (vb)
absolve
acquit
clear
free
uphold

expedite (vb)
ease
hasten
help
hurry
press
rush
speed
urge

explanation (n)
account
answer
comment
reply
tale
version

explosion (n)
blast
shock
spasm

F

fabrication (n)
falsehood
lie
tale
untruth

facilitate (vb)
advance
ease
expedite
impel
relieve
smooth

fallacious (adj)
false
untrue
wrong

fashionable (adj)
cool
stylish
trendy

foundation (n)
base
basis
beginning
charity

fraternise (vb)
befriend
help
mix with
side with

fundamental (adj)
basic
primary

G

govern (vb)
command

control
direct
manage
rule
run

government (n)
Britain (or nation where paper published)
Cabinet (if Cabinet involved)
country
minister's name is often aptest
ministry
nation
state
Whitehall
White House
(For provincial and state papers in federal country, the capital: London/Washington/Canberra/Delhi etc.)

grievance (n)
grouse
grudge
hardship
injury
injustice
wrong

guarantee
(nouns)
bond
mortgage
pledge
surety

(verbs)
endorse
go bail
insure
pledge
secure
support
sponsor
warrant

guillotine (vb)
chop
cut off
gag
silence

H

hallucination (n)
delusion
dream
illusion
mirage

harmonisation (n)
accord
bargain
compact
pact
peace
truce

harmonise (vb)
accord
agree
conciliate
heal
pacify

patch
settle
smooth

hazardous (adj)
bold
perilous
risky
unsafe

I

illegitimate (adj)
illegal
illicit
unlawful
wrong

illimitable (adj)
boundless
immense
infinite
no-limit

illustrate (vb)
explain
picture
reveal
show

immaterial (adj)
flimsy
thin
trifling

imminent (adj)
near
soon

important (adj)
big
grave
great
high
key
notable
prime
serious
signal
top
vital
weighty

improve (vb)
amend
better
bolster
ease
enhance
mend
patch
polish
promote
refit
refresh
remodel
renew
repair
restore
revamp
touch up

improvement (adj)
advance
betterment
progress
recovery

reform
relief
repair

inaccurate (adj)
false
untrue
wrong

inaugurate (vb)
begin
install
open
start

inauguration (n)
début
opening
start

incomes (n)
cash
money
pay
salary
wages

indemnify (vb)
balance
compensate
cover
make up for
redeem
set off

independent (adj)
free
impartial

neutral
unbiased

influence (vb)
induce
lead
sway

information (n)
advice
details
facts
news

injunction (n)
order
writ

inquire (vb)
ask
examine
look into
question
search
sift

instigate (vb)
impel
incite
provoke
spur
start

institution see **organisa-tion**

instruct (vb)
educate

guide
teach
tell

insurrection (n)
rebellion
revolt
riot
uprising

intercept (vb)
balk
hold up
impede
obstruct
stop

interfere (vb)
hinder
intrude
meddle
oppose
thwart

interrogate (vb)
examine
fathom
grill
probe
pump
question
quiz
vet

interrupt (vb)
delay
disturb
hinder

stop

interview (n)
dialogue
face-to-face
meeting
pow-wow
talk

introduce (vb)
guide
teach
tell
start

investigate (vb)
check
delve
examine
inquire
plumb
pry
scan
seek
sift
study

investigation (n)
analysis
check
hunt
inquiry
probe
quest
quiz
screen
search
study

invitation (n)
call
request
summons

invite (vb)
ask
beg
bid
call on
petition

J

jeopardise (vb)
endanger
hazard
imperil
risk

jewels (n)
gems (preferably specify:
    rubies, diamonds, pearls,
    etc.)
stones

journey (n)
hike
jaunt
outing
run
tour
trip
walk

judgment (n)
decision
decree

finding
result
ruling
verdict

justify (vb)
bear out
clear
confirm
defend
endorse
excuse
explain

K

kidnap (vb)
abduct
capture
carry off
grab
seize
snatch
steal
take

kidnapping (n)
abduction
capture
seizure
snatch

kingdom (n)
empire
land
realm
state

knowledge (n)
learning
skill

L

leader (n)
boss
chief
head
master
ruler
tsar

legacy (n)
bequest
gift
present

legalise (vb)
allow
enact
ordain
permit
warrant

legislation (n)
Act
bill
code
law

locality (n)
area
district
region
zone

luxurious (adj)
costly
cosy
lush
plush
rich

M

machinery (n)
machines
plant

magistrates (n)
Bench
court
JPs
justices

maintain (vb)
assert
back up
carry on
insist
keep up
support

maintenance (n)
support
upkeep

majority (n)
most

malefactor (n)
criminal
culprit
killer

thief
vandal

management (n)
board
company
directors
firm
owners

manager (n)
boss
chief
head

manoeuvres (n)
dodges
exercises
plots
ruses
tricks
wiles

manufacture (vb)
make
produce

manufacturer (n)
boss
maker

massacre (nouns)
butchery
carnage
genocide
killing
murder
slaughter

(verbs)
butcher
destroy
kill
murder
slay

maximum (adj)
biggest
ceiling
highest
most
top

measure
(nouns)
amount
size
(verbs)
assess
mark up
mete
rate
scale
size
weigh

mediate (vb)
fix
help
intervene
link

mediator (n)
envoy
go-between
good offices

meeting (n)
caucus

forum
talk(s)

merchandise (n)
goods

merchant (n)
dealer
trader

message (n)
letter
news
word

messenger (n)
courier
envoy
runner

minimum (adj)
least
lowest

miscalculate (vb)
err
fail
fall

mis-statement (n)
error
falsehood
fault
misreport

moderate (vb)
allay

control
lessen
limit

modification (n)
alteration
change
switch

N

nationalisation (n)
conversion
take-over

nationalise (vb)
acquire
grab
take over

nationalised (adj)
state
state-run

necessary (adj)
needed

negotiate (vb)
bargain
confer
discuss
haggle
meet
talk

negotiation (n)
haggle

parley
talk(s)

neighbourhood (n)
area
district
locality
place
region
town
zone

nominate (vb)
appoint
call
choose
invest
name
propose
return
term

nomination (n)
place
seat
ticket
vote

O

object to (vb)
abuse
attack
censure
denounce
dispute
fight
knock
protest

rap
rebuke
slate

objection (n)
attack
outcry
protest

objectors (n)
'antis'
critics
enemies
foes
rebels

observation (n)
eye
lookout
note
watch

observe (vb)
check
eye
inspect
note
spy
watch

obstinate (adj)
firm
hard
solid
stubborn
tough

occupant (n)
dweller

inmate
resident

occupation (n)
job
role
tenure
work

operate (vb)
act
control
run
work

operation (n)
act
action
deed
surgery
work

opportunity (n)
chance

oppose (vb)
bar
battle
block
censure
chide
clash
combat
decry
deplore
differ
fight

hit
lash
rebuff
reject
repel
rule out
slap
slate
veto

opposition (n)
'antis'
critics
enemies
foes
opponents
rebels
rivals

organisation (n)
institution (n)
board
body
club
corps
firm
group
set-up
society
unit

organise (vb)
call
develop
fix
form
join
knit

plan
pool
run
set up
tie
unite
weld

P

pacification (n)
compact
concord
cooling
healing
peace-making
settling/settlement

pacify (vb)
allay
calm
cool
heal
settle

performance (n)
action
display
exploit
show

permanent (adj)
abiding
constant
durable
lasting

give permission (vb)
agree
allow
approve
OK
pass
permit
say yes to

petition (n)
plea

plebiscite (n)
vote

population (n)
number
people

postpone (vb)
block
delay
hold up

precedent (n)
custom
habit
model
practice
rule
standard
use

preclude (vb)
forestall
hinder
prevent
stop

presentation (n)
gift
party
testimonial
tribute

procedure (n)
action
conduct
habit
practice
process

proclamation (n)
decree
edict

programme (n)
campaign
drive
effort
move
plan

prohibit (vb)
ban
bar
block
check
curb
embargo
end
forbid
halt
kill
limit
peg
prevent

stop
veto

prohibition (n)
axe
ban
bar
curb
embargo
end
halt
veto

promising (adj)
bright
hopeful

proposition (n)
idea
plan
thesis

prosecute (vb)
arraign
charge
cite
sue
summons

prosecution (n)
case
cause
charge
citation
suit
trial

pursue (vb)
follow

harry
hunt
search
seek
trace
track
trail

pursuit (n)
chase
hunt
quest
search

Q

qualification (n)
ability
art
craft
gift
skill
talent

quantity (n)
amount
number

question (vb)
ask
challenge
doubt
probe
query
quiz

quotation (n)
price

quote
tender

sedition
strife

R

ratification (n)
approval
consent
signing

realignment (n)
change
move
revision
shake-up
switch

reapportion (vb)
change
move
re-allot
switch

reapportionment (n)
part
share

reasonable (adj)
fair
right

rebellion (n)
mutiny
revolt
rift
riot
rising

reception (n)
party
welcome

recession (n)
slump

recommend (vb)
advise
back
boost
command
counsel
laud
pass
praise
propose
puff
push
suggest
urge

recommendation (n)
advice
backing
idea
plan
word

recompense (vb)
benefit
make good
repay

reduction (n)
cut
fall

redundant (adj)
needless
sacked
spare
surplus

referendum (n)
vote

reflation (n)
boost
spurt
tonic

regulate (vb)
control
run
vet

regulation (n)
code
rule

relinquish (vb)
abandon
leave
quit
resign

renounce (vb)
drop
forgo
give up
lay aside

quit
recant

renunciation (n)
about-face
desertion
disavowal
reversal

repudiate (vb)
deny
disclaim
rebuff
reject
repel
snub
spurn
throw back
unload

requisition (vb)
acquire
get
seize
take
take over

resign (vb)
give up
lay down
leave
quit

resignation (n)
abdication
departure

resolution (n)
motion
vote

responsibility (n)
duty
job
task

revenue (n)
cash
income
money
tax(es)

S

sanction (vb)
approve
OK
pass

satisfactory (adj)
adequate
enough
good
right

scrutinise (vb)
check
inspect
vet
watch

settlement (n)
bargain
bond
deal
pact

peace
treaty

significant (adj)
marked
notable
weighty

specification (n)
account
detail
plan

statement (n)
advice
news
notice
report
view

supplication (n)
entreaty
plea
prayer
request

support (vb)
aid
back
brace
feed
foster
help
prop
push
stand by
uphold

T

temporary (adj)
brief
short (-term)

terminate (vb)
end
stop

testimony (n)
evidence

tolerate (vb)
abide
allow
endure
let
live with
permit
stand

toleration (n)
leniency
licence

transaction (n)
affair
deal
process
trade

transformation (n)
change
shake-up

transgression (n)
offence

sin
trespass

treasure (n)
riches
spoils
wealth

U

unauthenticated (adj)
unproven
unsure

unblemished (adj)
clean
guiltless
spotless

uncompromising (adj)
unyielding (adj)
firm
fixed
game
solid
steady
tough
unmoved
unshaken

unconcerned (adj)
calm
quiet
unmoved

underestimate (vb)
err
misjudge

misprize
underprize
undervalue

undermine (vb)
belittle
burrow
damage
hurt
impair
sap
weaken

undertaking (n)
deal
mission
plan
plot
quest

unyielding see **uncompromising**

V

vacillate (vb)
demur
dodge
evade
hedge
wobble
wriggle

vanquish (vb)
beat
defeat
rout
scatter

vindicate (vb)
acquit
bear out
clear
justify
set right
uphold

vindication (n)
acquittal
clearance
defence

vulnerable (adj)
suspect
tender
weak

W

warranty (n)
bond
pledge
promise

withhold (vb)
ban
bar
deny
keep back
refuse

wreckage (n)
damage
debris
rubble
ruins
waste

Notes

1. *Writing English Prose*, by William Brewster (New York: Henry Holt, 1913), p. 171.
2. *The Art of Readable Writing*, by Rudolf Flesch (New York: Harper and Bros, 1949), pp. 106–17.
3. *Watch Your Language*, by Theodore M. Bernstein (New York: Channel Press, 1958), p. 126. See also *More Language that Needs Watching*, by Theodore M. Bernstein (New York: Channel Press, 1962).
4. *The Reader Over Your Shoulder*, by Robert Graves and Alan Hodge (London: Jonathan Cape, 1948), p. 51; (also published London: Mayflower, 1962; Cape Paperback, 1965).
5. *My Life and Hard Times*, by James Thurber (London: Hamish Hamilton, 1950), p. 150; (Harmondsworth: Penguin, 1948).
6. *Elements of Style*, by W. Strunk Jnr (New York: Macmillan, 1959).
7. *A Writer's Notes on his Trade*, by C. E. Montague (Harmondsworth: Pelican, 1949), p. 147.
8. *The Reader Over Your Shoulder*, by Graves and Hodge, p. 53.
9. *Usage and Abuse*, by Eric Partridge (London: Hamish Hamilton, 1954), p. 121 (also published Harmondsworth: Penguin, 1963).
10. *Plain Words*, by Sir Ernest Gowers (London: HM Stationery Office, 1948).
11. *Watch Your Language*, by Bernstein, p. 132.

12. *A Dictionary of Modern English Usage*, by H. W. Fowler (Oxford University Press, 2nd edition, 1965), p. 148.

13. *Concise Usage and Abusage*, by Eric Partridge (London: Hamish Hamilton, 1954), and *Doing it in Style*, by Leslie Sellers (Oxford: Pergamon Press, 1968), p. 166.

14. *A Dictionary of Clichés*, by Eric Partridge (London: Routledge, 1940).

15. *Watch Your Language*, by Bernstein, p. 223.

Index